Child of the Sit-Downs

Child of the Sit-Downs

The Revolutionary Life of Genora Dollinger

Carlton Jackson

Kent State University Press Kent, Ohio

Library of Congress Catalog Card Number 2008001510
ISBN 978-0-87338-944-0
Manufactured in the United States of America

Library of Congress Cataloging-in-Publication Data
Jackson, Carlton.
Child of the sit-downs : the revolutionary life of Genora Dollinger / Carlton Jackson.
p. cm.
Includes bibliographical references and index.
ISBN 978-0-87338-944-0 (hardcover : alk. paper) ∞
1. Dollinger, Genora Johnson. 2. Women labor union members—United States—Biography. 3. Automobile industry workers—Labor unions—United States—History. 4. Automobile industry workers—United States—Biography. 5. Labor unions—United States—Biography. 6. Women's Emergency Brigade. I. Title.
HD6509.D65J33 2008
331.88'1292092—dc22
[B] 2008001510

British Library Cataloging-in-Publication data are available.

12 11 10 09 08 5 4 3 2 1

Contents

Acknowledgments

Many people helped me to research and write this biography of Genora Dollinger, and I must express my appreciation to them. First, at the Archives of Labor and Urban Affairs, Reuther Library at Wayne State University in Detroit, Walter Lefevre, Patrice Merritt, Margaret Raucher, and Mary J. Wallace were helpful. Paul Gifford of the University of Michigan, Flint; William Glenn, Stony Brook University; Julie Harrada, University of Michigan, Ann Arbor; and David Kessler of the University of California-Berkeley found some much-needed materials, for which I am grateful. Thank you.

At Western Kentucky University I received considerable help from research grants and summer fellowships. I thank each member of that university's committees for their help. My graduate assistants proved so indispensable that I can truthfully say that this manuscript could not have been completed without them. John Paul Hill, Jennifer Kretzer, Melinda Jayne Squires, Evan Lambeth, Christopher George, Mary Bokkin, Jonathan Chilcote, and Phil Shaw provided unstinting help, cooperation, and encouragement. I thank also the former and present chairs of the WKU history department, Richard Troutman and Richard Weigel, for their support of this project. Nancy Marshall of the WKU library was extremely efficient in acquiring much-needed materials, as were Debra Day and Selena Langford of WKU's interlibrary department. WKU librarians Alan Logsdon and Olivia Fruit helped in the research, and I thank them. Professor Lowell Harrison of WKU's history department read the entire manuscript and gave useful advice. My friend and colleague Lou-Ann Crouther of the WKU English department gave the manuscript an extremely close reading and helped immensely with grammar, punctuation, and organization. I am most grateful for her assistance.

I would be remiss if I did not mention the assistance that came to me from Sol Dollinger, Genora's husband of fifty-one years. (Sadly, Sol died on September 12, 2001.) At my invitation, Sol read the entire manuscript. Although he corrected me on some factual matters, and while we did have some differences of opinion, at no time did he ever tell me how to write this biography (I cannot say the same about some of Genora's critics). When I interviewed Sol in 1997, I asked him what kind of biography he would like to see of Genora Dollinger. His answer was, "An honest one." This, to the best of my abilities, I have done.

Many other individuals besides Sol Dollinger supplied me with information. Their names appear in the text and in the endnotes. I thank all those persons who knew Genora personally and willingly talked to me about her.

Finally, I take pride in thanking my lovely family for their continued support of my publishing endeavors: my daughters Beverly and Hilary; sons Daniel and Matthew; sons-in-law Steve and Arthur; daughters-in-law Ling and Elaine; Grace; my grandchildren Colleen, Megan, Katharine, Travis, Patrick, Austin, Liam, Rowan, Carlton, David, Finn, and Alec. And, foremost and always, Pat.

Preface: Genora and Luther

Writing about the relatively unknown nineteenth-century politician Felix Grundy, historian Joseph H. Parks says, "The stories of the lives of the so-called great men of the nation have been told and re-told, but little has been done toward giving due credit to those who made them great." Leaders do not "spontaneously spring into national prominence. They owe much to those lesser figures who, for the most part, remain behind the springs of action."[1]

While Genora Johnson Dollinger would not have liked to be referred to as "remaining behind" the "springs of action"—almost always thinking of herself on the cutting edge of events—that is essentially the part she played in matters of unionism and feminism. She never became a forerunner in either movement, but she assisted enormously those at the very top. Who were they? The list includes John L. Lewis; Norman Thomas; Betty Friedan; George Meany; Owen Bieber; the three Reuther brothers, Walter, Roy, and Victor; and several other luminaries. Genora helped these people to get to the top of the list and to stay there.

If Genora helped the top to acquire and retain power and influence, her contributions also traveled in other directions. She could meet Norman Thomas at ten in the morning and "John Doe" at noon and be equally comfortable with both. She could relate not only to the rich and famous but to the common worker as well. Perhaps she could be called a pivotal figure between what was often intellectual unionism and real or practical unionism.

I raise these points because my father, Luther Jackson, was a coal miner in Alabama, and, like Genora Dollinger, he was a *worker,* not a theorist or intellectual. The two of them—and they never did meet each other—were the strongest of union people. In the house where I grew up, Jesus Christ came first, followed closely by John L. Lewis, head of the United Mine Workers of America, not all that much separated from the United Automobile Workers, the union with which Genora was most closely associated. As Luther—and perhaps Genora, too, at least in her earlier years—made his way to and from work each day, his mind, in all likelihood, was not on the esoteric niceties of the labor movement, either national or international. All he wanted to do was make a shift, go home to his family, and collect a paycheck every now and then. He was an example of how the working classes had, to a considerable extent, "absorbed the values of capitalist individualism."[2]

Neither Genora nor my father ever finished high school, and neither was born into the kind of family that garnered any kind of admittance into the world of philosophical adjudications of unionism or labor movements or, for that matter, any kind of academic and intellectual pursuits. She fought and gouged her way into whatever program she was espousing at any particular moment, making her in a real way a professional reformer.

Luther and Genora were born worlds apart: Alabama and Michigan. Yet their basic beliefs about the laborer and his or her importance in the world of workers were more in agreement than not. Although my father would not have worried himself about the scholarly nuances of the labor movement itself—at least as it was expressed in paradigmatic terms by experts all over the country and, indeed, the world—in reality, at least during the first part of her career, neither did Genora Dollinger. Her approach to the labor movement was pragmatic, head-on, even in-your-face, much like Luther's. They were the rank and file of the union, the heart-blood of the labor movement, the very people to whom theorists and philosophers seemed initially to ignore and then ultimately—and many times, it seemed, grudgingly—had to pay some attention.

As it turns out, some pretty heavy hitters in the labor movement agreed with both Luther and Genora.

James P. Cannon, founder of American Trotskyism, said, "If a revolutionary socialist party is predominately composed of non-workers it means that it can't . . . make its programs a reality." "Yes!" both Luther and Genora would have exclaimed. Separate the labor movement or the labor union from the people who actually do the work, and most of its constituency is lost. My father and Genora Dollinger saw this point clearly; the question ultimately was why so many top-ranking union, business, and academic people could not be as clever. Perhaps it was the difference between pragmatism and idealism. Cannon went further, saying that students and professional intellectuals—not the real workers in the fields of industrial endeavors—represented the first years of the Russian Revolution.[3] Leon Trotsky, who Genora came later to admire so much, weighed in on this significant matter. In a letter to

Cannon dated October 10, 1937, Trotsky wrote, "The task is naturally not to prevent the influx of intellectuals . . . but to orient the whole organization toward the factory, the strikers, the milieu of unions." He added, "I continue to be of the opinion that [the Socialist Workers Party] has too many petit-bourgeois boys and girls who are very good and devoted to the party, but who do not fully realize that their duty is not to discuss among themselves but to penetrate into the milieu of workers."[4]

The "milieu of workers" was the crux of the whole argument as far as Genora Dollinger and Luther Jackson were concerned. Luther—maybe he was a Trotskyist without realizing it—was a real-life coal miner. He went down into the pits and knew what a tipple and an adit were. Genora was a real-life worker on an automobile assembly line. She stood for hours putting little parts onto the developing automobile, and she knew how to read industrial blueprints and how to stir up workers for causes that she and, ultimately, they came to believe were just.

In some areas Luther and Genora parted company, because of both educational achievement and formal learning. Luther read, but mostly the Bible and other books of religious inspiration. Genora read, but mostly books by Karl Marx, Leon Trotsky, and other revolutionary leaders. Interestingly enough, my father's interpretation of the Holy Bible and Genora's take on Marx, Lenin, and Trotsky achieved a remarkable similarity. Leave out the religious connotations, and you'll find Luther H. Jackson of rural Dora, Alabama, and Genora Dollinger of urban Flint, Michigan, in almost perfect harmony with one another. That is because they were both frontline workers. One became a deacon of his church, the other a revolutionary.

Genora Dollinger was closer to Luther Jackson in her life's work than to, say, Karl Marx or Vladimir Lenin. Or, for that matter, Walter Reuther and many of the other tuxedo unionism leaders, as Genora called them. She had a prescience about labor unions and corporations: she was, as far as I know, the first activist to use the term "tuxedo unionism," by which she meant that labor leaders of the late twentieth century would become more like corporate executives than representatives of the rank-and-file workman. From Luther's and Genora's points of view, such attitudes predicted evil days ahead for unionism.

By the 1970s, a mere 15 percent of young people in the labor force joined a union, and by 2001, that number had been reduced to 5 percent.[5] At the turn of the twenty-first century, only 9 percent of the overall private sector was unionized.[6] Perhaps it could be said that the unions by and large were "victims of their own successes." Many of the things for which they had fought over the years had been realized: minimum wages, safety in the workplace, workmen's compensation, and sick and maternity leaves.[7] But, as Genora might argue, these accomplishments tended to overshadow the *real* differences and confrontations between labor and capital in the depression-ridden America of the 1930s. By the 1980s, Genora believed, the companies and the government had bought off union leadership—in effect, making it "one of their own." Complementing this thought was President Ronald Reagan's dismissal of the air traffic controllers, which had the effect of putting most other unions in line. This was tuxedo unionism with a vengeance. Genora feared that the old labor pioneers of Flint days were in danger of being forgotten, and not just what the men had done there, but what women—especially women—also had accomplished. She resolved to keep the memories alive; it is the purpose of this biography to show how and why she did it. Despite ridicule, personal tragedies, and balancing work and home, Genora Dollinger—by the time of her death in 1995—had finessed most of her detractors. I have chosen to discuss Genora's private life as well as her public life because I think we tend to create false divides between the two. Genora was a wife, mother, and jobholder who essentially melded these three duties into one. She generally tended to bring work home with her at night. She was not exactly a renaissance person nor a type A personality, though she exhibited traits of both from time to time. She had to be a participant in life, not a mere observer. These were the characteristics that kept this strong-willed woman going.

Genora Dollinger deserves a biography. So, one might ask, why hasn't it already been written? For one thing, her papers did not come together until fairly recently. Her widower, Sol Dollinger, owned a large collection of articles and travel diaries that shed light on her union and feminist activities, as well as her broader philosophies of life. To a greater extent, the Reuther Library at Wayne State University has a collection, which the Dollingers donated in the mid-1990s. From 1998 to early 2001, Sol Dollinger and I swapped e-mails on a regular basis. Sol's e-mails, which I have freely quoted in the pages ahead, are often fascinating for their insights into the world of big business, labor unions and their memberships, capitalism, and Socialism.

Over the years, many academics and other members of the intelligentsia (journalists, editors, broadcasters, etc.) may have befriended Genora and even corresponded with her on a regular basis. It worried more than a few of them, however, that as witty and intelligent as Genora seemed to be, she did not have the "proper documentation." Not only did she not have a college degree, she was, worse yet, a high school dropout. It was somewhat like a professional historian "wondering about the prowess of an amateur in the field who, though successful" in terms of having a following, had not earned any degrees.[8] Though the experts rarely came out and said it, they meant, "Yes, you are smart and knowledgeable, *but who are you?*" Many academics shunned her for this very reason; if they did not see any scholarly credentials, they were not going to write about her.

Genora Dollinger did not intellectualize or philosophize the interests and well-being of workers into some kind of esoteric oblivion. She was constantly on the front lines, from 1937 during the Flint strikes right on through the early 1990s, when the California teachers' strike made national headlines. Along with my father, she knew what it was like working for a living—no amount of theorizing or philosophical speculation can take the place of hard labor.

I have tried to strike a balance in this book between narrative and analysis, and I believe I have not stressed one to the detriment of the other. As all scholars know, one must have narrative before one can have any legitimate analysis. My main objectives in this book are the following:

1. To discuss unionism in the 1930s (especially 1937) and show its relationship to a rising feminism, as exemplified by the creation of the Women's Emergency Brigade during the sit-down strikes against General Motors in Flint, Michigan.
2. To describe unionism and women's work during World War II and how these two movements supported one another.
3. To examine the postwar attacks on unionism and the growth of governmental strictures because of the Cold War with the Soviet Union.
4. To explore the decline of the Socialist groups throughout the country and why they declined.
5. To explain the growth of a generation gap between older and younger unionists and discuss why Genora Dollinger and her followers believed there was a need to revitalize radical unionism. This theme is most apparent in Genora's railings against tuxedo unionism.

6. To offer some explanations of why mainline historians tended to bypass union and feminist participants like Genora Dollinger and of how things began to turn around in this respect by the 1970s.
7. To illustrate some of the disagreements between and among women's groups, particularly second-wave and third-wave feminists.

I would like my biography of Genora Dollinger to be read across a wide spectrum of the American public. I want intellectuals to read it and possibly learn something from it. I hope old-time union members of the United Automobile Workers locals in Flint, Detroit, and Los Angeles will read this book because in large part it is about them. Students, like those in professor Lauren Coodley's classes who are quoted at length in the last chapter, can learn much from the life and career of Genora Dollinger. I hope my biography of Genora will encourage high school and college students to learn as much as they possibly can about the connections between unionism and feminism and the fights for social justice everywhere.

I never met Genora Dollinger, but her husband, Sol, and I became good friends. When he visited me in western Kentucky and the idea was proposed of writing a biography of Genora, I asked him what I should call her: Genora Johnson? Genora Johnson Dollinger? Genora Dollinger? He said she would have been most pleased with simply "Genora." This is how I have addressed her throughout the manuscript. Far from showing any disrespect for her, the simple title of her first name is, as the person who knew her the longest and loved her the most told me, what she preferred.

An Introduction

Genora Johnson Dollinger gained fame in 1937 when she formed the Women's Emergency Brigade (WEB) to fight the police, Pinkertons, and other authorities in the sit-down strike against General Motors (GM) in Flint, Michigan. The WEB, or EB as it came to be called, was not intended to be another auxiliary responsible for making sandwiches and coffee for the strikers. Armed with clubs, stove pokers, crowbars, lead pipes, baseball bats, and auto-door springs, it became an integral part of the strike itself. Its activities contributed extensively to the United Auto Workers' (UAW) exertions and ultimate victory against GM in 1937.

Genora and colleagues dated the beginnings of the modern feminist movement to the role women played in the sit-downs against GM in the late 1930s and the coming of war in the early 1940s. This "emerging portrait of unionism as a vehicle for feminist aspirations"[1] in the 1940s "may have spurred feminism among wage earning women much as civil rights and New Left organizations did . . . in the 1960s."[2]

By 1930 one in nine women in the United States had cast off her role as the "mainstay of family life" to become a wage earner.[3] By the end of the 1930s, encouraged by increased automobile production, 15.5 percent of all married women were employed. There is no way that this percentage of women in the workforce (although, according to polls, public opinion was "lined up against them")[4] would not ultimately find its way into feminist movements. The two went together and go together. This was the message that Genora Johnson Dollinger tried to get across to both unions and corporations in her long years as a labor-feminist activist. It was only after several years of struggling that she felt any kind of success.

Historian John W. Jeffries asserts that "long term historical perspective suggests that many of the changes associated with the war [World War II] had long been under way—including new roles for women."[5] Arguably, for a lengthy period of time, unionism and feminism were, if not interchangeable, at least highly complementary of one another. Genora Dollinger was what sociologist Nancy A. Naples calls a "center-woman," a person who plays key roles in "linking . . . members of a community to one another."[6] This talent worked both ways because she was equally at home with the top echelons as well as the humblest workers. This ability was significant both in labor and feminist activities and the connecting of the two. Later in her life, Genora played important roles in many different communities in addition to labor and feminism, including civil rights, justice for schoolteachers, world peace, and politics. Her reputation as a center-woman caused her to be much in demand from many organizations of varied objectives.

After the dramatic events of 1937, Genora Dollinger spent the rest of her life (she died in 1995) supporting one Socialist cause after another: Trotskyism, social welfare, reform movements, and work with the National Association for the Advancement of Colored People (NAACP) and American Civil Liberties Union (ACLU). She was a professional reformer, looking for one cause after another in which to become involved. She was not, however, a flitter jumping from one reform movement to another, without serious motives behind the moves. Reform movements in which she participated were always in the context of Socialism, first with the Socialist Party and then as a member of the Socialist Workers Party (SWP). For the last forty-two years of her life, however, Genora was not a member of *any* political party, remaining a freelance or independent Socialist, meaning that all national and international problems to which she addressed herself had to be within the framework of Socialism. While an actual member of the Socialist Party and especially the SWP, she was required to take instructions from her leaders. At their behest, she stayed in Detroit after World War II, though it meant lengthy separations from her husband, Sol Dollinger. The leadership let it be known in no uncertain terms that it valued party advancement and successes more than family values. One may ask if there is such a thing as an independent Socialist, or if the phrase is oxymoronic. The answer is no, because philosophies like Capitalism, Communism, and Socialism can be approached on several different levels and from numerous directions. Within the framework of Marxism existed Stalinist Socialism and Trotskyist Socialism, and within these two major camps were many different sects. It was entirely reasonable for Genora Dollinger to be an independent Socialist. Differences of opinion do not necessarily reflect differences of principle.

Unlike most of her male counterparts, she had to balance all the conflicting dimensions of labor, feminism, civil and human rights, and

Socialist activities. She was a wife, a mother, a homemaker, and an assembly line worker, as well as an ideologue, and in all these roles she was like almost every other woman who has ever hit the campaign trail, so to speak. It was, after all, in the UAW as well as GM, a man's world, and she and women like her made the extra efforts required to be a part of the process. Genora was a pioneer in founding the EBs; she gained a reputation from the sit-downs of 1937 and, as a result, was invited to join reform movements, particularly those dealing with unionism and feminism, or she blatantly intruded herself into the process. Like other organizations, the EBs adapted verses to songs—some well-known, others not—that tended to symbolize their ambitions and intentions. This one was sung to the tune of "Marching Through Georgia":

> The women got together and they formed a mighty throng
> Every worker's wife and mom and sister will belong.
> They will fight beside the men to help the cause along,
> Shouting the Union forever.[7]

Genora was never passive: she would be a part of the action—even if she had to become strident. She would rather be told to go to hell than be ignored. She was not often ignored. But she was told to go to hell on more than one occasion. She always questioned the ideas and deeds of government officials, both local and national, why corporate welfare seemed to be more extensive (and expensive) than private welfare, and why women and labor movements and unions did not get their fair share of what is commonly called the American dream. She also questioned why the special interest groups, more than the man on the street, always seemed to get the ear of high-ranking government officials. As the saying goes, a rising tide lifts all ships. Genora was ready to see all ships rise and social and legal justice performed.

Ordinarily, many if not most American citizens would eagerly have agreed with these propositions. What fair-minded individual could oppose them? Genora, however, expressed her sentiments within the context of Socialism. Historically speaking, the average American will recoil in horror at the idea of Socialism, unaware that there are several levels of this political persuasion. Genora's ultimate persuasion was Trotskyist, and this caused her philosophies to be *persona non res* in the mainstream of American thought. Leon Trotsky was a Soviet; therefore he was the enemy. And his ideologies of permanent, worldwide revolution were not acceptable to most Americans, even during the drab years of the Great Depression.

Democracies must have dissenters; they cannot survive otherwise. Unlike in some other countries at the time (and into our own time as well), Genora did have the right to express her opinions, courtesy of the First Amendment—although in 1937 she was arrested during the sit-downs. Her crime? She distributed leaflets of the *Flint Autoworker*, edited by Henry Kraus (whom she came later to abhor), in downtown Flint, Michigan. It did not take long for the fiercely antiunion governmental authorities to realize that they had committed a serious violation of the Constitution. Genora was quickly released.

She did not advocate the overthrow of the American government. She may have gotten close to sedition on occasions but not to treason, as some of her enemies claimed. She wanted peaceful change if possible. She was ready, however, in 1937 and on some future occasions when the situation looked hopelessly bleak for the downtrodden, to man the barricades against both corporate and governmental forces in the name of social justice. Her greatest forte was the labor movement, strongly supplemented by feminist activism. From 1937, when she helped devise the plan that led to the union victory, to her death in 1995, her key word was "organize!" and close behind was "solidarity!" Her life encompassed several overarching themes: labor, women's rights, civil rights, Socialism, education, service to the unserved, health care and insurance for all, opposition to sending American jobs overseas, anticolonialism, a woman's right to choose between abortion and delivery, and, finally, the right of a human being to die peacefully, painlessly, and, above all else, with dignity. Genora carried out her activities in the context of these and other major societal movements of the time.

Beyond championing so many causes, Genora was a talented singer, writer, and speaker, and she possessed a love of the arts. She could be called to some extent a renaissance person, interested in learning simply for the sake of learning, not for some monetary reward or bragging rights at annual conventions. She never could get her fill of museums and art galleries or wherever the works of the great masters were exhibited.

Sadly, she suffered the tragic loss of her first two sons and battled one health problem after another, but she kept a cheerful countenance; so cheerful that her home in Los Angeles was often filled with well-wishers. Chapter 1 deals with Genora's early years in Flint, Michigan, and why the automobile industry decided to settle there in the early 1900s. GM was cordially welcomed to Flint because it brought economic prosperity. In time, however, rifts developed between GM and the workers to such an extent that Genora felt compelled to remark, "Once you pass the gates of General Motors, forget about the United States Constitution; workers had no rights when they entered that plant."[8]

Outside of her working life, Genora enjoyed piano lessons from her mother but endured hateful messages from her father, who joined the Ku Klux Klan. This trauma impacted her life significantly, as she continually strove to separate her own persona from that of her father. Later, as an adult, Genora joyfully joined the NAACP. Her motive here was to do well by a mistreated minority, but there could have been a subconscious rebellion against her bigoted father. It is probable that she loved her father, but she did not like him. Chapter 1 also shows the influence on Genora of Carl Johnson, father of Kermit Johnson, Genora's first husband. Carl was a "prairie populist," and his writings had an influence on Genora's young, developing, and impressionable mind. She became a Socialist by fifteen and remained one for the rest of her life.

Chapter 2 deals with the sit-down strikes of 1937 against General Motors, the most powerful automobile maker in American history. Genora's first husband, Kermit Johnson, was a strategic leader against GM, and Genora and her female colleagues wanted to work with him. But they refused to do the usual things in strike situations—such as making sandwiches and coffee and offering vocal encouragement. Genora was bound and determined that she and her ladies-in-arms be in the front line of these events. She and her followers joined the strike as equals with the sit-downers. Few labor histories have credited these women with major accomplishments, but it does seem clear that they were instrumental in bringing victory in 1937 to the UAW against mighty GM.

Chapter 3 discusses the lure of Trotskyism for Genora, especially during the heady days following the end of the sit-down strikes in February 1937. She was now famous on the local level, well-known throughout the state, and even noticed internationally when the photo of her and her son Jody standing in a picket line was printed in European newspapers. Her role in the Flint strikes further deepened the estrangement with her father because many of his friends began asking him about his "Bolshevik" daughter.

The Socialist Party in Flint, wishing to make the most of Genora's notoriety, sent her on an extensive speaking tour to industrial cities in

New England and along the Atlantic seaboard. She spoke to thousands of union people: here was a high school dropout lecturing the rank and file of unionism and giving advice to union leaders on how to win victories against major corporations. She always included discussions of the WEB, which had contributed so much to the victory in Flint.

With the Great Depression, many unemployed persons set up tents in Flint's Oak Park after being ejected from their homes because they couldn't pay rent. A confrontation resulted between several unemployed workers and the city of Flint. Genora and Kermit quickly joined them, eventually helping to win their case. The Johnsons were not totally altruistic: they did a bit of proselytizing for Socialism. But factionalism in the Flint Socialist Party led to the ultimate expulsion of the Johnsons. Immediately they became members and leaders of the Socialist Workers Party, positions they held for several months. This chapter also addresses the growing separateness of Genora and Kermit. No matter how famous one becomes, there is always the need for balance between career and family, as explained in chapter 3. The chapter ends with her introduction to a man named Sol Dollinger, to whom she would be married for more than a half-century.

Chapter 4 touches on World War II and the continuing problems of being a revolutionary on the one hand and a wife and mother on the other. Sol was away with the U.S. Coast Guard for lengthy periods, leaving Genora with two small children (from her marriage to Kermit Johnson), households to manage, and recruitment activities for the cause of Socialism. Blacklisted because of her activities against GM during the sit-down strike, she moved to Detroit where she hoped her name would not be as recognizable as in Flint. She was hired by several plants, but her past kept catching up with her. She did become, however, a chief steward and was fired three times. She continued to wrestle with the problem of the no-strike pledge of unions with the windfall profits that corporations seemed to be making during World War II. This chapter includes Genora's work on the Investigative Committee that looked into violence against union workers. Her labors here almost got her killed. She and Sol were viciously attacked on October 15, 1945, by two men. Genora spent several weeks in the hospital, where physicians worried that she would never recover her motor abilities. And then her youngest son, Jody, was killed, adding to the string of tragedies Genora suffered in the immediate postwar period. As the century reached its midpoint in 1950, Genora bounced back and looked forward to a new decade that could very well be dedicated to the new woman.

Chapter 5 discusses Genora's political bids, first as a U.S. senatorial candidate and then as a representative from Michigan's Sixth District. She barely registered any votes in either election. When she realized that she was not going to represent Michigan in any capacity in the U.S. Congress, she threw herself wholeheartedly into Socialist activities in Flint and elsewhere. During this time she had to contend with the death of Ray, her father: the love and affection that had been missing for her father in life came full force with his death. And then she had to deal with the death of her oldest son, Denny, from multiple sclerosis. Genora kept up a front here; the audiences who heard one fiery speech after another had no idea what kind of personal agony she was suffering.

By the mid-1950s she had attracted the attention of the Federal Bureau of Investigation (FBI). As it turned out, this governmental agency kept a watch—a very close watch—on both Genora and Sol Dollinger. Some of the things they had been saying during this time were not compatible with what the FBI thought was in the best interests of the country. Chapter 5 includes the ideological quarrels that began in the SWP between the Stalinists and the Trotskyists; the end result was the retirement of Sol and Genora Dollinger from the SWP to the Socialist Union of America (SUA), where they stayed for only a few years. The chapter ends with the opportunity for the Dollinger family to move to the Golden State, an offer they readily accepted.

Chapter 6 picks up Genora's activities in her new home state of California. Though she was no longer directly connected to reform movements in Michigan, in the NAACP, the ACLU, and as columnist for several union magazines she continued to find causes in California to champion. She was still in demand around the country for speeches; some labor leaders called her the grande dame of the union movement. Though at first it excluded blacks, Genora joined the National Organization of Women (NOW), apparently believing that she and like-minded middle-class individuals could positively change this situation by being inside the organization rather than outside it. Genora and Sol, along with their son, Ronald, continued to visit Mexico while the family lived in California, and, as had been the case for the past several years, their travels were closely scrutinized by the FBI, who had hopes of catching them in some sort of subversive activity.

"It Makes My Heart Sing," the title of chapter 7, derives from the fact that after so many years of talking, grumbling, and even shouting about the virtues of Socialism, several people and organizations now began listening to her. She addressed the annual meeting in Los Angeles of the Organization of American Historians and got a standing ovation from this learned group. Her speech was titled "What Is Radical History?" Because she believed that Los Angeles schools were deteriorating both educationally and physically, she helped to found the Los Angeles Advisory Council, which ultimately included Ralph Nader and Paul Erlich as members. She participated in the 1970 Los Angeles teachers' strike, opening her home on Queen Ann Place to those individuals in the picket lines. She helped to form the People's Lobby to get Los Angeles smog under control. She addressed students at the University of California, Los Angeles, not only on smog but also on women's involvement in the early union movements. She participated in what became known as the second wave of feminism, based in part on the idea of married women getting into the workforce. By the time of the third wave, Genora parted company with the "libbers," for reasons explained in this chapter. She began to make several trips back to Detroit and Flint, where she addressed the new members of the UAW. Always in her speeches she was careful to make the connection between the rise of unionism and feminism. She became a four-square supporter of the equal rights amendment.

The Dollingers made trips to England, Spain, Portugal, and other parts of Europe, where they met with many supporters of Socialism. They returned from these journeys with new insights about the status of Socialism throughout the world. This chapter introduces the discussion about the closeness that began to develop between union and management, a closeness that Genora later called tuxedo unionism. And then there was the movie, *With Babies and Banners.* Genora was thrilled with this recognition but disturbed about the filmmaker's inclusion of several women who had not actually participated in the sit-down of 1937 and the portrayal of the EB. Nevertheless, Genora asserted that women were becoming more than window dressing.

Genora became involved with Dr. Barry Commoner's Citizen's Party. Its platform suited Genora's philosophy: public control of energy industries, support for human rights both at home and abroad, a reversal in military spending, a guaranteed job for everyone, conservation with an emphasis on solar power, and adequate food, housing, and medical care for all citizens. Her euphoria with Commoner did not last long, particularly when it came to the foreign policy plank of his platform. And, finally, this chapter indicates once again the onset of several illnesses and diseases that plagued Genora throughout her life. Despite these, however, she was bound and determined to make her voice heard.

Chapter 8 is an explication of how Genora came to believe that the UAW might as well be working for GM itself. There was no conflict. Everything management wanted, union acceded. On July 17, 1980, bronze plaques were unveiled in Flint commemorating the sit-downs of 1937. The governor, the UAW Board, and the mayor of Flint were there. Who was *not* there? Anybody and everybody who had had anything to do with the Flint sit-downs of 1937! Genora was invited to attend, but she refused. The young historians of the 1980s, she asserted, may have been sincere, but they possessed no analytical skills and therefore could not assess the role of feminism in the context of the rise of labor unions. This chapter also explains the Dollingers' trips to Europe and to China and Genora's reaction to Geraldine Ferraro's nomination for vice president in 1984. Her initial enthusiasm, however, turned to disfavor when she concluded that the democratic ticket in 1984 was actually no different from that of the Republicans' in their approach to avaricious corporations.

One of the greatest honors for Genora, and, ironically, one of the greatest disappointments, was the fiftieth celebration of the Flint sit-downs. She was ill at the time, but she was invited to make the keynote speech for the meeting of the "pioneers." The only problem for her was that the commemorations were jointly sponsored by GM vice president Alfred Warren and UAW president Owen Bieber. How could a representative of GM, which had fought the 1937 sit-downs and hired thugs, goons, and Pinkertons to do everything they could to prevent them, now have the gall to be one of the endorsing agents of the fiftieth anniversary? They were simply cashing in, according to Genora. When she heard that Henry Kraus was to make a speech, Genora agreed to attend. She went into a rampage against Kraus at this meeting. She spoke about Kraus's book, *The Many and the Few,* and her conceptions of its flaws. Her speech this night not only summed up her alienation from Henry Kraus but also helped to create a split in the Socialist community of the United States.

Returning to Los Angeles, Genora vented her anger against UAW president Bieber because he cozied up to GM management. Despite all these heady events, and despite numerous health problems, she and

Sol departed for Moscow in 1987. Neither was prepared to see the paucity of accommodations in the Soviet Union. Genora suffered heart troubles on this trip, and the couple was alarmed, to say the least, by what they saw in Moscow hospitals. Apparently, the only thing that pleased the Dollingers about their trip to Russia was that at this time—the late 1980s—Leon Trotsky's reputation in the Soviet Union was in the process of being redeemed. Back at home, Genora continued a barrage of letters to anyone she thought might listen to her. The chapter ends with Genora's helping to form the Labor Party of America (LPA) for working people. This went nowhere. Two weeks before her death she was giving a speech for LPA and for Socialist causes in general. She died in October 1995.

Chapter 9 is devoted to a summary and analysis of Genora's life and her contributions and their meanings in the context of the major issues that affected and influenced the United States from the 1930s to the late 1990s. Her life spanned much of the twentieth century, from its progressive impetus to its negative connotations. She read widely, not only in labor history but in feminist history as well. Authors such as Nelson Lichtenstein and Sidney Fine in the labor field caught her attention. Ann Gordon, Eleanor Flexner, and Sherna Gluck in feminist studies are among those who enlightened her about second and third waves of feminism in the United States. Despite all these learned treatises, Genora still fretted that not enough attention was given by either labor or feminist historians (or a combination of the two) to the *foundations* of all these movements. A sense of the past, especially with third wave feminism, seems to have gone by the wayside.

In the belief that it is important to gauge the feelings of those who come after us, included in this chapter are some statements from the classroom of professor Lauren Coodley of Napa Valley College. She showed the film *With Babies and Banners* to her students and then elicited statements from them. They gave concise, often charming opinions of their take on this Oscar-nominated movie.

There are many ways a person can become a revolutionary: family influences, educational experiences, or circumstances. None of these conditions would necessarily apply to Genora. She was raised in a devoutly religious family, she never finished high school, and the circumstances of her upbringing were far from suggesting any kind of poverty-stricken environment to justify antiestablishment revolts. She entered the revolutionary life through the back door, so to speak. One can be a revolutionary by departing from family norms, by epiphany, by observation, and by a combination of all these factors. One frequently hears the comment, "Don't forget your upbringing!" Genora became a revolutionary on several fronts *in spite of* her upbringing. She possessed a minority mindset most of her life. This caused her to fight racism, poverty, religious bigotry, and ethnic hatreds and to support the idea of nobility of work in relation to fair treatment from the big corporations.

This book tells Genora Dollinger's story in the context of the major events that were happening in the country during her lifetime—the Great Depression, World War II, the Cold War, the civil rights movement, politics, liberalism, environmental and educational concerns, international affairs, and, above all else, labor and feminism. She felt deeply about social justice and spent her life trying to achieve it. She was a person to be reckoned with in the last century; she still speaks to us here in this one.

One Genesis of a Revolutionary

Genora Johnson and colleagues could cite numerous precedents of women's participation in the context of labor union activities in the 1937 sit-down strikes. In strikes of 1828 and 1834, women in a textile mill in Dover, New Hampshire, won higher wages, better working conditions, and the right to organize. Following the New Hampshire example, women textile workers in Lowell, Massachusetts, won important victories—including the reduction of the workday to ten hours—in the 1840s. In Lynn, Massachusetts, women in the shoe industry formed a union called the Daughters of St. Crispin. By the turn of the century, women workers had actually organized on several labor fronts.[1]

In 1909, twenty thousand shirtwaist workers walked off their jobs in New York City. Historian Nan Enstad explains the strike's significance: "The shirtwaist strike is famous in labor both because it was the largest female-dominated strike to that date and because it inaugerated [*sic*] a string of large women strikes in the 1910s that dramatically asserted working women's political participation and firmly established women's unionism." One major achievement of this strike was the formation of the International Lady's Garment Worker's Union (ILGWU) and the Women's Trade Union League (WTUL). During the early 1930s in the Great Depression, "Unions embraced a public agenda devoid of an overt gender rhetoric . . . but still with 'gender hierarchies.'"[2] Women workers were not considered equal partners in the labor movements of the 1930s, in part, because "labor propaganda described the movements as male, while women were portrayed either as victims of the industrial system or as loyal supporters of their worker husbands."[3]

One unusual aspect of the Flint sit-downs was that some participants, both men and women, had previously taken worker-education classes from Roy Reuther (later head of the United Auto Workers [UAW]) that ranged from labor history to parliamentary procedures. These classes had been funded in part by the Mott Foundation, whose founder was one of the largest General Motors (GM) shareholders in the country. Genora, noting this irony, wryly remarked, "The people that first built the nucleus of the strike were primarily people who had gone through Roy's classes."[4] By the time of the Flint uprisings in the late 1930s, then, there were numerous precedents for widespread feminist activity in labor events. The thing that set Flint apart from earlier labor experiences was that women's activities of the nineteenth century were confined almost entirely to female unions. One of the first women to take part in an otherwise male endeavor was Mother Jones in the coal industry. Perhaps a successor to Mother Jones was Genora Johnson in the Flint sit-downs of 1936–37. All three elements—women of the nineteenth century, Mother Jones, and Genora Johnson—surprised a large number of people, mostly males, when they showed that they had the same organizational capabilities, not to mention bravery, as men. Women worked on GM assembly lines and in other industries that supported the giant automotive manufacturer. But, as with the coal industry, the overwhelming majority of workers in making autos were men.

The most militant labor mood in the entire country in the late 1930s was in Flint, Michigan. The incipient UAW wanted job safety practices, a fair wage, and, above all else, recognition as the bargaining agent for the GM assembly-line workers. They had been met with hostility not only from GM but also from the city itself. GM, the Chamber of Commerce announced, had brought jobs to Flint; why rock the boat? The Depression accentuated these differences between the workers and management. Why should some have so much and others so little?

The Flint where Genora grew up—she was born in Kalamazoo and brought to Flint in infancy—was an amalgam of nationalities. Canadians, British, Polish, Hungarians, and Russians, to say nothing of Americans from other parts of the country, poured into this area of Michigan where lumbering and cart-carriage making were chief occupations. Quickly developing class distinctions represented the rich, the middle class, and mostly the poor, just as in hundreds of other American villages. Incorporated in 1855, Flint, by 1902, was becoming a chief automobile manufacturing center, second only to Detroit. In fact, GM, the largest automobile maker in the world, was established in Flint in 1908.[5]

Genora's grandfather, Jarvis Albro, a young man with a Scandinavian background, arrived in Flint in the 1840s. He became a farmer, a county supervisor, and a drain commissioner; later he served as an officer during the Civil War and became forever afterward known as "Captain Jarv" or "Silver Tongue Jarv" because many times he had defended people in court who could not afford an attorney. A shortage of licensed attorneys kept him busy in litigation. Famous for his political independence, he refused to run with the pack. Inheriting the trait, perhaps, from her grandfather, Genora liked to tell friends that "non-conformity is a strong tradition in our family."[6] As one might imagine, Jarv became a powerful influence in Flint and, indeed, the entire county of Genesee. In national politics, he was a Greenback and Populist and then a strong supporter of Socialist Eugene Debs. In 1913, the year Genora was born, he voted, much to the chagrin of many family members in Flint, for Socialist mayor John Menton.[7] By the 1930s, Genora lamented, there were no remnants in Flint of the old Debsians. "I could never find any old Socialists from that period."[8]

Jarvis Albro married a woman named Carpenter (Carpenter Road in Flint was named after her family) and, being a religious man, was a founder of the Court Street Methodist Church just after the Civil War. Here his granddaughter, Genora Gertrude Albro, taught Sunday school. Later, Genora attended the Unitarian Church on Clifford Street in Flint.[9] She became attracted to the Unitarians in part because of their propensity to discuss problems of the contemporary world rather than those of biblical times in the way of most other churches.

Raymond Albro, Jarvis's son, was born in Flint but, as a young businessman, went to Three Rivers looking for a place to open a photographic studio, and there he met Lora Fuller. Their friendship became serious, and he persuaded her to return with him to his hometown, just to see what it looked like. Around 1910 the automobile was already transforming Flint from a village to a boomtown. Its citizens argued, "Oh, Flint is going to be on the map of the world."[10] Lora got a job making spark plugs at the Albert Champion (AC) factory. She was probably still single, for at that time society in general, and in little villages particularly, looked askance at a married woman working outside her household.

Genora's maternal grandparents, the Fullers, who had New England antecedents, settled in Three Rivers. Adai Bine Fuller could repair anything mechanical. Everything broken was saved for him on his periodic visits to the Albros in Flint. Adai was Genora's favorite grandfather. "She loved his northeastern accent."[11] Alice Elizabeth Lane Fuller was her favorite grandmother. Alice Elizabeth bore nine children, was one of the first women in Three Rivers to bob her hair as a sign of modernity, and, worse yet, she drank beer![12]

There was talk of Native American antecedents in Genora's ancestry, from a tribe in New England, on her mother's side. Perhaps, some said, this was partly why Genora always seemed to be interested in minority struggles. An admirer said that she "never thought much of having a family that dated back to the pre-American Revolution. It was as natural as breathing for Genora to accept people for what they were rather than for their origins."[13] Alice Elizabeth frequently told Genora and the other grandchildren that "somewhere in the family tree" was a French Jew.[14] This information pleased Genora Albro.

Genora's mother, Lora Fuller, was the cultured member of the family. Born in Three Rivers and a graduate of the Chicago Conservatory of Music, she taught piano lessons in Flint. While a music student in her youth, Lora had lived in Chicago with her aunt, Genora Wilcox. The experience was so positive that Lora decided that her first daughter would be named Genora. Throughout her pregnancy, Lora knew that the baby would be large (Genora, at birth in March 1913, weighed ten pounds). Her mother was a midwife in Kalamazoo, and Lora was comfortable in having her deliver her own granddaughter.

In her earlier years, Genora remembered her father, Raymond Albro, as loving and caring, but as time passed, he became increasingly offensive, especially after having too much to drink. After the Buick foundry in Flint was built in the early 1920s, many blacks arrived from the South, settling in the Thread Lake area, and antiblack sentiment grew.[15] Raymond Albro exhibited it. Each time he took Genora and her brother and sisters for a ride through the north end of town, he made them crouch down, presumably because he was afraid they would be attacked by blacks as they rode through the colored districts of Flint, Michigan. Even then, at a tender age, Genora wondered, why—what's the problem? The question stayed with her for the rest of her life and helped considerably to turn her into a reformer. Later in life, she joined the National Association for the Advancement of Colored People (NAACP) to promote fairness and equality for blacks and other minorities. Her motive in joining the NAACP was to improve racial relations, but, in all probability, a subconscious response to her father's attitude toward race played a part.

Ray became a member of the Ku Klux Klan in the mid-1920s, a time in America when this group claims to have reached its height in membership. A proprietor of his own photographic shop, and in time branching out to operate several of them, Ray apparently thought that black migrants in the 1920s posed a threat to Flint society. Genora's relationship with her father helped her to become not just a reformer but an aggressive one. Ray apparently believed that a man was a superior being, with rightful power over his wife and children, even to the point of beating them from time to time. He made no secret about being disappointed when his firstborn was a girl. The detestation she felt for her father escalated as she grew older. "I felt . . . that never would I take a second place, in so far as I could help it, to any male—any boy, or any man."[16] She came to hate the machismo that her father displayed. A real man, she felt, was "kind and warm and affectionate and never macho."[17]

Jarvis Albro, Genora's brother, named after his paternal grandfather, worked for Chevrolet Gear and Axle in Saginaw, Michigan, but gained statewide attention by singing in a barbershop quartet. Like Genora, who had an alto voice, he always sang during festive occasions, especially at Christmas. Genora's sisters were Barbara and Beatrice, the two youngest in the family. Genora's father often commented on the odd family he and Lora had produced. Barbara married Dial Clifton, a "hillbilly" from Missouri who worked with AC Spark Plug and was a union man. Beatrice married Oscar Coover Jr., whose father, a confirmed Trotskyist, had spent some time in jail.[18]

Times had proven so well for Ray Albro in the booming 1920s that not only did he expand his photography business, but he also built a house on Garland Street—in an affluent neighborhood—for his family, with two apartments attached to rent. He made an attic apartment in the third floor of the house where, later, his rebellious daughter and her husband lived, causing a number of family rifts.

In due time, Genora was enrolled at Stevenson Elementary School in Flint, and she made some basic decisions that influenced her later life. One student never had the equipment the teacher asked him to bring: things like pens and paper on which to draw and write essays. The teacher failed to understand that the offending student was poor, not recalcitrant, and that he actually could not afford to buy what the teacher demanded. Genora took her weekly lunch money and bought the necessary supplies for the needy student.[19] This could well have been Genora's first overt action against what she considered to be injustice and unfairness. She began to believe that teachers, especially, should not jump to conclusions about the actions of people: opinions and situations should have factual bases behind them. She sensed that most of the problems in this world came from people—like her teacher—who expressed opinions without having any facts to support them. Surely, she reckoned, this accounted for most of the racial prejudice in the world, along with religious bigotry and ethnic hatred. She vowed never to fall prey to these human weaknesses.

Sixth grade students at Stevenson had opportunities for electives; however, the teacher made it clear that the boys should choose auto or woodshop, and the girls were to opt for cooking or sewing. Predictably, Genora picked auto shop, only to be denied. She then organized herself and four other girls into a demonstration, walking around and around the school, wearing overalls (unusual for that day—the early 1920s), until the principal, Mary Kelly, called them to her office. Miss Kelly contacted all the parents involved and told Raymond and Lora that they had better watch Genora, for she definitely had nonconformist tendencies. Though Genora did not get auto shop on this particular occasion, there were many assembly-line jobs in her future. After Stevenson Elementary, Genora enrolled in Central High School in Flint, where she excelled in English, drama, and music, playing both the clarinet and ukulele and having a full-sounding alto voice, for which she credited her mother.[20] In fact, Lora wanted her to be a musician, and for two and a half years Genora took piano lessons at the Baker Conservatory of Music. Tiring of the piano, Genora took acting lessons. She caught onto these right away and used them to good advantage in future activities.

She loved Sunday school at the Methodist church because it gave her a forum for advancing Social Gospel ideas to her young students. These ideas, propounded by the likes of Josiah Strong, Walter Rauschenbusch, and other major reformers who were at their pinnacle around the turn of the twentieth century, held that good governments do have a right and a duty to help the underprivileged and that big corporations should be controlled for the public interest. Like the Unitarians, the Social Gospellers had a sense of presentism. Human beings live in the here and now, and there were grievances in the community that needed attention not only from the government but from society itself. Why would a young girl raised in a Protestant Christian environment forsake almost everything that had ever been taught to her by both school and family and embrace what many Americans regarded as godless Communism or Socialism? It was a combination of love, life, health, and happenstance that caused such a drastic change in Genora Albro's outlook and philosophy.

Kermit Johnson, a year older than Genora, went to the same school, but they did not share many social contacts. Kermit was considered working class, while Genora's father, with his photographic shops, was upper middle class. Genora could not go out on weeknights, only on Friday or Saturday, and then only as late as 11 P.M. On some of these weekend occasions, she began dating Kermit, and she worried that her father would disapprove. Raymond did not foster a happy home life and was abusive, especially to his wife. "My father was a man you couldn't show any fear of. If he saw just a glimmer of fear in your eye, you were sunk. And he never saw that in my eye." These thoughts did not turn her into a man hater, but they caused her to think in terms of equality when issues of gender cropped up. This absence of fear—in addition to an impulsive nature—caused Genora to run away to Bowling Green, Ohio, and marry Kermit simply because—if we are to believe her—she lost a coin toss. One of Kermit's fellow band members had been going steady with a co-ed. Since the band usually traveled with the basketball team, the two couples told their parents they were going to a game in Bowling Green, where several justices of the peace married young couples without checking into their background, making Bowling Green, Ohio, popular among love-struck young people. Unknown to the parents, however, there was no basketball game that night in Bowling Green: Kermit's friend and his girlfriend were traveling to Ohio to get married. Kermit and Genora came with them to witness the event. Just after this couple exchanged vows, the bride in effect said to seventeen-year-old Genora, "Well, since we're here, why don't you and Kermit get hitched?" Genora agreed on a coin toss. She picked heads. It came up tails, which meant she'd marry Kermit. "Boy, I'm telling you," Genora later said, "I must have had spaghetti for brains." When the two returned to Flint, Kermit went to his home and Genora to hers. Raymond and Lora wanted to know how the basketball game had gone. She remembered, "I suddenly became physically ill, sick to my stomach." Genora and Kermit carried on the charade for several weeks. They continued in school just as though nothing had happened. One day at home, Kermit's mother said something derogatory about the Albro family, and Kermit exclaimed, "You can't talk like that about my wife."[21] The secret was out.

As could be expected, all hell broke loose in the Albro household. Raymond locked Genora in her room; she climbed out a window and contacted Kermit. Her father wanted to put Kermit in jail for what he considered to be a violation of the Mann Act, a federal law that forbade a man from taking a woman across state lines for sexual purposes. But Genora and Kermit had not yet consummated their marriage. Raymond talked with an attorney, who said he could get the marriage annulled. When Genora heard of this plan, she got word to Kermit that he and she had to get to a hotel right away. "And that's the first time that I had sex." Things finally settled down, primarily thanks to Lora, the peacemaker of the family. Raymond resigned himself to having a son-in-law, so much so that he brought the couple to his studio and had a "beautiful" photograph made of them, which he then had printed in the society column of the *Flint Journal.*[22]

The pair soon moved to Ypsilanti, where Kermit worked as a general laborer. When Genora became pregnant, they came back to Flint, and both Kermit and Genora returned to high school. He graduated, and Genora stayed for a half-semester of her senior year and then dropped out, largely because of the pregnancy. In later years, Genora expressed pent up bitterness about these turns of events. She had intended to go to the University of Michigan, but her marriage and subsequent pregnancy scotched these plans. Her later statement that she might have gotten an abortion had she known such a thing existed may have been colored by sadness over the loss of her firstborn son, Dennis, who died of multiple sclerosis. Even before Dennis, she lost her younger son, Jarvis, to a motorbike accident. He had been riding the handle bars, with Dennis steering, when they were hit by a speeding taxicab. Maybe her later talk of abortion was a way of coping with these tragedies. She told a friend that the deaths of her two sons was a dark time in her life, and she made every effort to block it out of her mind. Of course, she could not do this, at least not entirely; her lost sons were always with her in her thoughts, showing that one's personal life is always indelibly intertwined with one's professional activities.

Kermit Johnson's father, Carl, originally from South Dakota, had been a "prairie populist" before he found work at the Chevrolet division of GM.[23] In time he became an activist in Socialist movements and deemed Flint an excellent location to put his political, economic, and social philosophies into action. Although a longtime member of the American Federation of Labor (AFL), Carl gradually came to believe that it was not strong enough to achieve labor and social justice. An avid follower of the country's most noted Socialist of the day, Eugene Debs, he founded the League for Industrial Democracy and then the Flint chapter of the Socialist Party of America. He recruited members from GM and other industries in the area; helped to form a union newspaper, the *Searchlight;* and for years wrote a column for it titled "Only More Democracy Can Save Democracy."[24]

An important activity of the Flint Socialists consisted of small groups meeting each week and studying the history of past labor struggles. The members heard about the Molly Maguires (a group of militant coal miners in Pennsylvania in the 1870s), the Knights of Labor, and the Brotherhood of Sleeping Car Porters.[25] They discussed, among other things, the plight of the proletariat in America and why something should be done about it. They learned that doing the right thing always demanded a price be paid. In these study sessions, the Flint Socialists prepared themselves for the confrontation with GM they increasingly began to predict.

Genora was enamored of Carl's explanations of the world and how it should be fixed. Under his tutelage, she learned of the direct connections between economies and politics.[26] This became one of her first formal introductions to the world of Socialism. Why were Americans suffering through the Great Depression, which had begun with the stock market crash of 1929? Why wasn't President Herbert Hoover doing something about it? Government, she heard from Carl Johnson and other Socialists, comes into existence not simply to make people behave themselves but to help them in times of need. Where was help from the government? Not only was there not any, but also President Hoover seemed downright hostile to the idea that government should take care of its poor and needy citizens. The proletariat especially, Socialists believed, suffered hard times in the United States; they thought the Union of Soviet Socialist Republics (USSR) provided better for poor people than the United States did. Ultimately Genora outpaced Carl Johnson and other

Socialists in Flint in ideology; she was a fast reader who digested and retained the written word better than most of those around her.

To Genora, the best part of the Socialist Party was the way it treated women. Neither the Republicans nor the Democrats put a suffrage plank in their platforms until 1916. Yet, in 1901, when the Socialist Party was formed in America, women were present as delegates. Within a few years, women in the party were receiving grant monies and organizational support "for reaching women and agitating questions of special relevance to women."[27] Genora learned that "no other political party in American history has ever fought as consistently for women's rights" such as suffrage, employment opportunities, and equal rights as the Socialist Party. "The Socialist Party's conception of what women's rights were . . . agreed in all respects with those advocated by liberal feminists."[28]

Genora landed a job as an assistant to a Flint pediatrician and worked in his outer office as a receptionist. It seemed appropriate employment for her as she was expecting a child herself. The physician received many magazines, and one of them, *American Guardian,* was published by well-known Oklahoma Socialist, Oscar Ameringer.[29] Someone, Genora reckoned, had seen *American Guardian* in the pediatrician's office and had thrown this "offensive" journal into the wastebasket. Out of curiosity, she retrieved it and began reading. The articles in this magazine reinforced what she had been hearing from her Socialist colleagues. Justice for the working man? What right-minded individual could not be in favor of such? It certainly was not unusual for such subjects to be readily available for discussion in Flint, Michigan, one of the flashpoints of the twentieth-century labor movements. She read the articles in the discarded magazine with increasing interest and wondered, first, why it had been discarded and then decided to find out the realities behind the articles. In the magazine an advertisement appeared for the *Socialist Call,* and Genora subscribed.

With her elopement, having a baby, and getting a job, 1931 and 1932 were momentous years for Genora Johnson. All through this period she suffered from a mild cough, to which she gave little thought or attention. One night at home after supper, however, she and Kermit were having coffee when suddenly and without warning the cough worsened. "I must have coughed up a cup of blood."[30] Trying to control her panic, she telephoned Dr. Stevenson, the pediatrician for whom she worked, and calmly announced that she had coughed up blood. The physician came immediately to her apartment and diagnosed tuberculosis (TB).

Genora's affliction surprised no one in the Albro family. Her father's brother and sister had both died of tuberculosis, or consumption, as it was generally called at the time. Knowing how contagious the disease was, her relatives gave Genora all kinds of excuses why they could not visit her in the hospital. Genora was skinny and accustomed to being out in all kinds of weather. Perhaps the physical and emotional stresses she had encountered in recent months had aggravated the situation.

Whatever the cause, it was serious. At Hurley Hospital in Flint, physicians found two cavities in her lungs, one "as big as a nickel and another as big as a quarter." She stayed in the hospital for three months and was treated experimentally with a revolutionary medical technique. Twice a week doctors injected air through the chest cavity to the outside of the offending lung to collapse it, a laborious and painful procedure. With the lung collapsed, they could treat it. This was a frightening experience for Genora because she came close to death on several occasions. The physicians did not know how to determine how much air to pump into a lung; the amount for a man, for example, sometimes differed greatly from that for a woman. According to Sol Dollinger, "Many mistakes were made and the unlucky patients paid for the error with their lives. She [Genora] saw many large men carted out of the hospital ward because of the trial and error method."[31]

Unfortunately, this was just the beginning of Genora's health problems. In 1933, at the age of twenty, a relapse of TB caused her to spend another three months in a medical treatment center, this time at the Ingram County TB Sanatorium. Genora fussed at her mother for writing letters to her using her maiden name: "Now mother, you know I'm married, so why do you keep sending letters to Miss Genora Albro?"[32] She recovered somewhat during 1934, particularly after spending three months in the rarefied air of Denver, Colorado.[33] Kermit renovated an old car and built a makeshift bed for the trip. Neither Kermit nor Genora found gainful employment, so the State of Colorado—to avoid welfare—paid their expenses back to Michigan. Genora became pregnant with Jarvis (Jody) on this trip. At this stage of her life she knew nothing about birth control, and it would have shocked her friends even to have mentioned the subject. "They thought I was so far ahead in all my political ideas anyway, and racial ideas. . . . [I]t was a part of your private life and you just didn't talk about it with anybody."[34]

Because complications arose when Genora gave birth to her second son in 1935, Lora took care of Jarvis for her. Genora chafed at being absent from her two sons, especially her newborn, writing to Lora that "it seems like I get all the hard part without any of the fun that goes with having a little teeny new baby." She worried that a "bottle baby never has quite the chance against colds and disease." Fluid built up in her chest, requiring a thoracentesis for relief. The attending physician, Dr. A. Froelich, was a refugee from Vienna who had fled Hitler's Austria. He was all business and did not communicate well with other people. Genora needed some kind of diversion from the painful needle insertions into her chest, particularly since the needle sometimes missed the mark as it tried to find the pockets of fluid. Each time this happened, the doctor had to reinsert the long, sharp needle. Hoping to liven up things even just a little, Genora said to Herr Froelich, "I hear you are from Vienna. What do you think about the Karl Marx apartments?" "What do you know about the Karl Marx apartments?" the astonished doctor asked. "I am a Socialist," she said quietly. "I read about the resistance made to Hitler's army at these apartments in 1934."[35] The Karl Marx Hof, designed by Karl Ehn, was constructed between 1926 and 1930. The tenants were "socially homogeneous" in a "protective enclave" where they propounded upon the life and principles of Karl Marx. Individual apartments and courtyards were connected through a central building where all their meetings took place.[36] A rapport now developed between the famous Austrian doctor and the young neophyte Socialist. Froelich gently nursed her back to health and sent her home to Flint. For the next two years she continued to have pneumothorax treatments as an outpatient at the county hospital. During this time, her attending physician, H. Winchester, arranged for the county government to supply Genora with an extra quart of whole milk a day, believing that it would help in the curative processes. The long periods of treatment gave Genora plenty of time for study, reflection, and reading.

Always the most religious member of the Albro family, she taught Sunday school at the Methodist church and participated in church socials and singing events. While confined to bed during her bouts with TB, she read everything she could find about the world's religions. She wanted to know how and why religions were created. She read lives of Zoroaster, Christ, Mohammed, and the Buddha, and she studied Bahaism. Steadily she came to realize that the founders of the world's great religions were simple—not simplistic—people who created beliefs that were noncomplicated. Later, these religions were institutionalized to include beliefs and requirements that had nothing to do with the founders. Human beings created dogma, she reckoned, and dogma was not a perfect persuader. Interspersed with her religious readings was Genora's study of the various Socialist movements in the world.[37] As she read Marx, Lenin, and Trotsky and learned of women labor reformers such as Rose Pesotta, Elizabeth Gurley Flynn, Rose Schneidermann, and Rose Pastor Stokes, she discovered totally different religious and philosophical worlds from the comfortable one in which she grew up. When she read and heard about the events of the day, including so much labor unrest at GM and elsewhere throughout the country, she began to see what in her own mind was the hardboiled capitalist attitude of management toward labor. Accordingly, she plunged herself into the Socialist activities of the time.

She had been involved intermittently in the Young People's Socialist League (YPSL). Now she began to attend meetings of the League for Industrial Democracy, where discussion topics ranged from the Molly Maguires to Terence Powderly's Knights of Labor. Genora, who soon became a mover and shaker of the organization, began to alternate the places where the group met, setting up a chautauqua-type circuit of sending speakers to various locales. These speakers included Norman Thomas, who became the national head of the Socialist Party, and Walter Reuther, who later headed the UAW.

The conditions in and around Flint in the early 1930s were conducive to many labor-management upheavals. Threats of strikes were a daily concern. Political, economic, social, and philosophical ideologies multiplied on a regular basis. Genora recognized the plight of blacks from the South: they lived in corrugated metal huts and tarpaper shacks with no inside plumbing and only primitive toilet facilities. "You wouldn't think of raising animals in such places," she snorted, "let alone children."[38] Fie on a government that allowed such conditions, whether it be in the North or the South. If capitalism under Hoover and Roosevelt could not fix the problem, then perhaps some form of Socialism could. Socialism offered many forms from which to choose. Reform Socialism sought to change society without overthrowing government. Revolutionary Socialism, expounded in various ways by the followers of Karl Marx, taught that old forms of government had to be wiped out completely so that a new order could be created.

Genora was a Socialist by the time she was sixteen and ultimately came to believe in the philosophies of Leon Trotsky, a leading member of the Russian Revolution of 1917. Trotsky believed that the revolution could start in Russia, but its continuing successes depended on extending it to the industrial countries of the West. Russia was to be the "pacesetter" of the revolution, but its ultimate victory would come only if the proletariat in other European countries supported it.[39] "The battle cry of the party," Trotsky had written, "must be 'The Revolution in Permanence.'"[40] The defeat of the German revolution in 1919–23 led his opponent, Joseph Stalin, to expound the belief of building "Socialism in One Country,"[41] a slower method of world Communism than Trotsky envisaged and the leading cause of rivalry between the two Russians.

Genora was never a "card-carrying Communist,"[42] though, of course, she was frequently accused of it. She was, however, a lifelong Socialist of one variation or another. For the last forty years or so of her life, though still imbued with Socialist ideals and activities, she did not affiliate with any one branch of Socialism.[43] To most Americans, however—at least historically—Socialism equates with Communism. Americans fail to realize that several layers of Socialism exist and that one can be a practicing Socialist without being a Communist.

After many years of study—although she never did get a high school diploma—and deep reading in religious and political philosophies, Genora was prepared to embrace the cause of Socialist advances. She could not predict how she was going to do this, except that she knew—and had known for a long time—that if she ever did become involved in a major labor-management confrontation, she would not be in the kitchen making sandwiches and coffee for the men. She would be on the front line, as an integral part of it all.

The UAW strike against GM in 1937 was a culmination of grievances that had been brewing for years—brought on in no small way by the deleterious effects of the Great Depression—not only in Genora's mind but in those of many of her contemporary colleagues. What became unique about the strike was the sit-down technique and, most importantly, the role women played in it. The 1937 sit-downs were the first defining moments, if not *the* defining moment, in the life of Genora Johnson and, by extension, thousands of other women around the country. One could say that this was the impetus from which a great reform movement began to grow.

Two **Genora and Friends—Standing By Their Men**

The stock market crash of October 29, 1929, "Black Tuesday," heralded dark days ahead for the 1930s and social and political influences on American life that lasted for the rest of the century.[1] Unemployment grew to a steady 25 percent, with some cities like Cleveland and Toledo suffering more than twice that amount. Entire families from coast to coast "slept in tar-paper shacks and tin-lined caves and scavenged like dogs for food in the city dump."[2] By-products of the Great Depression included malnutrition, especially in the American South, and alarming increases in the crime rate as bank robbers like Bonnie Parker and Clyde Barrow terrorized the Midwest and outlaw John Dillinger became public enemy number one.

The crime rate could very well have taken a significant swing upward on Monday, January 11, 1937, because, as it turned out, that would have been a good day to rob a bank in Flint, Michigan. City and corporation police were centered in just a few places—leaving other public and private concerns vulnerable—as talk of a Communist takeover consumed the opinions of company and town folk alike.[3] Genesee County sheriff Thomas Wolcott and his deputies were out in full force. The Flint fire department provided ladders for invading police to scale the heights onto the second floor of Fisher Plant Two, where most of the striking sit-downers were located.[4]

Since New Year's Eve 1936, some 2,000 automobile workers at the GM plants in Flint had been striking, many of them adapting the sit-down technique (i.e., just sitting down at their places of work and doing nothing; in effect, closing down the plant) to air their grievances.[5] Both outside lines as well as inside sit-downers complained about police harassment and taunting of the picketers. Walter Bergman, a Detroit professor sympathetic to unionism, telephoned some clergy friends and talked them into coming up to Flint to join the picket lines. If police saw the clerics, Bergman reckoned, they would back off out of respect for the church. The plan worked: the police, while not stopping their harassment, reduced it.[6] Sometimes GM representatives and Pinkertons infiltrated the picket lines in an attempt to provoke violence among the strikers. Some jujitsu experts were hired by GM to flip a man onto the pavement to make it appear that a unionist had done it. Men and women fought police and plainclothesmen on Kearsley Street. One woman received a seriously twisted arm by a policeman and another's face turned black and blue from a beating by the "authorities."[7]

Rumors had it that newly installed governor Frank Murphy might call out the National Guard, although there had been no overt violence during the twelve-day standoff.[8] On January 2, 1937, GM won an injunction against the sit-downers; the UAW, however, invalidated the order when they showed that the judge in the case was a major GM stockholder. Six days later, as an omen of things to come, GM announced that it would cut off the heat (it was sixteen degrees above zero, Fahrenheit) in the plant and would not allow any more food deliveries. Hundreds of policemen gathered directly in front of Fisher Two, on Chevrolet Avenue, fully intending to drive out, first, the picket lines, and then the sit-downers. Neither picketers nor sit-downers numbered more than a hundred persons.[9] In late afternoon a large number of UAW men tried to enter Plant Two to bring food, despite GM orders, to the barricaded strikers. The plant protective force denied them entry. The captain said he had lost the key to the entrance. The Union men gave him a count of ten to find it; when nothing happened, they took down the door themselves. As *Life* magazine reported, "It was a shouldering, pushing affair, and none were injured. The door lock was sprung and food brought in."[10]

At this minor confrontation, the uniformed men surrounding the plant fired buckshot and tear gas through the second story windows where the strikers were located; occasionally, a rifle was discharged. Simultaneously, numerous law enforcement officials tried to get through piles of overturned cars Chevy workers had left on the grounds leading to Plant Two. The police were met with paving stones raining down on their heads, as well as auto-door hinges (some of which weighed well over a pound), causing a retreat and keeping the picket lines intact. As this battle raged between police and striking sit-downers and picketers, the event got full coverage from the newly developed techniques of radio reporting. Households all over Flint—and, for that matter, Michigan and a fair part of the country itself—heard of the confrontation; many listeners had husbands, sons, fathers, and brothers in the midst of the battle. Much to the chagrin of the police and deputies, Flint citizens began to converge on the battle site. One such listener was a diminutive—at five feet four inches—slim woman with an alto voice (which carried a long way) named Genora, whose husband, Kermit Johnson, worked for GM and had taken a leading role in calling the strike in the first place. Genora reported, "This was my first experience with violence. I had heard about it. I had read about it. I thought I knew how to act under such circumstances, but coming into this situation I was terrorized."[11] Her terror soon mixed with anger. For the past several months she had worked with Kermit, trying to gain a rule against "speedups"—that is, running the assembly lines so fast that some workers could not keep up; they wanted better pay (more than their $1,296 annual wage), safer and less strenuous working conditions, and recognition of the UAW as their bargaining agent.[12] She deemed these demands reasonable: nothing to warrant getting shot at or possibly killed. With some bravado, she said, "I am going to walk right up to that firing line and let them shoot a woman and then maybe Flint will wake up and they will find out just what is happening here."[13] Many men, including Kermit, sought to dissuade her. "There is no point in a woman becoming a martyr to the labor movement," one person told her. She was both pleased and piqued at this assertion: pleased that someone cared about her safety and a bit angry because she thought it "sexually insulting." Why couldn't a woman be a martyr if she felt the need? Was this why, sometimes later, actually to her displeasure, many writers and commentators began to call her the Joan of Arc of the labor movement?

When the strike started on December 31, 1936, the usual "auxiliaries" were called forth. Women went to work cooking meals in the strike kitchens on Saginaw Avenue for the workers on strike and in the picket lines. Coffee and sandwiches came from the Pengelly Building, which housed UAW headquarters. Genora's idea, however, right from the beginning, was that skinny men can peel potatoes just as well as skinny women. To hell with expected household duties; women this time were going to join the strikers. This thought produced an odd agreement between the company and the strikers. GM did not want to risk women being hurt or even killed in the violence that seemed increasingly predictable. The strikers considered "their" women to be domesticated, ready and willing to do the housework. Genora said later that even the best men in 1937 "had no concept of what a woman could contribute, either in ideas or in action."[14] Even those in society who "spouted rhetoric" of family values and wifely devotion looked askance at domestic jobs, dismissing them as woman's work.[15] The work women did was "naturally" biological. They bore the children and had the primary responsibility of nurturing them. Women activists were restricted, generally, to the outside of the plants. Neither labor nor management would permit groups of women, even if they worked there, inside a plant. Sit-down organizers feared that the presence of large numbers of female workers would cause employers to exploit the situation "to their own advantage, sensationalizing the sharing of living quarters and discrediting the union in the eyes of the public."[16] GM agencies broadcast throughout the city that the sit-downers played cards, listened to music and programs on the radio, and were, it was actually reported, visited more than once by *senoritas de la noche.* Some women still at home were so distraught by these reports that a few actually threatened to divorce their husbands if they did not return to their households. Genora's group of the Women's Auxiliary spent much time convincing the wives of Flint to discount such corporate propaganda and support their husbands and sons.

Genora spent most of the late afternoon and early evening of January 11 shouting encouragement to the strikers and urging them to maintain resistance to the combined law enforcement agencies. At one point she needed to use the bathroom to wash the wisps of tear gas from her body. She walked from the picket line while some of the picketers accompanied her inside the plant and to the women's restroom. They found it locked; this was strange because during the strike there weren't supposed to be *any* women in Fisher Two. All eight of the company guards, part of the so-called plant protective force, had locked themselves into the women's toilet—apparently to escape the violence they feared would erupt—and refused to move all night long. Of course, they later received the opprobrium of friend and foe alike for their timidity, if not cowardice. Genora used the men's room.[17] Fisher Two's restroom entrance had swinging doors: one for entry and one for exit. Genora remembers a man coming out as she was going in, and his habits were so ingrained that, right in the midst of the conflict, he tipped his hat to her.[18] Refreshed and washed, Genora Johnson came out of Fisher Two and resumed her role as number one strike supporter. "They [the police] were firing buckshot and rifles at me" she said; it was at this point that she realized, "This is for real."[19] Fortunately, she was wearing a leather helmet, so the hits were mostly symbolic. She saw a friend, Fred Stevens, a Socialist and a president of the local bus drivers' union who had come to Fisher Two to help the sit-downers, jump over a pool of water that turned red as he was shot in the leg. Other bleeding men passed by her.[20] One eyewitness to these events was Robert Morss Lovett, a stockholder in GM. He wanted to see for himself how his "property" was faring at the hands of the sit-downers. "I saw . . . holes in the glass [of Fisher One] and dents in the metal sides. I thought these indicated wanton violence against my property, and asked how it occurred. Gun fire by the police, was the answer." These shots had been fired toward the second floor of Fisher One, "endangering the lives of my employees, whom I was beginning to like though they were on strike."[21]

These sights infuriated Genora as much as Mr. Lovett, but mostly she railed against the indignity of being fired upon. She ran up to a youthful Victor Reuther, who stood by a car with sound equipment in it. He had been using it to bolster the morale of the strikers. Now he told Genora that the batteries were running down, and it appeared that the strike action was going to be lost. "Please, Victor," she asked, "if they [the batteries] are going down, let me speak." She said to the police and other law enforcement officials, "Cowards! Cowards, shooting unarmed and defenseless men!"[22] And then she spoke to the women of Flint, most of whom, up to this time, had been spectators (among some 3,000 on the scene) of the confrontations:[23] "Women of Flint! This is your fight! Join the picket line and defend your jobs, your husbands' jobs and your children's homes!"[24] Further: "Do you know that these cops who are cowards enough to fire into unarmed men are also cowards enough to fire into the mothers of children? There are women down here. There are mothers of children down here that the cops have been firing into. I am making a plea for all of you women up there [in the crowds] to come down and stand beside us. . . . Break through please. For God's sake, come down here and help us."[25] And they did—nearly a thousand of them—one by one at the start. The first woman was grabbed by a policeman and she pulled out of her coat, but then the women joined hands and walked down the hill toward Fisher Two. The police dared not shoot a woman, especially in the back.

Some histories, including Sidney Fine's brilliant study, *Sit-Down: The General Motors Strike of 1936–1937,* refer to this situation as the "Battle of the Running Bulls."[26] According to some eyewitnesses, however, this is misleading.[27] The slang term for policemen in many areas and subcultures, including labor, was "bull." The insinuation in Fine's book, and others, was that the police or "bulls" left the confrontation in flight. This was not exactly so. They had guns and did not have to run. The women marching on Fisher Two apparently inspired a lot of better instincts that day, and the police and deputies holstered their guns and walked away. They did not wish to be remembered as the killers of children's mothers. The more accurate title is the "Battle of Bull's Run," Genora later said, although who coined the phrase is problematic. It was actually an "echo from the past."[28] Genora had heard stories all her life about the Civil War; after all, it had ended only forty-eight years before her birth in 1913. Her father and grandfather regaled their families with stories about the war. Included in these descriptions were the disastrous battles—for the Union—of Bull Run, in Manassas, Virginia ("run" in Virginia and some other southern states means "creek"). Because the policemen were already known as "bulls," it was a simple transposition to "Bull's Run."[29]

The police retreat brought union rejoicing. Genora, Kermit, and her younger brother, Jarvis, built a huge fire in a metal drum and stood around it, making up new words to familiar songs.[30] One was a parody of *That Old Gang of Mine:*

> Not a cop down on the corner,
> It's a pretty certain sign
> Our Union men are holding fast
> That Old Union Line.
> All the boys are singing strike songs,
> They forgot "sweet Adeline"
> Those Union Men are holding fast
> That Old Picket Line.[31]

Another parody came from "A Hot Time in the Old Town Tonight":

Now this scrap is o'er
the boys are sticking fast
We'll hold our Grounds
and fight here to the last
And when this strike is o'er
We'll have our contract fast
We'll have a hot time in the old
town to-night.[32]

And finally:

Oh, it was a jolly sight on that wintry chilly night
When the bulls came out to throw us from the fort,
But with bruises, bumps and jolts,
From the storm of nuts and bolts,
They just turned about and made a line for port.[33]

Such heady feelings made some in the crowd believe that the strike was over and that the union had won. Nothing was further from the truth: the Battle of Bull's Run, if anything, was prophetic of things to come.

Bull's Run enlarged women's roles in the strike. The women at Bull's Run came to a "mature conclusion" of what must be done "if they and their children [were] to have a decent life," and they were "behind their husbands as long as there [was] a need."[34] Nearly a month after Bull's Run Genora wrote an article for *Socialist Call,* in which she boasted that "women from 16 to 65 went into action that would have made a cattle stampede on a ranch look like an afternoon stroll. . . . Yes, we women are as brave as our men any old day, and they'll fight to the finish and so will we."[35] This declamation was largely hyperbole. She had rejected the title of Joan of Arc of the labor movement and began making it clear that although she was happy at the uplifting of feminism during the strike, she was hesitant to lead a gender revolution. She insisted that the home be infused into the union and the union into the home, with the woman still in charge of the latter. It was revolutionary in 1937, from both the viewpoint of the striker and that of his adversary, that a woman would actually get out of the house and do something publicly controversial. Perhaps this was why newspapers began to refer to Genora Johnson as the Mother Jones of the Automobile Workers of

America. What Mother Jones had done earlier for coal miners, Genora Johnson was now doing for the auto workers. She much preferred this designation over Joan of Arc. She never forgave Sidney Fine, however, for saying in his 1970 book that the "participation of the women in the strike was probably more important for them than for the men."[36] Fine's statement, Genora believed, missed the point altogether. She avowed frequently that the Women's Auxiliary was not out to proclaim a sexual revolution; however, it was making a statement that women were just as capable as men, perhaps in some instances more so, of taking on dangerous situations.[37]

Noted labor writer Henry Kraus got some of the same cold-shoulder treatment when his book *The Many and the Few: A Chronicle of the Dynamic Auto Workers* referred to the auxiliary's work as "defensive feminism" that protected husbands in the Flint sit-downs and called these women "the girls."[38] But writing for the *Flint Auto Worker* the day after the strike, Kraus faulted the police for using tear gas and rifles against "peaceful pickets." Not a single city ordinance, he reported, had been violated when the police, deputies, and specially hired agents from the Pinkertons attacked. Kraus noted one event in particular: "One of the highlights of the evening was the speech of a young wife of a striker who blasted police for firing on unarmed women and children. It shamed the police temporarily into not shooting promiscuously into the strikers." The "young wife," of course, was Genora Johnson. Her speech also had the effect, insinuated Kraus, of causing the citizens of Flint to ask whether or not their police, supported by tax money, were not in fact shooting down taxpayers themselves. Some bystanders who came to the scene began shouting, "We don't pay you to shoot down people." "This night," wrote Kraus, "will be remembered long in the history of the labor movement both in Michigan and throughout the country. It was almost unbelievable."[39]

Shortly after the Battle of Bull's Run, the Michigan American Civil Liberties Union (ACLU) called a special meeting at Flint's Durant Hotel to hear the strikers' side of the story. The ACLU invited Genora to speak. "I went directly from the picket line. . . . My shoes were old and muddy. My hair was stringy and I was tired and exhausted." She explained the conditions of work in Flint as she saw them and described Bull's Run. She got a standing ovation.[40]

There were strong forces against the strike. First and foremost was GM itself. The Flint Alliance made up of chamber of commerce followers thoroughly objected to any and all labor organizations. Much to Genora's consternation, Flint churches also opposed the strike. The pastor of her own church, Court Street Methodist, adjured his flock into an antistrike position. Her father, Raymond, said he was ashamed to continue going to this church because of her activities in the strike. She later reported that it had been the pastor at Court Street who signed up her father in the Ku Klux Klan. Because of her pastor and congregation's attitude, she explained, she discontinued all of her relationships with the Methodist Church.[41]

Genora thought that a force was needed to counterbalance the antiunion biases in Flint.[42] She had heard that there were 40,000 GM workers in Flint (80 percent of the adult population in 1936),[43] with thousands out on strike. Surely such numbers could not ultimately be ignored. Genora formed what became known as the Women's Emergency Brigade, or EB, designed distinctly as a paramilitary group to help the Flint sit-down strikers.

The day after the Battle of Bull's Run, Genora called for women to join as a part of the strike rather than as a supplement to it. More than 100 women enlisted, and within a fortnight the EB had more than 400 members.[44] Genora was quickly elected as captain, not wanting to be general (for reasons she never made clear). She selected five lieutenants (Ruth Pitts, Fisher Plant One; Nellie Besson, A.C. Sparkplug; Sybil "Teeter" Walker, Redman Parts Plant; Inez Chapman, Fisher Plant One; and Tekla Roy, whose husband was fired from GM for wearing a union button) to help her run the group. Most of the officials of the EB either worked in GM plants themselves or had men in their family who did. They let it be known from the beginning that their work would not be in the kitchen; it would be on the front lines of the battlefield.

On January 19, 1937, the WEB was established in Flint, Michigan. Members of the press were called in, and they took photographs of this first meeting. After a few remarks from Genora and some other women, the meeting went "into a showing of Charlie Chaplin's *Modern Times*."[45] This movie personified the auto workers' adversarial relationship with GM: Chaplin becomes a "part of the mechanical process. He continues to turn nonexistent bolts after the assembly line has shut down." Watching the movie caused one Flint striker to exclaim, "Where you used to be a man now you are their cheapest tool."[46] The women wore red berets and red armbands with "EB" sewn into them as official insignias. There was to be no mistaking who they were. When the Women's Auxiliary membership shot up to 1,000 and the EB to 500, Genora became concerned: "We had a little grandmother in her sixties that insisted upon signing up. She wanted to be in the Brigade any hour of the day or night. And we had a young girl, she was about sixteen, I think, and she insisted." In fact, Genora began to make the EB's job sound more drastic than it actually was because she felt that elderly and younger women should not sign up. So strong was the feeling among the ladies of Flint, however, that not even Genora could dissuade them, even with a stark warning:

> Remember, when we go into a situation and if the police come out . . . and start shooting or throwing tear gas or clubbing, you stand at your post of duty. You do not move, and if your sister beside you goes down in a pool of blood, you do not get hysterical. You cannot join the Women's Emergency Brigade if you are going to lose your head and get hysterical. Do not sign up in the Women's Emergency Brigade, take your role in the strike kitchen, take your role in the first aid station.[47]

She also kept reminding would-be members of the EB that in the Battle of Bull's Run sixteen workers and eleven police had been injured.[48] Membership in the EB was not child's play.

Genora's speech was the first time the press started taking her seriously. One headline spoke of housewives going into battle with their brooms and mops. Even that was not accurate: they would more likely carry baseball bats than cleaning implements. Or, if not bats, clubs and blackjacks braided with upholstery leather, with wristlets to keep them in place. Some women carried soap bars wrapped in socks and sometimes filled with nuts and bolts. The picket signs they used were deliberately nailed onto two-by-fours that, if necessary, could be used as weapons.[49] "Whenever you saw one of those women," Genora proclaimed, "you knew she was ready for action . . . morning, night, or any time."[50]

The qualifications Genora outlined for membership in the EB "could easily have curdled the blood of most men." The pledge to the EB required women to "be prepared to stand in front of the men if shooting broke out." The severity of the pledge was designed to discourage all "but the bravest and boldest" of women. "This was War," Genora pronounced, "and we meant business! We weren't fooling around!" Auxiliary and EB members made at least ten times the sacrifices of men to participate in the strike. A woman had to take care of groceries, cooking, and laundering; find a babysitter; and see the kids off to school in addition to strike work. Some mothers brought their children to the Pengelly Building, where they were looked after by Wilma McCartney, a mother of eight who, at the time, was seven months pregnant.[51]

In addition to the child care center in the Pengelly Building, the EB also started a speaker's bureau and conducted short, intensive classes in labor history—particularly about women's roles—for whomever wished to attend. They dispatched "flying squads" to aid and comfort the unionists in nearby towns also affected by labor strife, inspiring the coining of the phrase "Flint is Coming."[52] A first-aid center was established, with trained nurse Bertha Simmons in charge, accompanied by a midwife and several assistants.[53] They conducted raffles to raise funds and even organized a couple of Saturday night dances! These activities were in addition to their main tasks of running picket lines and helping the men gain footholds in the continuing troubles. "Events moved so quickly," Genora later asserted, "and yet we did all this without any outside help—completely autonomous and independent of the male leadership!"[54]

Again, a strange coalescence of company and union ensued: the women of Flint who just a month or so ago were pictures of domesticity now came out in militant force. "We women don't want violence," Genora claimed. "We don't want trouble but we are going to protect our husbands."[55] Their motto was "Always ready for emergencies!"[56]

Genora told a Detroit paper, "I realized during that trouble women could and should play a prominent part in any future emergency. The idea of the women's battalion was born then. We will be ready in the future to have 200 at the scene of trouble in ten minutes." She added, "Any hard boiled cop will attest any one woman can give lots of trouble to those she doesn't love during a good free for all. . . . If there's a fight, we'll get in it. I was in my first one [during the Battle of Bull's Run] and police bullets don't bother me. . . . If we go into battle, will we be armed? Yes, with rolling pins, brooms, mops, and anything else we can get. You see, we're fighting the cause of the ones we love."[57]

Membership in the EB was electrifying for the women of Flint. As one of them said, "After this [joining the EB] there was no returning to dismal, pessimistic thoughts of before." New member Violet Baggett attested, "I found a common understanding and unselfishness [in the EB] I'd never known. . . . These people are real people and I'm glad I'm one of them. . . . I only wish I'd gotten mad long ago and investigated, but I didn't have time for anything outside of my small circle. I'm living for the first time with a definite goal. . . . I'm ready and glad to wear my beret and Women's Emergency armband anytime, anywhere I'm needed." She was glad to be among women who "help[ed] men in their fight for decent wages and working conditions."[58] It was like a "new breath of freedom," Genora exulted. The women in the EB were being emancipated from homes as well as poverty.[59]

Beyond physically and morally supporting their husbands, brothers, fathers, sons, uncles, and nephews in the continuing sit-downs at Flint, the EB asserted that it also had other important duties. One was to offer classes by teachers from nearby schools on parliamentary procedure, public speaking, and the history of the labor movement. Graduate students from the University of Michigan in Ann Arbor came in to teach classes in journalism and creative writing.[60] Another was to form a speaker's bureau to sponsor notable individuals to speak out on the labor conditions in America, with specific attention to GM.

Cornelia Bryce Pinchot, whose husband, Gifford Pinchot, was a conservationist during the Taft administration and a former governor of Pennsylvania, argued before a group of Flint EBs that the first entity in the country to use the sit-down as a way of protest was GM itself. The corporation, she said, had used it recently to denounce the regulations from President Franklin D. Roosevelt's National Recovery Administration. As a stockholder in GM herself, Mrs. Pinchot denounced its "defiance of the law" and "setting themselves above the law-abiding stockholders they are supposed to serve."[61]

Another speaker was a member of the British House of Commons. Speaking to the EBs, Ellen Wilkinson, or "Red Ellen" as some of her countrymen called her, was "amazed at the political and social backwardness of General Motors." The corporation's labor policy, "if it has one, is still in the nineteenth century. . . . British workers told me before I left for America that I must be sure to visit Flint and report on the American phase of the sit-in campaigns that are sweeping the industrial world everywhere."[62] Ellen Wilkinson was not just *any* member of Parliament. The previous year, 1936, she had participated in the famous Jarrow Borough Council's petition to Parliament in London and the subsequent 300-mile march from northeast England to get it there. Widespread unemployment was the motivating factor, but the march also highlighted the general unhappiness with the Unemployed Assistance Board that was not doing enough, it was universally proclaimed, to ameliorate negative economic conditions.[63] Wilkinson's appearance before the EB gave the organization an international boost and, for the most part, favorable publicity. After Wilkinson's speech to the EBs, professor Walter Bergman escorted her to Fisher Two. They were forced to climb up the ladders to the second story because management had locked the doors to the bottom floor.[64] She gave a tub-thumping philippic to the sit-downers, emboldening them to continue the strike.

Other EB-sponsored speakers included Mary Hillyer, wife a New York City official. She spoke to a mass meeting of the Women's Auxiliary at the Pengelly Building and mentioned—unfortunately without documentation—a confrontation that had occurred between workers and GM president William Knudsen just before Christmas. Because the workers were "a bunch of slobs," he reportedly said, they would not get any Christmas bonuses. The workers supposedly told him what he could do with his bonuses and began shouting "Knuts to Knudsen!" Rose Pesotta, an official with the International Ladies Garment Workers Union, also spoke to the EBs, and novelist Josephine Herbst told the EBs to "hold the line!"[65]

GM spokesmen fought back against these descriptions and charges. Alfred P. Sloan Jr., GM president of the board, wrote a general letter to the Flint workers telling them, among other things, not to worry about claims that if the union won, nonunionists would be out of a job. This was propaganda, he said, of the worst sort. "General Motors grew up on the principal that a worker's job and his promotion depend on his own individual ability—not the say-so of any labor union dictators."[66] Some of the sit-downers showed their opinions of Mr. Sloan by writing this little ditty:

Oh Mr. Sloan, Oh Mr. Sloan
We've known for a long time
You would atone
For the Wrongs that you have done
We all know, yes everyone
Absolutely Mr. Sloan
Positively Mr. Sloan
Oh Mr. Sloan, Oh Mr. Sloan

Our homes are what we all now wish to own
But living costs are high
So we are out to do or die
Absolutely Mr. Sloan
Positively Mr. Sloan.[67]

Sibyl N. Walker, a member of the EB, gave her opinion of the top leadership at GM:

Wishie Washie
Wishie Washie
Give them soap
We've got old Sloan's
and Billy's [Knudsen] goat
We'll wash 'em and scrub 'em
And bring 'em to time
Then hang 'em to dry
On the old picket line.[68]

The UAW leadership also struck back at Sloan's assertions. Homer Martin, president of the union, despite having been described by his enemies as a "drunken butterfly" who "didn't know from one minute to another what he was going to do,"[69] wrote clearly to Sloan that at 78.6 cents an hour at forty hours a week, the average GM employee did not make enough money to buy even the cheapest GM product.[70] This was social vision? Not likely, scoffed Martin and the vast majority of his membership.

In addition to bringing in speakers and publicizing the opinions of strike and corporate officials, the EBs also launched an all-out effort against what they perceived to be a continuing program of propaganda and intimidation sponsored by GM. They began to deliver letters to the sit-downers from their wives, and many of these letters painted stark, realistic pictures of what it was like to be an industrial worker during the Great Depression:

"Patient wife and baby" needed to pay the house rent. "If you will sen[d] me your badge I can get your check. . . . I am going to welfare tomorrow. Are you getting enough to eat? And are you warm? . . . Well honey, I wish they would hurry up and settle it. I want you to be home."[71]

"Dearest Joe: . . . I will send your banjo and other things. . . . I hope you have enough clothes. . . . I sure am glad to hear you miss me and Melba. We all miss you. But don't give up. It won't be long."

"Dearest Vess: Heard there was flu and dysentery in the plants. If you are sick, come home. Don't stay there and get worse. There is work at the union to do without staying in there. . . . Sure hope with all my heart the union wins and show[s] some of these people a thing or two."

"Dear Dad: Crowds at the Pengelly: thick and fast they come. . . . 1–2–3–4 who are we for? Sitters in! Sitters In! Boy oh boy! Hold the fort, for we are with you . . . heart and hand and soul we're with you. . . . Lots of Love to Daddy; Marja."

"Happy birthday, hubby dear. Keep up the good work. I was in the big workers parade yesterday. Wish you could have been with me. . . . Wife and daughter Minnie and Ann. P.S. The strike is almost won for us."

And the men wrote home, in particular about the GM tactic of telling the women that their husbands were ill:

"If anyone goes to the house ask him their name. We will do the rest. If they don't want to leave, shoot the bastard. . . . They'll do anything to get us out."

Sam wrote to Lorene that "if anyone comes around and says that I am foolish for staying in you just order them out. I am fighting for a good cause."

Harold told Mable that "we are one happy family. . . . We are peaceful Chevy workers." And Tony apologized to Emma because "I cannot keep my date with you on Thursday." He was, however, "pretty safe with all these soldiers around."

On and on these heartfelt letters came from the strikers' wives, daughters, and sons, and letters to them, delivered by the EBs, showed that the workers, while determined to endure, still missed their families and home routines. In their entirety, the letters show that prolonged strikes come at a cost—not just in profits, wages, and salary but also in emotional expenditures.

Finally, an important result of forming the EB in Flint was that women in other strike-torn cities did likewise. Some fifteen GM plants were on strike in the early part of 1937, most in Michigan. "The news went out about the role women could play"—Detroit women wore green berets and armbands; Lansing wore blue; Pontiac, orange.[72]

The EB soon got into the dangerous business of confronting management thugs. Two years earlier, in 1935, GM had switched its Parts and Services plant from Flint to Saginaw. At the same time, it formed a "loyalty league" to combat unionization.[73] Also, apparently, GM hired thugs to use strong-arm tactics against any Saginaw worker who might want to join a union. One worker, Earl A. Parks, testifying before the LaFollette Committee investigating violations of free speech and rights of labor, quoted the chairman of the loyalty league, Daniel Robbins, as saying, "These organizers will find that Saginaw is a hot town; in fact, we will make it so hot they won't be able to stay. We might treat them to tar and feathers or run them out of town on a rail. We might send them home in a pine box with a bunch of Saginaw Forget-me-nots on top."[74]

In the middle of January, after the Battle of Bull's Run, a carload of union people went from Flint to Saginaw to bolster strikers' spirits there. On this first occasion, UAW members took a taxi from Flint to Saginaw. On the way back, corporate thugs ran them into a telephone pole, causing one of the passengers to suffer a concussion. Saginaw had "been impossible" for the union, Genora concluded. Robert Travis and other leaders in the Flint UAW thought that Flint speakers could substitute for Saginaw speakers to keep them from GM retribution if they appeared publicly. On the second trip to Saginaw, Kempton Williams, UAW organizer and active member of the Socialist Party, drove the new Pontiac of Merlin Bishop (the UAW educational director) "because we felt they [Pontiacs] had more power to get away than any of our little old cars." The other four who went with him were Bishop; Fania Fish, wife of the Flint Socialist Party (SP) organizer in Flint (who later became Mrs. Roy Reuther); writer Mary Donovan Hapgood; and Genora. Speaking to about fifty strikers in Saginaw, Genora noted that many of them wore bandages on their eyes, heads, and arms "from being beaten up." After the speeches, the Flint group left, accompanied to the city limits by cars full of Saginaw unionists armed with clubs. After a few blocks, however, "a great big black limousine zoomed in ahead of our car and another black limousine zoomed in back of us." Their intentions were clear. But driver Williams was a quick thinker. He turned off the lights to his Pontiac and sped up to eighty miles per hour. The group "went all the way to Flint and a good share of it with our lights off, zooming in and out, passing cars," in what Genora described with considerable understatement as "the most dangerous ride of our lives."[75] Inside Flint city limits, the group knew they had reached safety. The tension had been so high on the journey that no one actually spoke. Now they began to laugh and even cry some and sing because they knew this was their "little victory."[76] Hapgood began a union song, "When a scab dies, he goes to hell, parlez-vous,"[77] and everyone exuberantly joined in. They also rendered robust versions of "Solidarity Forever."

The strike wore on. GM would not negotiate with the UAW until all of its plants were free of sit-downers, and the UAW refused to negotiate with GM until its union had been officially recognized. Such stalemates brought public officials into the picture. Frances Perkins, FDR's secretary of labor, tried to get the sides together, to no avail. Other public figures urged that once again court injunctions be sought against the strikers.

In late January, GM offered nationwide employment on a part-time basis in any strike-free plant that had been idled by the stoppage in Flint. Some 40,000 GM workers around the country went to work; in Flint, about 11,000 resumed their employment.[78] These actions worried the UAW leadership as well as its principal advisor, the Congress of Industrial Organizations (CIO), headed by John L. Lewis. Ultimately, they decided that their best strategy was to enlarge the strike, and this meant taking a Chevrolet building that had previously been struck but had resumed work under GM's enticement. This was Plant Four, the sole producer of engines (as well as other equipment) for Chevy and "thus one of the two or three most important units in the entire GM complex."[79] In fact, it was the largest unit of all the Flint GM buildings; in normal times, it employed 4,000 workers, 2,000 on each shift.[80] If the UAW could capture this huge entity, its members felt sure they could win the strike.

From one point of view, Plant Four was logical because it had only two main entrances, first to take and then to keep. The plant was, however, only a third of a mile from the GM personnel building, which housed a "virtual arsenal" of company police, Pinkertons, and other officers.[81] A diversionary scheme had to be cooked up to get the attention of the lawmen away from Plant Four, at least long enough for the unionists to occupy it. Kermit Johnson, Genora's husband, worked in Plant Four and was the leader of the strike committee against Chevrolet. One night he came home with a "greasy little piece of paper in his hand."[82] It was a complete plan by which to take Plant Four. Workers in Plants Six and Eight were numerous enough to take Plant Four *if*—and this was a big *if*—the lawmen could be gotten out of the personnel building and sent to a distant place.[83] That distant place was Plant Nine. Put out the word that strikers were moving against it, and the police would flock to it. While they were away, the UAW would take Plant Four.

The plan was put to a vote by the SP in Flint (Kermit was a longtime member of the Socialists). Walter Reuther was up from Detroit, and he opposed the plan without giving any distinct reasons. He created ill will by making it appear that he was the big city guy, up here to show the locals how to do things. He obviously thought the plan had been put together too hurriedly, mentioning how long it had taken the American Federation of Labor to become powerful, and that nothing, not even bold union plans, could be done overnight. He told Genora that this was her first strike and that she was still "wet behind the ears." The UAW would have to learn how to "creep before we could walk."[84]

Genora typed a two-page, single-spaced letter to Norman Thomas, leader of the National Socialist Party, and outlined her husband's and his colleagues' plans to take Plant Four. Thomas, who believed the sit-downs symbolized a challenge to capitalism and that the Flint strikers were "harbingers of a new society," wrote to the SP secretary, Frank Trager, in support of Kermit's plan.[85]

At the next meeting of the Flint Socialists, Trager spoke strongly in favor of Kermit's proposal. Those assembled in Flint on January 21 certainly did not want to be at cross-purposes with national leaders. This time the voters approved Kermit Johnson's plan.[86] Walter Reuther (who had organized the Kelsey Hayes Plant in Detroit and from this action derived his authority as a union leader)[87] still adamantly opposed the scheme, again without saying specifically why, and he told Kermit that if the strike failed, it would be Kermit's fault.[88] Kermit and Roy Reuther (Walter's brother) were charged now with taking the plan to the strike committee for its members' approval, which they got in quick order. One wonders how the plan could have been discussed in so many meetings, committees, and letters (from Genora in Flint to Thomas in New York and back) without some kind of leak about their true intentions. It was the Socialist wing of the UAW who presented this plan, and their meetings were so small that infiltration by the police and company spies was minimal. The union people as a whole knew that company infiltrators were in their midst and apparently claimed in meetings that Plant Nine was targeted. The union deliberately leaked information to a corporate "spy" at a meeting that discussed only Plant Nine. "Nothing was mentioned about Plant Four."[89] That is apparently why Kermit's plans were never fully discussed at most meetings; it was only in secret sessions that Plant Four was mentioned in the context of Plant Nine. "We wanted GM to put all its guards on Plant 9 and leave Plant 4 free to be taken."[90]

On February 1, at the shift change around 3 P.M., the action started. Genora and her EBs appeared just outside the gates, wearing their red berets and red armbands. They were equipped with clubs of various sizes. When the police—who had been gathered at Plant Nine for some days, expecting an attack—saw them coming they formed a ring in front of the plant. The police pulled their guns and Genora ordered her followers to lift their clubs in defiance. Company officials quickly shut off the heat in Plant Nine. Suddenly Genora heard breaking glass and looked around to see Tom Kasy, a prominent auto worker, with blood all over his face and his head out a window, screaming, "They're gassing us in here!"[91] Immediately Genora and her entire brigade—about 100 of them—ran for the plant, pushing policemen aside, and began to knock out all the windows to let in air for the besieged men. Things cooled off for a little while, and company authorities apparently thought the incident had ended with a GM victory. Only Genora knew that the real action was taking place a half-mile away, down the hill, at Plant Four. She ordered all but five of the EBs to go back to headquarters at the Pengelly Building.

A group of union men, led by striker Ed Cronk, stormed Plant Four.[92] The union men at Plant Four got into a big fight with nonunionists and some of the foremen. The police had not yet caught on to the ruse; most of them were still at Plant Nine. William Carney, a union organizer from Ohio, called to Genora from inside the plant: "Hold that gate! Whatever you do, don't let the police get through that gate!"[93] The six EBs locked hands and threw themselves over the gate to the main entrance of Plant Four. The police arrived quickly, realizing now that Plant Nine was a diversion. They asked the ladies to leave; when they said no, the police wanted forcibly to evict them. "Over our dead bodies," Genora called out.[94] She said that they themselves probably had relatives inside that plant, and were they willing to put them in harm's way? In return, two or three of the policemen told Genora that GM was the "lifeblood" of Flint, furnishing livelihoods to large numbers of its citizens. Genora told them that she and her followers had a special name for the policemen: scissorbills, to denote any person "too dumb" to know that the union was for their benefit.[95] This dialogue was intended as a delay tactic to buy enough time for the entire EB to arrive on the scene.

And they did. A telephone call to Pengelly alerted the EB to the developing situation, and they marched down the hill, carrying a huge American flag in the belief that police would not fire on Old Glory (they were correct) and singing "Solidarity Forever." Genora instructed them over a sound truck to lock arms and form an oval picket line to prevent the police from entering the plant.[96] An eyewitness gave this account:

> Down the hill came the procession preceded by the American flag. The women's bright red caps showed dramatically in the dark crowd, as they were singing "Hold the Fort." Their return to the picket line was a moving sight to that crowd which knew the women had been gassed only a short time before at Chevy 9 in defense of their men. The line of bright capped women spread itself out in front of the high barbed wire gate. Clasping hands, they struck up "We Shall Not Be Moved."[97]

By now Michigan governor Frank Murphy had called out the National Guard. (In fact, he had activated the state's military units shortly after the Battle of Bull's Run.) Genora walked by one of the guardsmen, a young boy, whose "finger was actually trembling on that trigger."[98] He was, she averred, about as scared as she was. She wanted to get by him, to visit Kermit inside Plant Four. "I just want to go through and talk to my husband, and I will come right back out." The young guardsman told her sternly, "I have orders to shoot," and Genora backed off. "This is one battle I did not win. He was a very, very nervous young man."[99] She noted, too, the machine gun emplacements on top of the personnel building.

All over Flint in the early days of February, picket lines were in great abundance. Some of these lines—around Fisher One and Two—were motorized, with cars slowly driving around the buildings. The picket line continued at Plant Nine, and most of the EBs stayed on the scene at Plant Four, "while the police looked on sheepishly." City police, sheriff's deputies, and the National Guard threw a cordon around the plant, not allowing anyone in or out—not even for a cup of coffee, a toilet break, or food. Only after twenty-four hours, in the early morning of February 2, did the authorities in the plant permit any contact with the outside world.[100]

From inside the plant, Kermit Johnson wrote testily to Robert Travis, apparently believing that Travis and the local UAW were not giving him enough attention. "Is there some reason why you can't write to me? I find time to write to you and I haven't slept over three hours a nite [*sic*] since I've been here."[101] Some of his men were getting restless, probably because they weren't certain of what was happening on the outside.

On February 4, Johnson again wrote to Travis: "There is considerable dissension among the men in regards to messages from the outside concerning families, etc. . . . This will have to be remedied." He and his men wanted to be kept informed about their families and whether mail was being received for them in the personnel building. If so, "Why don't we get it here?" Above all, Johnson wanted to confer with Travis about further strike strategies. "Bring some cigarettes," he suggested, "as an excuse to come here immediately." He added forlornly, "Actually we need them anyway."[102]

Meanwhile, GM called for a "special payday" on February 4. All a worker had to do was come to the personnel building and collect his regular pay. If a worker did not present himself, he was assumed a "sit-in" with nothing in his pay packet. The company was accused of forwarding letters to the women back at home saying that if they could see who was keeping company with their husbands, they would know why many did not *want* to come home. There were prostitutes among them, it was said, and the sit-downers were indeed happy.[103] Nothing of this sort was ever proved, but the charges had a powerful influence. Reports were bandied about to the men inside Plant Nine and others that their wives were "ill," some seriously. Many men left the sit-downs to see to their womenfolk.

In the midst of the sit-downs, on February 3, 1937, a "Woman's Day" was proclaimed by the UAW to recognize the work and meritorious services of the women of Flint who had come to stand by their men. It wasn't just the Flint women: when word got around that this recognition was being planned, women's brigades from Detroit, Lansing, Pontiac, Saginaw, Bay City, Cleveland, and Toledo poured into Flint. It was their day, too, and they meant to observe it.

Defying all law and order (there was to be another injunction announced against the strikers) the congregated women—about 700 of them[104]—marched through a tense Flint with their children and carrying placards that read, "Our Daddies Fight for Us Little Tykes."[105] Genora formed a child picket line even before the Battle of Bull's Run, after convincing their mothers that the striking men would protect them. She wanted press coverage other than from the *Flint Journal,* which she deemed unfriendly to the sit-downers. The strategy worked.

It was not long until Detroit papers and even some foreign ones began to note the activities in Flint.[106] Four abreast, they came through the Flint business district to show the world that these "were simple hard-working American wives and mothers." They sang,

We're the Wives,
We're the Mothers
Of our fighting union brothers.
We'll fight for our kith and kin
And when we fight we fight to win![107]

Flint city manager, John Barringer, whose metal casting factory was a chief supplier to Buick, was frustrated. The state police and national guard had decided to "lie low" during Women's Day, and he did not want those who favored the strike to gain any momentum. Barringer deputized 500 special deputies to force the sit-downers out of the factories.[108] With the Women's March, however, and the continued occupation of GM factories not only in Flint but in many other industrial towns across the country, a sense that public opinion was turning in favor of the strikers caused the deputies, or "vigilantes," as they were commonly called, to have virtually no influence.

After the march, a mass meeting was held. "By six that evening the hall was full of women—even men—standing in a solid ring around the [Pengelly] hall." Many there believed that they were seeing history in the making, "a movement in its moment of creation."[109] The "taking" of Plant Four and Women's Day in Flint were clear indicators that the sit-downs were in their final days and that GM was not going to be the winner. Many of the assembly lines depended on the products (engines, mostly, but also crank shafts) coming out of Plant Four for continued operations. In this respect, time was on the side of the strikers.

The day after Women's Day, at the time the court injunction against further union demonstrations was to take place, a dance started in front of Fisher Plant One. A ten-piece orchestra had been allowed—as a gesture of goodwill—by the authorities to go inside the plant; they used amplifiers to pipe their music to the outside. Some 10,000 union members, men and women, danced on the hard, cold ground in front of the building, where a light snow was falling. It was not a grand ballroom, but the exuberance and excitement of the moment could hardly be duplicated elsewhere. As the dancing continued the crowd built a huge fire, coffee and sandwiches were served on the lawn, "and the dancing continued way into the night."[110] The union definitely sensed victory.

All during the strike, federal mediators brought company and union together, or at least tried to. They faced tremendous pressure from FDR's White House and Governor Murphy's state house in Lansing to bring these difficulties to an end. Not the least of the factors considered was the economic damage done to capitalism and labor. The two sides, it was widely held, were destroying each other. Finally, however, GM offered a settlement.

The GM contract—written on a single page—recognized the UAW on February 11, 1937, as the official representative of the Flint workers. The strike was over. It had lasted forty-four days. About a month later, March 13, 1937, GM and the UAW signed a formal, albeit inconclusive, contract with one another. It did not, for example, provide for a steward system, but it did allow union committeemen, according to the size of the plant. Chevy was large enough to warrant seven committeemen.[111] This was the first labor contract GM had ever signed. It was indeed a historic moment.

Genora claimed later that the sit-downs had been an "educational process" for several workers up from the South. In one plant, they had shown disdain for the only black member present. His name was Roscoe Van Zandt, and as the strike continued, everyone emphasized their common cause rather than color of skin. When the strike ended, Van Zandt was chosen to carry the victory flag out of the plant and into a waiting public.[112]

As news of the GM recognition of the UAW spread, the "winds of freedom roared down Flint streets, filled with the mighty outpouring of its working people." Chevrolet Avenue was packed with some 5,000 people singing "Solidarity Forever," sending helium-filled balloons aloft, shooting fireworks, honking horns, and yelling, "Join the Union: We are Free!"[113] The multiple repercussions of the union victory included a Chrysler-UAW contract in April 1937, an increase in UAW members from 88,000 to 400,000, the creation of Local 152, and the takeover of the Flint city government. Moreover, "in the first two weeks after the Flint victory there were eighty-seven sit-down strikes in Detroit alone."[114] Throughout the rest of the nation, in March 1937, there were 170 sit-down strikes "involving 167,210 workers."[115] Organizers in the steel industry had refused to "stick out their necks" while the sit-downs in Flint were in progress. Once the UAW victory was accomplished, steel workers flocked to the unionist standard.

Non–auto unions were affected, too. At the Ferry-Morse seed factory in Detroit, 300 workers walked off their jobs, demanding wage increases and union recognition. At the Conant Factory Lunch, sixty high school boys who delivered food to local factories sat down and won a pay increase from $1.00 an hour to $1.25, and fifty-five charwomen who cleaned the Penobscot Building won a pay raise after a two hour sit-down. It was not long before Woolworth workers in Detroit and elsewhere began sit-downs as well. Clearly, sit-down fever was in the air.

Who won the strike for the UAW? The men? The women? It was a combination of the two. There is no doubt that the changed roles of women in Flint during that forty-four-day period helped ultimately to bring about a settlement between company and union. Even with the aid of its own security guards; city, county, and state police; and Pinkertons the company did not want the reputation of being "women killers."

The members of the Women's Auxiliary and the EB exulted when the strike ended, and they sensed that they had been an important part in bringing about a happy conclusion. One said, "A new type of women was born in the strike. . . . Women who only yesterday were horrified at unionism, who felt inferior to the task of organizing, speaking, leading, have, as if overnight, become the spearhead in the battle of unionism."[116] The role women played in the strike showed an elevated purpose in their lives. "They had the satisfaction and wholeness that people have when they are using all their powers instead of letting four-fifths of their talents rot unused."[117] Genora exclaimed that "just being a women isn't enough for me anymore. I want to be a human being with the right to think for myself."[118] Once "freed," the women of Flint did not return to their former roles as only homemakers. Even union men, who had disdained "their women" taking part in the labor strife, now recognized how valuable they had been in bringing about the ultimate victory. In a newsletter, *Women Today,* established by the Flint women, one of its contributors, Eva Stone, penned an article titled "Women in Auto Organize," in which she wrote, "We must build our Auxiliary, carry on our educational and cultural functions. We must make our union our social center, and it is up to the Women's Auxiliary to make all this possible."[119]

Travis noted the transition of the women's attitudes from the strike's beginning to its ending. At the beginning, many wives had given ultimatums to their sit-down husbands to come home. During the strike, they redirected their ultimatums to GM, with resounding results.

Did the Women's Auxiliary and the EB, then, create a "new woman"? To a considerable degree, yes. It caused more women than before to agree with Genora that *all* human beings are entitled to get the most they can out of life, that there is dignity in work, and that the wives and daughters of the workingman could also have careers.

When the Great Depression struck in 1929, Genora Albro was sixteen years old and had already committed herself to the idea that government should be helpful to people in need. As the dark years of the Depression creeped by, she began to feel that neither Democrats nor Republicans were ready to take on these domestic responsibilities. Genora Dollinger spent a great many years of her life looking for a party that was ready to take them on.

Three **The Lure of Trotskyism**

The union victory intensified Genora and her colleagues' philosophies concerning the roles of huge corporations and big government in American life. Why should it even be necessary for groups of determined workers to *have* to take on the giant companies to obtain labor equality? Beneath the naïveté of the question lay longtime concerns among social reformers about human nature itself. Was competition or cooperation uppermost in the lives of human beings?

Companies like GM argued that they were involved in capitalistic competition. Reformers, however, going back to sociologist Lester Frank Ward of the late nineteenth century, could argue that if true laissez-faire—which corporations said they wanted—was to be accomplished, the government would truly have to stay hands-off. This meant that the government would have to not only refrain from regulating big business but also cease helping it in the forms of protective tariffs, strike breaking, and tax incentives, particularly on local levels. Corporations did not wish to be regulated by government at any level; but when it came to governments *helping* them, they were much in favor.

Corporate collusion, which included widespread price-fixing practices, was not, in Genora's and her followers' eyes, illustrative of capitalism, for over the years she felt that corporations had tried to destroy capitalism's main ingredient: competition. Instead of actual competition, there seemed to be a strong adherence to the Machiavellian doctrine that the ends justify the means. Big government gave every appearance of allowing corporations to get away with it. Union people came to believe that trickle-down prosperity, which argues that government support of big business results in financial prosperity seeping down into the economy and smaller businesses, was no more efficacious under Franklin D. Roosevelt than it had been under Herbert Hoover. Under the facade of kindness and helpfulness, the bottom line for the New Deal was trucking to the interests of giant corporations.

Another question growing out the Depression that troubled Genora and her unionmates concerned the purpose and function of the government, especially the federal branch. Was government brought into existence only to regulate its citizens, to make them behave themselves? Or could or should there be a modicum of benevolence? Should government come to the aid of needy citizens, or just simply ignore them? Should it be, as former president Grover Cleveland once said, that "the people support the Government, the Government should not support the people."[1] Here was a Democrat (Cleveland) of the nineteenth century giving sustenance to a Republican (Hoover) in the early twentieth century.

It was within these political and philosophical parameters that Genora spent the immediate post-sit-down, pre–World War II years. She sought answers to the questions promulgated by her father-in-law, Carl Johnson, and to her newly found interests in the revolutionary ideas of Leon Trotsky. She put her version of the answers into the context of continued activities on behalf of unionism (primarily the UAW) and what she considered to be social justice. As the sit-downs ended, she was famous throughout Flint and, because of so much press coverage and photos, was known throughout the state and many industrial parts of the country. As her notoriety increased, she was to pay time and again for her fame. First was an estrangement from her father. She may have loved Raymond, but she did not like him. He was abusive to her mother, Lora, macho toward his son Jarvis, and bigoted against blacks. Then, to beat it all, when his daughter became a "Bolshevik," as he put it, and not only joined the sit-downers but formed the EB as well, it was just too much. Genora came from a fairly well-to-do family, and here she was cavorting with the Socialists, either on the picket lines (frequently with her two sons, although Genora's mother and two sisters, Barbara and Beatrice, took care of them most of the time) or leading large groups of shouting women down the streets of Flint.[2] From Ray's capitalistic point of view, his daughter had become wayward, and over time he tried many tactics to get her back on the straight and narrow.

In all likelihood with Lora's prodding, he rented the top apartment of his house on Garland Street to Genora and Kermit, and before long a sizeable portion of the Flint community stuck their noses into his business and asked why he allowed his "Communist" daughter to continue living at his house. The banks put the squeeze on him in 1937 for numerous unpaid debts. One bank official told him, "As long as [Genora] is living there we're going to cut off the water, your loans, and your money." Ray told Genora and Kermit to vacate the premises. She angrily refused. "I'm not moving and if you try and evict us I'll have a big announcement to the press that this is the way you treat your daughter."[3] She also threatened to call the city health department and "expose him to the public for mal-treatment of his own children." Raymond Albro could only shrug his shoulders and shake his head over his rebellious daughter. His capitalistic mind simply could not understand her. When one of her kinsmen, Charles Wetherald, a Flint vice president of GM, offered her a job (or bribe, as Genora interpreted it) with a respectable salary, she would not accept it.[4] It was both bull-headedness and deep conviction that caused her to stand so faithfully with the Socialist and union causes. The "bribe" that hurt the most, however, was from within the union itself. Much factionalism existed in unions and between the Socialists and Communists. Genora came to believe that Dorothy Kraus, whose husband, Henry, later wrote a seminal study of the sit-downs, *The Many and the Few: A Chronicle of the Dynamic Auto Workers,* tried to push her out of the Women's Auxiliary and hand it over to the Communist Party. According to Genora, she was "taken aside" by Dorothy and told that she (Genora) should not be out in such inclement weather, especially since she had received weekly treatments for tuberculosis, requiring the ejection of air from one of her lungs to keep it collapsed. Genora wore a pair of high-heeled shoes with holes in them; in fact, she put playing cards in the soles for some sort of dryness and warmth. If Genora would just be "reasonable," that is, not object to Dorothy's ascension to power as head of the EB, Genora could have warm shoes and coats and even gloves. It did not take long for the fiery Genora Albro Johnson to tell Mrs. Kraus what she could do, and where she could go. By a vote, the EB ousted Dorothy, effectively keeping it within the realm of the Socialist Party instead of using it as a Communist front, as Dorothy and Henry desired.[5]

During the forty-four day sit-down strike, Genora and the Socialists in Flint got full press. The new role of women in the industrial world received coverage all over the world, generally with Genora Johnson headlined more than anyone else. Heady stuff, this, for a woman still in her twenties. The Socialists in Flint, wanting to take advantage of the enormous publicity they and the EB had gained, asked Genora to go on a speaking tour of several East Coast cities; the tour included the May Day (1937) parades in New York. Her appearance, it was reckoned, would bolster incipient union movement all over the eastern United States, from Philadelphia to upstate New York and some parts of New England. Although she had never taken any formal speech classes and, in her opinion, had not spoken in public often enough to convince people of her cause, she gladly accepted the invitation.[6]

Needing appropriate dress for the occasion, she went shopping with Fania Fish and bought a gray suit for her trip, realizing as soon as she got home that she did not like it. She did not take it back, because a negative reaction from a TB treatment at her physician's office caused her to postpone her trip for a day. She left Flint on April 28, heading for Philadelphia. Her train went through areas of Canada, and she was impressed with the destruction that the floods of 1937 had caused all over the United States and Canada. In Canada alone, to say nothing of the United States, more than 6,000 homes were lost.[7] Seeing the aftermath of nature at its most destructive, she reflected that the New Deal government of President Franklin D. Roosevelt was neglecting flood victims all the way from Kentucky to Pennsylvania.

In Philadelphia she toured Fairmont Park and Germantown and attended a conference of the United May Day committee, where she spoke to several members of the YPSL and told them about what she considered to be the virtues of a Socialist approach to the country's problems. She also told a large Socialist gathering of all ages that the Soviet Union seemed to be solving problems of the Depression better than the United States. Arriving in New York City on May 1, she spoke at Union Square to the masses of labor union members in the metropolitan area. The Women's Socialist Guard honored Genora for her work in the sit-downs and presented her with a check for the furtherance of Socialist causes.[8] She watched the annual May Day parade with several Socialist dignitaries. Thousands of union people filled Fifth Avenue from curb to curb, and monitors were lit with Socialist slogans. Members of unions came in work clothes indigenous to their trades. The painters wore white shirts and caps, and sailors wore blue denim shirts and Levis. Each group carried its own banners and posters. The Communists had the largest contingent. The Socialists bore banners that read DOWN WITH WALL STREET, and they sang "Hold the Fort" and "Solidarity Forever."[9] The parade lasted the entire day.

Genora welcomed the time she could spend as a tourist. She went to Central Park, St. Patrick's Cathedral, and Radio City Music Hall, and she attended a reception in her honor at the home of Corliss and Margaret Lamont. On May 3 she went to Norman Thomas's home for a press conference, primarily with the city's Socialist press. She lunched with the editor of *Woman Today* and then in the afternoon visited the Empire State Building. That evening she was named the honorary chairwoman of the Women's Guard of New York City.[10]

On the morning of May 4 she went shopping with Vicky and Eda Trager for dresses. In the afternoon Mary Hillyer drove her along Riverside Drive and the banks of the Hudson River. She saw the HMS *Queen Mary* in dock, and later that evening she addressed 1,000 auto strikers in Yorkville Center, telling them of her experiences in Flint and that the best way to win was to persevere.[11] On May 5, in Poughkeepsie, she addressed a number of Vassar College girls and sat up until 4 A.M. with them, singing union songs and telling the young ladies, many from "capitalistic" homes, about the virtues of industrial democracy. The next day, back in the city to arrange a flight to Cleveland, she spoke to a mass gathering of United Auto Workers and to the United Labor Congress. Her message had now become a set speech: nothing comes free, you always pay a price, you have to be brave and proud, and, above all else, persevere. In Cleveland she had a long talk with Wyndham Mortimer, a well-known Communist functionary, although he did not admit to being one until years later. Bert Cochran, a leading Trotskyist at the time but later a Stalinist, drove her to Akron for her next appearances.

Back in Cleveland she overslept, missing the morning train to Philadelphia; on the later train she sat up all night reading Knut Hamsun's *Growth of the Soil*. In Philadelphia she addressed the fruit packers union in the afternoon of May 11 and early that night gave a rousing speech to 1,000 members of the United Distillery Workers of America;[12] afterward, she was guest of honor at a "swell" reception. Interspersed with these social and Socialist activities, Genora also found time for a bit of politics and culture. She went to Harrisburg, the state capital, to hear lawmakers' discussions on various labor bills; she saw the movies *Café Metropole* and *A Star Is Born* and went on a daylong excursion to Atlantic City.[13]

At Camden, New Jersey, Genora spoke to shipyard workers, receiving an honorary membership in the Camden Women's Auxiliary, which hosted a banquet in her honor. In Jersey City she spoke to the International Union of Machinists and addressed a special meeting of the women's committee. These gatherings continued: Temple University students in Philadelphia, as well as that city's Painter's Union; National Convention of Office and Professional Workers Union; and others. She bolstered so many failing labor movements, the saying "Flint is Coming" came to mean that Genora Johnson was on the way.[14]

After six weeks of as arduous a trip as Genora ever took, she returned to Flint and collapsed, suffering a relapse of TB brought on by the strenuous activities of the last month and a half. Bob and Max Delson raised funds from sympathetic unions in various industrial cities for her to spend six months at the Trudeau Sanitarium in the Adirondacks in upper New York state. During this stay at the hospital, she learned that she no longer had the use of her right lung, yet she continued to smoke cigarettes for many years to come.[15] While on her speaking tour, Genora's friend and colleague, Teckler Roy, was left in charge of the Women's Brigade in Flint. When Genora found that she would have a further absence of at least six months in the TB sanitarium, the EB began to fall apart. It had become full of factions in her absence, reflecting the general state of the UAW itself. All sorts of political ideologues vied for power. At the first meeting upon her return, Genora's "nerves were shot," and she realized that the EB was just about to pass into history. Anyway, she consoled herself, there was no "further need for an emergency military organization like that."[16]

Returning from Trudeau as the momentous year of 1937 came to a close, Genora squeezed in the UAW convention in Milwaukee. Although Kermit was a delegate, Genora was not, but she represented numerous women's organizations and was authorized to sit in on all the caucus meetings.[17] Milwaukee Socialist mayor Dan Hoan held a banquet for Socialist members of the UAW in attendance and presented Genora with the keys to the city.[18] Though the EB no longer existed, Genora had no intention of remaining idle throughout the new year. In February 1938 she faced one of her most sensitive and compelling campaigns yet. It revolved around a large group of poor workers' families, many of whom had just arrived from the South. Before it ended, she attracted the attention of state officials in Lansing as well as FDR's Works Progress Administration (WPA) in Washington, D.C.

The WPA was a New Deal agency designed to help down-and-outers and contribute to ending the Depression. Apparently, however, WPA locals could and did get caught up in governmental bureaucracy and red tape. Such was the case in 1938, in Flint, Michigan—so much so that Kermit and Genora Johnson organized the Unemployed Workers Union, Number Twelve.[19] Unemployed workers were evicted from their homes and sent to "shelters" after banks foreclosed on them. One shelter housed males and the other, women and children, though separating families ran counter to official New Deal policies.[20] As the WPA functionaries placed families' furniture out on the street, Genora and Kermit, with a specially created unit of Local Twelve came right behind them and returned the furniture to the houses. This ploy could not work long, so the local unionists erected large army tents in Oak Park on Industrial Avenue, just across the street from the WPA office itself. Genora and her allies moved all the dislocated people to this place, an action that attracted the attention of city government as well as that of the press. One local newspaper ran a story about a "leading Communist" in Flint bragging of being in a position to poison the city's water supplies. The leading Communist was identified as Genora Johnson. Genora denied the statement, saying that she was not and had never been a member of the Communist Party. She also denied ever having tried to contaminate any water system, in Flint or elsewhere. Genora and Kermit posted signs on each corner of Oak Park, "inviting the public to come out to see poor people with hungry, starving children—to watch people die." They ran taps into the street wires to get electricity and used hot plates to prepare food. The people within this encampment were forced to live their private lives in public. Women washed clothes in huge tubs and hung them out on tree branches. For warmth against the cold February nights, little children huddled around fires in huge oil drums. Altogether it was not a pretty sight: some two or three hundred people living in the open in the middle of winter right in the heart of industrial America. One of Genora's signs read, "This is the Death Watch." Another proclaimed, "If you want to see people in the city of Flint die, here they are."[21] Yet another announced, "If Flint workers must starve to death, let them do it publicly."[22] These ploys attracted much attention, as cars full of curiosity seekers drove slowly by every day and into the night.

City officials quickly reminded everyone in the camp that they were breaking the law. Oak Park was public and not for the benefit of a "select few." Welfare officials threatened to take, forcibly if necessary, all the children from their mothers and put them into juvenile detention centers. The police (who remembered Genora all too well), on orders from city hall, threatened the group with jail. Union people began to stand guard on the periphery of the park. A nearby Buick plant was full of UAW members, and their leader, Pat Murray, swore that "if any cops come up anywhere within the district, we're going to come out with our pipes and our hammers and our wrenches and we'll take care of them." Such threats actually helped to keep the peace. As an indication that demonstrations, even those that threaten violence, are effective ways to show disaffection, the "Death Watch" ultimately got what it wanted. The spectacle grew increasingly embarrassing to the city of Flint, especially as lawmakers in Lansing and Washington, D.C., asked what was happening. Finally, under the auspices of the WPA in Washington, federal officials came to the camp, sat down, and talked with the women about their needs. Afterward, they walked across the street to the welfare office and ordered that these mothers and children be given everything they wanted. Large shipments of surplus food arrived, and, for the first time in many weeks, these displaced citizens filled their stomachs.[23] Genora and Kermit had put three or four families in each tent to symbolize and dramatize the plight of the laid-off workers. Laborers, along with all other groups in society, have rights to dignity and security. She discovered that many of these individuals allowed themselves to be downtrodden because they did not know they had rights in the first place. Genora set out to teach them differently. She inspired the out-of-work men and their wives and children to take on the establishment and win the rights and privileges to which they were entitled. If such actions meant creating a "sensational nuisance," as some observers dubbed the encampment, then so be it. Kermit and Genora were not beyond a bit of proselytizing for the cause of Socialism during this campaign. One by one, they felt, was the way to gain new membership for the party, and they were successful. More than one person left that encampment with the thought that "all the government wanted me to do was starve to death, but the Socialists—well, they helped me, and I will not forget."

Genora, and by extension Kermit, roused jealousy in numerous parts of the Socialist Party (SP). Factionalism always seemed to affect labor movement as much as, or more than, capital endeavors. With Communists of two or three sorts and various shades of Socialist ideology, it's little wonder that unionists were frequently at each other's throats. All these people believed intensely, almost evangelically, that their system was the best for solving national and international problems. The SP in Michigan and throughout the nation rose and fell according to economic indicators. During World War I, the SP prospered, although "like the IWW [International Workers of the World, or "Wobblies"], the Socialist Party was preoccupied with defending itself against . . . wartime repression" and "provided no national coordination for the upsurge of new unionism."[24] As a result, in the 1930s, the party was a "mere skeleton of its former self. The appearance of prosperity had seemed to refute Marxist claims of the decline of Capitalism."[25]

As the Great Depression intensified, with high rates of unemployment, scarcity of money for most people, and an almost total lack of social services, the philosophies of the SP once again became attractive to thousands of people sympathetic to the workers' movement. By the late 1930s, however, there were at least partial economic recoveries, and the fortunes of Socialism in America once again began to plunge. Kermit and Genora got caught up in the vicissitudes of the SP and its ideological conflicts. Having made enough enemies with the SP by 1938, the couple was either expelled, or left voluntarily, depending on who tells the story. Their continued Trotskyism, which ran counter to the beliefs of many Communist and Socialist followers of Joseph Stalin, did not sit well with many party members. The Johnsons' most intense Trotskyist period occurred from 1934 to 1938, during which, according to Martin Glaberman, the objective of the Trotskyists was to capture the left wings of the European social democracies.[26] This policy was known as "entrism," by which the SWP (Socialist Workers Party) would infiltrate into the Socialist or Communist parties with their messages of Trotskyism.[27] Accused of sabotage toward the SP (which in Michigan was on the verge of collapse) and a general disruption, Genora and Kermit issued this statement: "After seven years' membership in the Socialist Party, striving for the true path to socialism . . . the facts have shown us that the Socialist Party had not and can not provide the leadership necessary." They added further: "We are leaving the Socialist Party and joining the Socialist Workers Party to build the vanguard of the coming revolution unhampered by reformist maneuvers, petty intriguers, opportunists and careerists."[28]

Though no precise definitions or explanations were given here, in all likelihood, the attention Genora received for her part in the sit-downs, her speaking tour, and, above all, the Death Watch, created jealousies and resentments hard to overcome. With only two dissenting votes, the Flint SP deprived the Johnsons of membership despite the fact that they had already resigned. Bruce Sloan, for one, rejoiced to see them go. He wrote scathingly to George Clarke that "I cannot resent your party [SP] relieving us of Genora and her carbon-copy Kermit . . . and I have watched the amusing tantrums of the SWP . . . but by the beard of Leon Trotsky, if what the SWP does is revolutionary, then I'll eat the beloved beard."[29]

The Third Communist International of 1919 had been described as the first group with the distinct objective of worldwide revolution, thus introducing Trotskyism.[30] In America, Trotskyist origins go back to the Sixth Congress of the Communist International meeting in Moscow in 1938. An American, James P. Cannon, attended this congress and was converted to Trotskyism.[31] The SWP was formed in December 1937–January 1938, in part to protest the SP's expulsion in June 1937 of many left-wingers. One of its major founders was Cannon, born in Rosedale, Kansas, in 1890. His father was a Socialist and a partisan of *The Appeal to Reason,* a popular Socialist journal. Cannon joined the SP at eighteen and three years later became a member of the Industrial Workers of the World (IWW). Later he was hailed as the "founder of American Trotskyism," the leader and teacher "of three if not four generations of revolutionists." He strongly believed in "practical politics," opposing the "nationalist theory of Stalin and his gang of 'Socialism in One Country' argument. Internationalism was the most important consideration in the world because, "in reality, we live on one planet, and all the countries and parts of it are joined together in mutual independence."[32] The SWP sought to "mobilize the American masses" and lead them in the overthrow of the capitalist economic system. It proposed to recruit "among the middle classes, Negroes . . . unemployed youth, trade unionists, and 'colonial people.'"[33] From its inception in the late 1930s, the SWP "recruited women comrades on a scale never seen before in the radical movement"—40 percent "of our staff members are women."[34] In 1938, 4 percent of the convention's delegates were women, the next year it was 8 percent, and the trend grew in the years ahead.[35] Cannon was "angry at injustice, inequalities, special privileges, and exploitation. He was angry at poverty. He seethed over the crimes of Capitalism . . . its wars, its reactionary ideologies . . . its police, its courts, its prisons, its fascism, its tendency to drop back to barbarism."[36]

These philosophies and outlooks were exactly what Genora wanted to accept in 1938. A chapter of the SWP was formed in Flint (the main party headquarters was in New York City), and Genora, after her expulsion from the SP, became a member (by the early 1950s, Genora rose to the post of state secretary). The SWP in New York had been trying to recruit the Johnsons for some time; that the couple did not repel such advances was another reason the Flint Socialists removed them from their party. Its official newspaper, *Socialist Call,* had printed numerous articles about the Flint EB, almost always highlighting Genora's Socialist roles in Flint. These articles did not sit well with the Flint Socialists, either. An immediate SWP goal was to instill members' responsibilities to the party and the need for regular contributions for its maintenance. It wanted to involve "comrades" not in the auto industry, although GM and other car manufacturers appeared the most fruitful field for recruitment. What role SWP militants, who called themselves the vanguard of the working classes, should play with the UAW was a subject of intense debate. Of special interest to the Flint SWP were the newly arrived black workers—the SWP went house to house in the black neighborhoods, preaching the virtues of a Socialist America. Discussion groups met regularly in members' homes and held symposia and sponsored lectures on not only GM's treatment of the working person but also on the need of the federal government to set up training centers for laid-off workers to "retool." In the meantime, in 1939, Genora and Kermit attended the annual meeting of the SWP, held at Irving Place in New York City. Unknown to Genora at the time, as she walked down the center aisle with Kermit right behind her, a young man in the audience admired her: "Genora came smartly down the aisle dressed in a jacket, blouse and slacks. . . . Many people can make an entrance and never be noticed, but with Genora every head was turned in her direction." The young member of the SWP felt certain that now, with the Johnsons, the party could go in a new proletarian direction. But watching Genora come down that aisle made it difficult to stick to politics. "At that moment I had to confess, if only to myself, how lucky a man would be to have a companion like Genora."[37] The young man was Sol Dollinger, and Genora would be his companion for over a half-century.

In addition to difficulties with her father because of her fame and expulsion from the SP, there was another price to pay. By 1939, Genora and Kermit were seldom seen in each other's company; the trip to New York was an exception. Since the sit-down of 1937, Genora had been either on the road promoting unionism or convalescing in a TB sanitarium. Lengthy separations between the two began to take a toll, particularly on Kermit. On a moment's notice, or so it seemed, Genora could be called away to some union hotspot. In December 1939, Riley E. Males, of Kokomo, Indiana, wrote to Genora that he needed her help in organizing the Delco Radio Plant. He had "about 1400 girls" who "need some women to work with them a while to prove to them that there is really a place in the labor movement for them."[38] Genora was always happy to honor such requests because it was an important way of bringing incipient women's movements into line with labor concerns. But again, such departures meant leaving husband and children behind.

Not unmindful of the home life she was creating with her numerous extended absences, Genora vented her feelings in poetry. One poem indicated her personal feelings about leaving home so often. It was called "Goodbye Again:"

Goodbye again, goodbye again
Is it always to be like this?
A goodbye smile, a goodbye sigh
And then a goodbye kiss
Fleeting moments of happiness
Is not all that I desire
The ecstasy of a weighted heart
Caught deep and fast in the mire
Of life's bewilderment—and then
Goodbye again, goodbye again.[39]

Apparently, all of her friends knew of the impending breakup before she did. She penned this poem when she realized the situation:

Say it isn't so, say it isn't so
People say that you don't love me
Say it isn't so
Everywhere I go

Everyone I know
Tell me that you're growing tired of me
Say it isn't so
People say that you
Found somebody new
And it won't be long before you leave
Say it isn't true
Say that everything is still OK
That's all I want to know
And what they're saying
Say it isn't so.[40]

It was true. Kermit was lonely. A sensitive person, he was jealous of the attention Genora had gotten in the past several months. And, too, there was the bottle, which underscored the loneliness. Furthermore, there was Winifred Bauman, or Winnie, as her friends called her, who began to comfort Kermit in Genora's absence. Genora and Kermit—after a dozen years or so of marriage—formally separated in 1941.[41]

Shortly after the separation from Kermit, Genora and her sister Barbara traveled to New York—mostly for a vacation. This was Genora's first visit since 1939, when she and Kermit had attended the annual meeting of the SWP. Naturally, the two sisters attended several functions sponsored by the SWP. One night they went to a social at party headquarters and were surrounded by admiring men. One was Sol Dollinger (later known as Solly or Jerry Kirk—primarily when he was in trouble with a government), who had been enchanted by Genora just two years before when he saw her enter the room at the SWP annual meeting.

Some might call it too much a coincidence for Sol once again to find himself in Genora's company. Actually, it was quite predictable. Sol, born in Youngstown, Ohio, in 1920 (he was seven years younger than Genora), but raised with a brother and a couple of sisters in New York City, was a merchant mariner. He had committed himself in his youth to Socialist principles and found membership in the SWP amenable to his political and social ideologies. When in port, he usually attended the party's meetings, including those of a purely social nature. Sol was thrilled once again to have spotted Genora. He bought three bottles of beer and headed for her group. He gave one bottle to Barbara and the other to Genora. Although he already knew who Genora was, he waited for formal introductions. He learned that the two had come to New York by car, and Genora asked if there was anyone around who could escort them on their sightseeing tours. Sol had never moved so quickly.[42] The next day the trio saw *Citizen Kane* and then headed for a Greenwich Village nightclub, where Sol bought corsages for his two beautiful companions. The band began to play "Stardust," and Sol saw tears streaming down Genora's face. Embarrassed, he asked Barbara for a dance. "Why is Genora crying?" he wanted to know. "Stardust was Genora and Kermit's favorite song. They are now separated. She made me promise not to tell anyone that they are getting a divorce. She came to New York to get away from it." Before the dance ended, Barbara told Sol that her husband was pressing her to return to Flint. Would Sol please keep an eye on Genora while she was in New York? Well . . . Yes![43]

There were several days of sightseeing, art museums, movies, and Broadway shows. Genora also found a picket line or two that were as exciting as the cultural events she witnessed. She joined Sol in a picket line on Staten Island, where merchant mariners were demanding wage and safety improvements. She gave a speech to the assembled men, many of whom remembered her work in the 1937 sit-down. As Sol and Genora continued to travel around New York City, his feelings for her deepened: "With each passing hour I knew I was helplessly in love. I intended to propose marriage at the first propitious moment." When he introduced Genora to his two sisters on Long Island, he referred to Genora "as my intended wife."[44] Genora did not contradict him, though (she told him later) the biggest stumbling blocks were the seven-year difference in their ages and her two sons, Dennis and Jarvis.

Genora and Sol always celebrated their marriage anniversary on September 19, 1941. "That is the day we agreed to be man and wife. We did not need a certificate from a bourgeois court to affirm this decision."[45] (Her divorce from Kermit was official on February 24, 1942.) They formally and legally married in December 1942, although Genora continued to use the name Johnson for some time.

Genora took Sol back to Flint with her. He fascinated the Albros, who loved his New York accent, especially when he dropped his *r*'s and said "corna" for "corner," or "borda" for "border."[46] By this time, Genora's father, Raymond, largely ruined by the Depression, made a mock lament that his elder daughter had "married a Jew." Sol learned later that Genora's father told her that marriage to him was "all right," but they "shouldn't have children."[47]

Just a few weeks after Genora and Sol's declaration of marriage, the Japanese attacked Pearl Harbor, and their lives, along with those of millions of other people, were changed forever. Both Genora and Sol thought the war "imperialist,"[48] and Sol did not wish to be drafted. As long as he sailed regularly with the merchant mariners, he was deferred from the draft. Whenever he finished a job with a particular vessel, its owner notified his draft board, located in Flint. He then had a month to get work on another ship. Without a new assignment, he was vulnerable to the draft.[49] The young married couple prepared for a long and grim war with Japan and Germany and their allies.

If Genora had thought that the 1937 sit-down was the climax of her personal and professional life, she was wrong. The Death Watch and expulsion from the SP in 1938, separation from Kermit in 1939, and then marriage with Sol Dollinger in 1941 gave her life a number of new perspectives. She had moved far from the Methodist girl who taught Sunday school to an ardent supporter of Trotskyism.

Four Genora's Wars

The sit-downs of 1937, World War II, and their immediate aftermath marked the beginnings of the modern women's rights movement in the United States. These events fused feminist activism with progress in unionism, and Genora Dollinger played a role in the merging of these two movements. Feminist progress was made by women activists of the late 1930s who were UAW members (and this list included Genora Johnson Dollinger), "when the wartime mobilization drew them into auto factory jobs."[1] The war, symbolized for women by Rosie the Riveter, led millions of females into large factories to build tanks, guns, airplanes, and other materiel. Women proved to be as capable as men in producing the goods that helped lead the Western allies to victory in 1945, although they were never paid as much as men for their quantity and quality of work.[2]

Women exulted in newfound freedoms as a result of World War II. Margaret Wright said, "When factory work opened up, it was like a Godsend. . . . [I] was earning pretty good money . . . [and] I thought that was so terrific that I had a Social Security Card," and Lola Weixel exclaimed that "men had been telling us all along the line that oh, it takes six years to become a welder. . . . They had been sold a bill of goods in their lives, you see. It wasn't true at all."[3] Despite these outpourings of jubilation at the "new woman" in 1945, the government, corporations, and even labor unions tried to put women back into their kitchens after the war. But the women would have none of it; they had had a taste of freedom, independence, and self-esteem, and they meant to keep it.

On the one hand, the war had brought an exhilaration to Genora, augmenting her role as feminist heroine in the sit-down of 1937. As women increasingly entered the workforce, they sought Genora's opinions, for she was reckoned to be a leader who knew what to do. On the other hand, the war brought turbulence, loneliness, and tragedy to the young woman who had recently made labor history in Flint, Michigan.

After Sol got another merchant marine assignment in early 1942, Genora stayed for a time in Flint. Sol wanted her to come to New York to be near him, telling her that when she arrived, "we will be two happy Bolsheviks."[4] He still addressed his letters to G. G. Johnson, 1908 Ridge Street in Flint.[5] Onboard ship during periodic voyages, Sol carried on the work of the SWP, talking to shipmates about the advantages of socialist solutions to world problems. He exulted in a letter to Genora that "I can tell all . . . my wife, too, is a Bolshevik! She is a leader in her own right. None can deny it and no one can take it away."[6]

By May 1942 Sol was in Scotland. Addressing Genora as his "bonnie lassie," he wrote to tell her that he probably would not be stateside until September or later.[7] Genora wrote in the margin of this letter that "her plans were dashed at this moment." She told Sol in September that "our anniversary [September 19, the date of their declaration of marriage] was both blue and happy."[8] Always one to air her feelings in poetry, Genora wrote,

Today I smiled, Today I sighed; Today I shed a tear; Today I laughed, Today I cried.
Today has been a year.[9]

She penned this remembrance of their declaration of marriage:

And then that day—that day of sighs; He held me in his arms.
Our vows exchanged, his lips met mine.
Last moments of his charm, He sailed away on oceans blue,
To gird the earth around. Through war and death and dangers grim;
Oh rush the day he's homeward bound.[10]

She could, however, see a bit of humor in the situation:

Oh, Freud says this, And Freud says that. I know it all by heart.
When Sol comes back from off the seas I'll demonstrate the part![11]

Sol returned to Flint in late 1942. He had to spend a few weeks there to regain full use of his legs. His ship, the SS *Olopana,* had been sunk by a German submarine in the icy waters of Barents Sea, off the island of Novaya Zemlya, and he'd waited several hours in frigid waters before being rescued. With only seven hundred dollars in his pocket, he knew that he would not be able to support them through the winter. (Jarvis, or "Jody," Genora's youngest son, lived with her and Sol; Dennis, or "Denny," stayed with Kermit.) Blacklisted in all the GM plants in Flint, employment for Genora in that city was out of the question. Moreover, GM had not converted all that quickly from automobile to defense production, so, ironically, a rather high rate of unemployment existed in Flint. Genora, Sol, and Jody went to Detroit, which, compared to Flint, was a boomtown. In Sol's absence, Genora learned to run a lathe, a drill press, and milling machines. By now she could also read complicated blueprints used by tool and die makers.[12] Sol wanted to work while the Great Lakes were frozen over, and he planned to find a ship in the spring of 1943. Both he and Genora got employment at Budd Wheel in Detroit.

One of the first women ever to be hired by Budd Wheel, Genora tested eighteen-inch shells manufactured for the war effort. Her back-breaking job, testing for leakage by forcing a white, milky fluid into the shell to see if any of it oozed out, required that the heavy shells be moved around and sometimes lifted. She went home, a one-room attic apartment that was a "dirty old firetrap," every night with an agonizing backache and blistered hands.[13] Years later she told an interviewer about how she had been treated at Budd by all the male workers: "Those men were so 'gracious' that when women came into the plant they [the men] were resentful that they took all the hard jobs and left them to women and they picked their other jobs. And I had a job that was so hard that I just came home every night and didn't know if I could go back the next day."[14] Sol explained the men's behavior this way: "The men thought the women should be home tending the kids and mending the socks. A decent job meant a prolonged life in the industrial plants. Why should women get decent jobs? They would soon be turned out, thought the Budd men, to make way for returning veterans."[15]

Genora had to perform satisfactorily on a ninety-day probation period before her employment at Budd could become permanent. She got through the probation period and then some, so she was surprised when she received a pink slip. She had, the personnel officer told her, falsified her application for employment because she used the name Johnson. Michigan, she and Sol believed, would not recognize their marriage of September 1941 for things like health insurance and unemployment benefits, so they deemed it in their best interests to keep her first married name of Johnson. Furthermore, Budd officials had now heard of her activities in Flint dating from 1937 to the present. Sol explained the dismissal: "Detroit plants were hiring the lame, the halt and the blind, but Budd had no hesitation in getting rid of a union strike leader." The incident caused Genora to comment, "Well, it looks like I have gone as far as I can with the name of Johnson. Now it is time to use the name of Dollinger."[16] And so they legalized their marriage in December 1942, before a Detroit justice of the peace.

Assuming her rightful name of Dollinger made it easier for Genora to get a job than if she had retained Johnson. The name Genora Dollinger was not yet as recognizable as Genora Johnson; it would take a few months for "Dollinger" to be instantly recognized in labor and management circles: in the one instance, as a heroine, in the other, as a notorious troublemaker. She applied for employment at Briggs Manufacturing, which, before the war, employed 18,000 workers who made bodies for the Chrysler Motor Company and now mostly manufactured B-27 aircraft for the government.[17] The employment manager asked her why she wanted to work at Briggs. He was so impressed with her "dress, diction, personality, and good looks" that he wanted to hire her as a receptionist in the front office.[18] She responded, "Because of the war effort, you know. Everybody's supposed to do their part."[19] She did not mention her ambition to participate in the activities of Local UAW 212, which, under the leadership of Emil Mazey, was the most militant local in Detroit, so militant that its members were frequently referred to in union circles as the "Dead-End Kids."[20]

Refusing to accept the receptionist job because she thought it patronizing, she worked at a drill press at Briggs; it was not as strenuous as working with the shells at Budd but hard enough. She told her manager that she knew how to operate lathes and would like a transfer. He assigned her to the inspection department on Mack Avenue, where her job was, among other things, interpreting tool and die blueprints. She noted right away that most of her coworkers—about 500 of them—were women who lacked union representation. She kept her head low, however, not wanting to be recognized by anyone in the sprawling Briggs plant. Not having completed her probation period, she knew she would be fired instantly the minute management learned her true identity. Some women with grievances called a meeting and pressured Genora to attend. Sitting in the back of the room, she saw none other than her friend and comrade from sit-down days in Flint, Emil Mazey—who had just been drafted into the army—approaching the platform. He gave a rousing pep talk to the women and ended by saying, "I don't know why you [women] have to . . . get any advice from us. You've got one of the leaders of the union sitting right back there. . . . Genora, why didn't you stand up?"[21] All eyes turned to her, and she could hide no longer. "Emil," she said angrily to him after the meeting. "You son-of-a-bitch. You blew me out of the plant. I've only got about three or four days to go [before finishing probation]." Mazey responded, "Don't worry, Genora. I will leave word with Jess Ferraza. He succeeds me as president. If they fire you, he will be instructed to shut down all eight of the [Briggs] plants."[22]

They did fire her, and Local 212 did shut down the plants. She was quickly rehired, and the rank and file elected her as chief steward in the inspection department, a powerful position within the Chrysler work system as she would now direct and coordinate union activities, including grievances, as well as collect dues and negotiate with management. She and other stewards in the Detroit area represented about 8,000 workers. "Their [the stewards'] moral authority lay in the ability to maintain a unity of purpose with their workmates."[23] She began to work with chief stewards from other Briggs plants, and collectively they became known as the "Aisle-Way" caucus because informally, in the aisle of the plants, they talked over the affairs of the day and heard new grievances.[24] There were plenty of these, for Briggs management was known for its antagonism toward organized labor. Genora's stature as chief steward grew at Briggs, and her reputation as a militant feminist-unionist increased throughout Detroit, the state, and the country. According to historian Nelson Lichtenstein, "The greatest militancy in most factories came not among the alienated . . . workers of the main assembly line, but among those employees who maintained a high degree of verbal interaction."[25] In other words, the person who spoke the loudest got the attention. Genora Dollinger was no slouch in this category.

Before Genora left Budd Wheel, Sol shipped out again. Genora's son, Jody, became a latchkey kid (a child who comes home from school each day before his mother or father are home from work) and was thus on his own for several hours without any direct parental supervision. It took Genora an hour or more to get from her fire-trap apartment to work each day, and an hour back, so, after she started at Briggs, she found a place on Gladwin Street where she could walk to and from work. The place was in ill repair: its oak floors were painted black, there were holes in the plaster, and "tons" of debris was piled up.[26] Sol had many seamen friends who belonged to the SWP. A dozen or so of them arrived at the house on Gladwin and put it back together. Over the next several months the place became a haven for merchant mariners and labor activists, a second headquarters where they plotted strike strategies and lauded union accomplishments. At this residence Genora tried to raise her two sons, as Dennis had now come to live with her in Detroit. Her family life was painful at this time, and any thought of union work for the socialist cause had to be subordinated to interests of survival. Genora and Sol (and to a lesser extent their birth father, Kermit) doted on the two young boys. The older of the two, Denny, wrote a poem to his mother:

From early morn till set o' sun
Her tasks of love are never done
She shares our hopes, our dreams, our plans
Believes in us and understands
And even when we're far apart
She keeps our interests at her heart
Her life's a perfect symbol of
Enduring and unselfish love.[27]

Kermit wrote to Genora on April 9, 1943, that he had been reclassified in the draft as One A, making it necessary for Denny to stay permanently with her. (He had lived for some time with his paternal grandfather, Carl, or "Dad," Johnson, as well as with Genora's mother, Lora.) As he sent Denny to Detroit, Kermit reminded Genora that "the government is rather slow in making remunerations on collateral dependents." Kermit had always been derelict in sending child support payments, and Genora thought this letter another ruse to avoid responsibilities. She wrote, "Kermit sure got out of a lot of headaches [by being drafted]."

She complained that Kermit made a "splurge" by sending both boys five silver dollars each, making him the hero in his absence and Genora the tyrant for trying to discipline them.[28] In a separate postscript to Denny in one of his letters to Genora, Sol asked Denny to see that his mother got three square meals a day and that he continue to obey her.[29] But this was the big city, and Genora's work at Briggs with the union, and living in a house where dozens of people were coming and going on a daily basis, often left Denny to his own devices. He skipped school, was accused of stealing a radio, and sassed Genora to the point that she sometimes used corporal punishment. Concerned about the theft charges, Sol wrote to Genora that "if he took the radio and the police find out there won't be anything that we can do. They will ship him so fast we won't know what has happened. If it does, I'll feel sorry that we didn't send him away on the charge of skipping school rather than to have let it drift into a charge of robbery."[30]

Jody, born in 1935 (Denny was born in 1931), learned from Denny and began playing hooky from school. Genora knew nothing about it, but she suspected when both sons came home with dreadful report cards. When she asked Jody about the bad grades, he began "lying as fast as a horse can trot." She learned that back in Flint, Jody had a practice of bumming cash from drunks in the beer garden just across from Lora and Raymond's house. In Detroit he was accused of stealing jewelry at school, and then somehow he came into possession of an unregistered gun.[31] Even if it had been registered, as a minor, it was illegal for Jody to have it.

Several unionists and merchant mariners moved into the house on Gladwin Street and not only neglected to pay the rent but also did nothing to keep up the place; repeated requests and even warnings of forcible evictions produced no apparent effect. Genora's temperament was such that she began to write testy letters to Sol about his lengthy absences and his periodic visits to Detroit. (Did she ever think of Kermit when she was in these moods—that she had left him alone so often?) She wrote to her parents asking if they could take Jody; they could not. Her experiences in wartime Detroit to some extent resembled those of Harriett Arnow's fictional character Gertie Nevels in *The Doll Maker* in terms of adjusting to war work, running a household, and raising children all at the same time.[32]

Back in the Briggs plant, Genora attended to business and rarely let on to coworkers the turmoil of her life on Gladwin Street. She lunched regularly with two African Americans, Thelma Hawkins and Bill Wardlow, both stewards in other departments at the huge Briggs complex.[33] Befriending African Americans earned her the enmity of some fellow workers, but she shrugged off their complaints. (Much of the race riot in Detroit in 1943 was caused by bigoted whites, many who came up from the South and objected to what they considered to be equal treatment and benefits to black Americans.) When Genora spoke to Local 212, "several Negro outsiders" were present and they seemed to "come alive." On the whole, however, African Americans did not trust Socialist representatives of the UAW. Charles Denby wondered why "the [Socialist Workers] Party had no resolution on the Negro question. They had one on Trade Unions, on the American question, on Europe and many other subjects. . . . The leadership never mentioned that Negroes had ever done anything progressive."[34] Nevertheless, Genora exuberantly wrote to Sol that she was "so hyped up" after this meeting that she felt like "cooing, and I don't know how to coo with only a piece of paper and pen in front of me." The only two things she'd never had enough of, she said to Sol, were "you and black olives."[35]

Detroit was a buzzing city during the war, "open" twenty-four hours a day. By order of the federal government, a worker could not unilaterally move himself or herself to another job, in effect freezing most laborers into their positions. The only way for them to move up to obtain a better-paying job was to get themselves fired. The job market was so good that they would be reemployed almost immediately.[36] Thus there were numerous, deliberate wildcat strikes, or walkouts as the union called them, illegal by government definition. Many of those who participated were fired, and they got better paying jobs elsewhere. The wildcat strike became an instrument for working people to show their disapproval of unions who entered into no-strike pledges for the duration of the war. With the no-strike pledge, labor and management promised the government to work in harmony as long as the war lasted. The companies, though, according to labor opinion, did not live up to their side of the bargain. They used all sorts of techniques (such as speedups, denial of time-and-a-half by cutting out Saturday shifts, forced work on nonwar products, shortened lunch periods, and following workers on toilet breaks) to violate at least the spirit if not the letter of the law. The movement against the no-strike pledge was greatest in Detroit because the vast hinterland was "more conservative and so much more controlled by the [FDR] administration." Nevertheless, the opponents of the no-strike pledge could secure no more than a third of the votes for its removal.[37]

The most vocal opposition to the no-strike pledge came from Trotskyists in the SWP (with only 110 members in the UAW) and from the Workers' Party, led by Max Schactman. To acknowledge the no-strike pledge, they believed, was to recognize the legitimacy of the war itself. At the 1944 UAW convention in Grand Rapids, the main subject was the no-strike pledge. Walter Reuther wanted a "reaffirmation" of the pledge until Germany was defeated. The subject was so intense that fistfights broke out on the convention floor.[38] Genora was caught up in the activities of wildcat strikes and no-strike pledges. She spent much time as chief steward listening to worker complaints that dealt with what they considered unfair labor practices. Most of the workers in Genora's department were women, who worked in "cribs," or sections with chicken-wire partitions. One was a "navy" crib, another "army," and a third "marine," all working on different parts for the planes and tanks as they were being built. Each crib was restricted, but it was easy for someone in army to see what was happening in navy. Genora was upset at the way crib foremen treated women. They kept speeding them up on the assembly lines, teasing them about menstrual periods, and, in particular, targeting women who had just left school or their households to work at Briggs.[39] Many of these foremen had come up from the assembly line; they knew how it worked and, once arriving at their new positions, got everything from it that they possibly could. "Bring 'em on, bring 'em on," became one of their mantras, meaning a speedup beyond some workers' capacities. "I'll tell you," said one GM veteran, "it was just like what you've seen in . . . chain gangs and prisoners. They [the foremen] just about operated that way."[40]

Genora called a wildcat strike over these and other grievances. Her first tactic was to tell "her" women not to check out so their pay time would continue, making it clear that this was a deliberate walkout. Genora went into the superintendent's office and complained about Eddie, the army foreman, "who had a nasty mouth." In addition to Eddie, she railed against the navy and marine foremen and even the general foreman, causing the superintendent to call them into his office. While Genora was "yelling and hollering as hard as I could—like you had to do with those kind of foremen, charging them with all kinds of things," the army foreman looked out the window and exclaimed, "My God, the department is all gone!" The women had walked out, and "none of

[Genora's] stewards were fired."[41] She and her union made a point here, although she had used questionable tactics: treat the women better or walkouts will increase. Things did improve—at least for a time. During the two years or so that Genora worked at Briggs as a chief steward, she was fired three times. Each time, however, Local 212 president Jess Ferrazza got her hired back.

As the war was ending in Europe, in May 1945, Genora got into some squabbles with various representatives of the Briggs Corporation. She needed to appoint an assistant steward for one of the cribs and asked her friend Vida Ash to take the position. She declined, and Genora approached several newly returned veterans. As she talked to one of them, Harold Zwirmer, a foreman, interrupted the discussion and remarked, "Don't you think this social visit has gone on long enough?" This tactless remark almost started the war again. She told Zwirmer she was discussing the appointment of a line steward and a grievance that some workers had brought. "You are out of line," he said, "discussing a grievance before informing the line steward of such"; she retorted that how the hell could a grievance be taken up with a line steward if there wasn't one. Zwirmer ordered her out of his area, and Genora "reminded him that I was the elected chief steward of the . . . cribs and I was only there in the line of duty." He demanded to know the grievance under discussion. Genora told him it was none of his business, at least not yet. He was, she told him, violating the contract between union and company by trying to intimidate her. After "further nasty and threatening remarks," he left but told Genora "to make it snappy." Genora was "shocked and angered" by the confrontation but at the same time exhilarated. She and Zwirmer had gotten along in the past, and she could not understand his attitude on this occasion. She went to see him and said she would not report the incident to the shop committee if he would explain himself. "I have my orders," was all he would tell her. Things did not improve between the two. Later in the day, near the end of the shift, Zwirmer walked through the plant and yelled out to the army crib foreman: "Hello, Sister Bellamy." Bellamy called back, "Hello, Brother Rat." He walked over to her and said, "What's the matter—has your chief steward been talking to you?"[42] Zwirmer apparently now wanted to antagonize Genora further, and, to be sure, she answered in kind. A feisty woman, she would take little guff from anyone, especially when it came to defending her union.

The next day, May 2, she became involved with what she considered to be an unauthorized attempt by both union and management to upgrade wages for war veterans who had returned to the plant. She did not object to the raises as such, but rather that she, the chief steward, had not been consulted on the matter. She spent the rest of the week dealing with one complaint or another. Even on VE (Victory in Europe) Day, May 8, 1945, she entered the plant superintendent's office to represent the opinions and grievances of numerous crib workers.

The stewards at Briggs started their own news bulletin, *On Guard,* subtitled *Instructions for Committeemen Chief Stewards and Stewards.* Written and printed by the Educational Committee of Local 212 UAW-CIO, issue number 4 contained a complaint from Faye Taylor, personnel director for Briggs, that "there certainly aren't any thoughts conveyed in this Bulletin which would create harmonious relationships" between management and labor. Genora shot back that this statement showed that Taylor and his company cohorts feared an "enlightened steward body." The union's educational committee, she said, "is responsible to the [union] membership," and it was "up to the membership" (not the company) to "determine whether ON GUARD is creating unharmonious relations with management."[43]

Detroit was the industrial heart of the nation during World War II and led the way in producing war materiel and provided a breeding ground for conflicts between management and labor. Any union activity against the company was labeled by stockholders and government as "traitorous" to the cause. If the companies had behaved, unionists claimed, and had not monetarily enriched themselves by the war, things might have turned out differently. Genora censured capitalism for its profit-gouging ways and led many like-minded people to ask who the real traitors were: unionists or capitalists? She opposed the war from the beginning, believing that its inspiration came from imperialistic politicians, but that did not mean she acted disloyally toward the fighting men and women in the armed forces. By the same token, she took care that her nonmilitary unionist colleagues—the ones not in uniform but who nevertheless worked in factories during the war—received fair treatment.

The war over, the SWP sent Sol to Flint as a recruiter, for it reckoned Flint the most promising city in the country for gaining members. Sol lived with Genora's parents, and her father at last came to have a begrudging respect for his "wayward" daughter. Genora stayed in Detroit, at Gladwin Street, still working for Briggs and increasing her union activities on a daily basis. Detroit was "such a fertile field of contacts—what a golden opportunity for the party!" Both the UAW and the SWP were pioneering in the postwar period because there were no "emergencies" that had to be handled. "We are breaking new territory" in relations between management and labor, Genora said, "and other generations" will benefit from our experiences. "This is a new period for us all; we are becoming recognized as a force by our friends and our enemies."[44]

She threw herself—or tried to—into the labor union activities of Detroit, especially as they applied to Local 212. An aisle caucus meeting with 800 people present came up with the following concerns at the Briggs plant: the matter of seniority throughout the departments and the entire plant; settlement of all grievances, no matter how trivial; and immediate negotiations on a 30 percent pay raise for all workers. If no actions were taken on these matters, they promised a strike within a fortnight. None were taken—at least in Detroit. GM in Flint was struck for several weeks in 1945. The union felt that the day President Harry Truman said the war with Japan was over, the no-strike pledge ended. Genora kept working on a speech she planned for the Educational Committee of Local 212 titled "How the Workers Took Power in Russia," dedicated to union members everywhere. Sol pressured her to join him in Flint. "For both of us to do our best for the party, we should be together. Do you agree?"[45] No, she did not agree. She wrote, "Ernie [Mazey] wants me to stay here [in Detroit] as long as I can." One person, it was adjudged by the Detroit SWP, was enough for Flint—and that was Sol. As time passed, it seemed as though Genora never again wanted to see the town where she grew up. In Detroit at the end of August 1945, there were 150,000 workers newly unemployed, 30,000 of whom were women. Genora joined other members of Local 212 protesting against "returning to work in the kitchen" and the wiping out whole Briggs departments, particularly those with a history of vigorous labor activity.[46] Genora was one of those to go.

Historians Leila Rupp and Verta Taylor remark with some understatement that "women active on behalf of women's rights in the post-1945 period perceived the social environment as an inhospitable one."[47] They quoted a woman as saying, "My husband is a firm believer in 'woman's place is in the home.' . . . He . . . belittles most women's groups. . . . I get the impression that what he wants is a good housekeeper . . .

[but] I feel morally obligated to take part [in community affairs] in view of my education and some capabilities."[48] Activists believed that there was nothing wrong with a woman worker returning to full-time domestic duties. Problems arose only if they were forced to do so. There should be a choice on the matter by each individual woman.

Postwar realities included management arguments that hiring women entailed increased costs. Additional facilities had to be installed, such as toilets separate from men (although bathrooms during the war had been shared by men and women). Also, absenteeism of women workers was greater than that of men, especially if there were children at home. Even the postwar president of the UAW, R. J. Thomas, seemed to be against women activism when he said, "I think it is pretty well recognized that it is an additional expense to a management to have women."[49] Employers argued that it was not cost-effective to train women for work (especially in skilled jobs) because women workers were only temporary. And, of course, there was always the fear that "women would displace male workers at lower rates of pay."[50] Women, however, were already in the workplace and had been for years. Most of the arguments against adding women turned out to be more contrived than legitimate. "The attitudes toward working wives reflected firmly entrenched ideas about woman's proper place, not the reality of the job market." In 1936, for example, 82 percent of the American population "felt wives should not work" if husbands had jobs.[51] Sherna Gluck writes that "eventually, half of the women defense workers were drawn from the ranks of women who were already in the work force before the war."[52] It is clear, then, that postwar opposition to women employment was more socially than economically motivated.

The "woman of the house" could either continue her present employment or seek public work, that is, a job outside the home. Historian William H. Chafe notes that "at just the moment when husbands and wives were planning to build new homes, buy new cars, and purchase improved appliances, a series of arbitrary price hikes stood in the way. Many couples found it impossible to fulfill their quest for a higher standard of living on one income."[53] Genora and Sol barely had a *single* income in the immediate postwar period. She helped to print and distribute nearly a thousand pamphlets to protest the postwar industrial actions in Detroit in general and at Briggs specifically. In numerous speeches she tried to bolster union morale and worked with several committees to plan upcoming Labor Day parades in September. She found it necessary, however, to register for unemployment benefits from the federal government (as did Sol in Flint). Genora said that the unemployment lines were so long that the jobless had to stand in them all day; some applicants, she said, lined up at midnight and slept on the sidewalk. She took Denny with her to hold her place in line while she went for food and restroom breaks.

Genora's health grew tenuous again. She wrote to Sol on August 20, "Couldn't sleep for the pain . . . in . . . my chest. And I always get a bit jittery when that happens." She had to come home from a rally because of an attack. "I can't figure out the 'waves' of these pains," she said, "unless it's related to my physical strength giving out."[54] Sol mentioned her attacks of pleurisy, related to her previous bouts with TB, and urged her to take three or four weeks off somewhere in the country before the Detroit winter set in. She promised to get some X-rays taken.

Her work with the investigative committee to look into increased violence against labor union members at Briggs since the war led to personal grief.[55] UAW president Walter Reuther was especially vulnerable to attacks by various thugs and had been beaten at least twice over the years and shot once. Union activists Roy Snowden and Art Vega also were assaulted. When the committee was formed to find the source of this violence, only two people volunteered to serve on it, and one was Genora. "Old dumb-bell me!" she later exclaimed.[56] She had known for years how dangerous it was to cross swords with big corporations. "You could get beaten up walking home or in a beer garden if you talked union in the shop." Corporations, she claimed, actually put a lip reader an aisle or so away from "troublesome" workers to see what they were saying and report to management. "You'd wind up in the hospital the next day."[57]

Contract negotiations were pending with Briggs, and though Genora no longer had steady employment with the company, she still conducted speaking classes to union people, encouraging them to refuse Briggs' offers because she thought they were not generous enough in the post–World War II economic boom. Usually Sol came to Detroit every weekend, arriving late on Friday and returning to Flint on Sunday. On one particular weekend in October 1945, he called to say that he would have to come on Sunday and go back the next day. Thus he was at home with Genora on Gladwin Street during the early morning hours of Monday, October 15. At about 5 A.M. two men—who obviously did not know that Sol was at home—broke into the house through the backdoor, which opened onto an alley. Genora heard them, thinking it was either Denny or Jody returning home. The men maneuvered in the darkness straight to the bedroom without knocking over any chairs or furniture (causing later speculations that they knew their way around the house),[58] and began to beat Genora on her head and body with lead pipes. Sol awoke and threw himself across Genora to stave off the blows. "If he hadn't put his arm over my head," Genora reported later, "I think I would have been injured . . . beyond help. He tried to climb over me, and they clubbed him on his legs so bad that when he tried to stand up against them, he collapsed."[59] When they were finished, the two men walked calmly out of the house and disappeared into the darkness.

Sol was finally able to call an ambulance and then get in touch with Ernie Mazey in Grosse Pointe, informing him of the attack and demanding a thorough investigation. Genora had a fractured collar bone, and blood from gashes in her forehead poured down into her eyes. Her right side was paralyzed by a brain concussion, and she suffered nerve damage on her face. The couple was taken to Detroit's Grace Receiving Hospital, "a cockroach infested place."[60] Genora, in a plaster cast from rib cage to shoulder blades, remained in the hospital several weeks to recuperate from her wounds. A photo of her in one of Detroit's widely circulated newspapers caused consternation among friends and acquaintances. Elaine Roseland wrote, "What a terrifying experience it must have been! How desperate the bosses must be to commit such terroristic acts."[61] Another woman wrote that she was frightened when she saw Genora "all taped up. Whoever did it [the beating] must have been a gangster to beat up a woman." Another wrote that Genora knew "the grim feeling of hate we have for the rats that pulled such an act." After seeing her photo in the papers, a woman named Henrietta wrote to Genora that "we know they couldn't batter down your spirit but they did a hell of a job on your body." Another friend penned, "I guess this is a sample of what we must be prepared for when the bosses become really desperate at the crescendo of militancy the workers will exhibit in the current and coming struggles." Blanche Straub wanted the "hours to be short" and the "days few" until thirty-two-year-old Genora was totally restored to health. And Mildred Oreson said that Genora had "plenty of courage and pluck."[62]

On her release from the hospital, Genora faced several weeks of rehabilitation. Her sister Beatrice, who lived in Detroit, watched after her when Sol returned to Flint. Some years after the attack, Genora told her mother that her face "was still pretty crooked." The big questions for Genora and her friends and family were whether she would ever regain her motor facilities and what brain damage she would have. These questions were answered only in the months and years ahead. There is no doubt that the beatings intensified the health problems Genora already suffered. But this intensity emboldened her further in union work and social reforms. She let it be known that even beatings would not stop her quest for social justice. Detroit police blamed the beating on union leaders, intimating that Genora was getting too "high" in union circles and had to be taken down a peg or two.[63] Local 212 shot back at the police department, citing its lack of progress in investigating any beating of union people that had occurred since the end of the war. Genora and Sol and dozens of their associates put the blame squarely on the Briggs Corporation. First and foremost, it was a vigorous antiunion entity. Second, it was clear that Briggs's leadership detested Genora and her unionism.

Ironically, a few days before her own beating, Genora had led a delegation to ask R. J. Thomas of the UAW to offer a reward for recent assaults on Snowden and Vega. Thomas was out of town, so the group visited Walter Reuther instead. Reuther took her lightly, saying, "Come on Genora. Let's not get dramatic."[64] (Years later, in February 1954, Genora wrote an article for *The American Socialist* titled "I Warned Reuther.")[65] It was only after Reuther was shot—three years after Genora's beating—that he favored serious reward money for bringing assailants to justice. Vincent Dunne of the Minneapolis Teamsters, a union that had suffered much violence itself, visited Genora in the hospital. From his experiences, he surmised, the culprits were thugs hired by the corporation: this was a pattern that had followed almost without fail in past labor strife.[66] According to reports, Briggs had awarded a scrap metal contract to a son-in-law of Michigan mafia leader Santo (Sam) Perrone. In return, Perrone would supposedly "take care" of "uppity" union leaders. This lucrative contract, Genora believed, "resulted in at least five violent and potentially deadly assaults on [various] members of Local 212."[67] Though Perrone had run afoul of the law on past occasions and would again in the future, he and his accomplices were never, beyond a shadow of a doubt, placed at the scene of Genora and Sol's beating in October 1945. At the 1951 hearings of Senator Estes Kefauver, Perrone denied knowing anything about the beatings. Neither, he said, was he aware of any Trotskyists in the Briggs plant, and he had never heard of Genora Dollinger.[68] Genora slowly recovered during the remainder of the year, gradually resuming her activities in Local 212 and the SWP.

On the domestic front at Gladwin Street, one of the lodgers volunteered to redecorate the place. He began to "splash stuff on the walls," and when Genora offered to help, he condescendingly told her that "this is not women's work." She called him a chauvinist. He replied, "For Christ's Sake . . . I'm protecting women more than you are!" Genora wanted to know why he thought this was. "It ruins a woman's insides," he averred.[69]

Also at this time Genora worried because her two sons continued to get into trouble. Denny found a quart of whiskey and got very drunk with some young girlfriends. From time to time Denny suffered numbness in his tongue and face, and Genora wondered if there might be something mentally wrong with him. "No matter what he does," she stated, "I love him and I hate him. I feel sorry that circumstances have turned him into something that he would never have been under a different environment." Jody found and spent $8.00 in dues money that Simon Owen had paid to the union.[70] On another occasion, her pent-up feelings of frustration led her to "whale hell" out of Jody for going to a show without telling her. She hit him so hard when he walked in at 11 P.M. that "she broke the slat and was immediately repentant." She did not have enough money to buy Denny a birthday present. Jody's shoes were so worn out that one of his teachers gave him a pair. Jody was hit by a car and hurt slightly. Denny broke into a house and was subsequently dragged into court. Genora's frustration was apparent when she wrote to Sol, "Bills, bills, bills. No money. No job yet. And your answer: Come to Flint, come to Flint!"[71] It was well and good to be a young and well-known, even important, labor-feminist and social reformer, but Genora paid a price for it.

She was asked to run for a seat on the SWP's executive committee in Detroit. She did not know whether to seek the office or not; her indecision was triggered by living apart from Sol. Genora told her supplicants that she and Sol did not "want to continue being separated." The couple could not reach an agreement on either his coming to Detroit or her going to Flint, and so they asked the party to decide for them. The party claimed that it could not "make any such decision." Genora and Sol would "have to iron out this problem for themselves," although the party made it clear that it did not want Sol to leave Flint because "no one could replace him," and it wanted Genora to remain in Detroit. One party wit suggested that the two arrange to meet periodically in Pontiac, a place equidistant between Detroit and Flint.[72]

Although she relished the thought of serving on the SWP executive committee, Genora chose not to run for the office. She would have been separated from Sol for even longer periods, and, though not admitting it publicly, she yearned for some stability in her life. "I have truly attempted to push my personal wishes and longings into the background," she wrote to Sol, "and I appreciate the work there [in Flint] to the movement." With some sarcasm, she wrote, "It [the separation] has been good for you—it has been good for the party. . . . But I cannot see where it would be good for me."[73]

Extremely busy in Detroit during the early spring of 1946, she and her colleagues looked forward to a visit from socialist activist Farrell Dobbs. They rejoiced when a court ruled against Briggs for short-paying certain workers who did not meet various production standards. The corporation was ordered to pay $100 to each worker who had been illegally docked.[74] Genora educated a union "faction" on its "duty in recruiting and soliciting contributions" for the fund drive.[75] Personality clashes had to be dealt with, as unionists and socialists alike showed that they were as capable as any capitalist of getting into political squabbles. Genora—when she was not politicking herself—acted as a peacemaker (an unusual role for her) on more than one occasion. Unemployed but active in Local 212 in Detroit, she lived largely off compensation checks from the federal government. Did she feel any compunction collecting a check from a government whose policies she disagreed with so much? Not at all. This was the "benevolent" side of government; this was what government was supposed to do: protect and defend its citizens in their times of need. On May 6, 1946, Genora went to collect her last check but could not produce her social security card; she had lost it.[76] It would take several days, she was told, to get a new one.

The next day, May 7, 1946, she hired on under the name Johnson at Burkharts, a textile firm, using Budd Wheel as a reference but definitely not Briggs. Ingesting huge amounts of cotton dust into her lungs each day, Genora worked ten hours a day at seventy cents an hour.[77]

This bare subsistence intensified her life on Gladwin Street. She "sure as hell" was not going to "get up every morning at 5:30 and slave away for those stinking wages" so that some of the merchant mariner residents could sleep "till noon and then go shoot the breeze with the boys at the local . . . come home, read the papers, drink coffee and then crawl into bed to read . . . and smoke"—"My bitterness," she told Sol in understatement, "is beginning to get out of control."[78]

A friend told her that Sol's recruitment for the SWP in Flint would take several years. That, Genora told Sol, was a problem "for [Sol] and the party to work out," for she made it clear that she was not soon coming back to Flint. Having found her niche in the SWP and the UAW in Detroit, she intended to stay. "I am serious," she told Sol, "about wanting some time to do some reading. . . . If we're ever going to be back together again, I'd like to know it. Our marriage, even though it isn't the major consideration, certainly looks pretty hopeless right now, doesn't it?"[79] Sol replied the next day: "Ever since I first met you it hasn't been easy to decide which way we were going."[80] He believed her "refusals to consider Flint at all delays our getting together for a long period of time. The only way I will get out of Flint as I see it is when I am needed in some more important center of activity." Uppermost in his mind was Trotskyism for world revolution and "the establishment of the Socialist Republic of Labor, for the American worker." He added, "Capitalism with its slave wage system must be abolished and dictatorship of the Proletariat must be instituted if the complete emancipation of [workers] is to be a reality."[81]

Sol and Genora loved each other; that is clear. Nevertheless, each put party interests before the welfare of the other. Could their mutual love survive loyalty to the party? Genora told Sol when he went to New York in mid-May 1946 to "put the problems between us out of your mind so you can concentrate on the bigger party problems." Was it loyalty to the party or personal pique that caused Genora to write in such a manner? She was "deeply hurt" by Sol constantly characterizing her as a "flighty person" and blamed such behavior on his "pride."[82] She asked him to stop classifying her disagreements with him as "psychological reactions."[83] Responding, Sol asserted that "we have interests that don't coincide." They had been married now for nearly five years, and he told Genora that "as long as you have the feeling that you can be happier elsewhere without me we can never be happy. It will always be between us." He regarded his proposed visit to New York as a "sort of swan song" and looked forward to it "with regret" because he knew their love had been blind; but with her eyes wide open, Genora had perhaps found a "better and happier life" than the one she'd had with Sol.[84]

The upshot of this dialogue was that Sol would remain in Flint (except for occasional visits to New York, Detroit, and other cities where labor activities were intense), and Genora would stay in Detroit. Both made this decision on matters of principle; maybe their marriage was strong enough to sustain lengthy separations, but, then again, maybe it was not. The overriding allegiance of each was to the party; the triumph of the proletariat through the SWP became the thought that consumed both of them.

Relations between Sol and Genora reached a stalemate by summer 1946. Sol remained in Flint, and Genora was "sticking to the Briggs' boys" in Detroit, many of whom had the "DTs" from too much alcohol consumption.[85] Among the comings and goings on Gladwin Street, a stray Boston bulldog, which Genora named "Bozo," took up residence. Sol was pleased with the canine because he thought it might give Genora extra protection at home.

About the boys, she wrote presciently that "I think I made a mistake in getting the bike. They are gone constantly and won't do anything around here." In September 1946, Denny and Jody were riding their motorized bike, with Denny guiding and Jody riding the handlebars. Apparently, Denny went through a stop sign, and although cabbie Merton L. Mace tried to dodge them, the two boys were thrown off the bike, and Jody suffered serious head injuries. Rushed to Hurley Hospital, he died two days later. A distraught Genora swore that Mace had been speeding and so could not stop in time. She sued for $25,000 damages but later dropped the charges.[86] Denny survived the crash with minor injuries.

Genora took Jody's body back to Flint to the Reigle Funeral Home, where several of his classmates were pallbearers. Condolences came in from all over the country. Her old friend and fellow union activist Ernie Mazey wrote to Genora, "Dear Comrade, you certainly have had more than your share of the hard knocks of life."[87] Another friend wrote that Jody "was a wonderful kid, with a class consciousness and a revolutionary spirit which he got from you, and which a lot of us could go a long way to emulate."[88] Oscar Coover, her brother-in-law, wrote, "I think I know you well enough to know that you will bear up under this as heroically as you have the ones in the past and that you will be on the fighting line again soon." But it took a while, for Jody's death subdued her. A few months later, her mother, Lora, died.

The late 1940s and early 1950s were not happy years for Genora. Her oldest son, Dennis, was admitted to a Flint hospital in 1947, suffering numerous ailments, including what was apparently an early stage of multiple sclerosis. He kept running away from the hospital and returning to Detroit to be with Genora and his friends. Kermit would come and get him one time, Sol another. Denny entered hospital after hospital; then, apparently making a secret of all his illnesses, he enlisted in the United States Army in 1949. Almost instantly, he went absent without leave (AWOL), a situation that became chronic with the young man.

In mid-1948, Genora had begun—after her near-fatal beating—to get back into full swing with union and SWP activities. She endorsed an idea from her friend Bert Christensen, a member of the Local 598 Education Committee. He suggested an annual "White Shirt Day" in Flint to commemorate each year the February 11 anniversary of the UAW victory over GM. Christensen "wanted workers to wear white shirts traditionally worn by managers to show the company they were equally important people." The shirts represented equal respect and treatment for blue-collar workers. "Workers try to keep their shirts as clean as the bosses."[89] White Shirt Day quickly became a tradition throughout the UAW, and it continues to be celebrated into the twenty-first century.

In mid-1949 Genora was in New York—her first extended visit since 1939, when she was married to Kermit—for the May Day celebrations that year. She wrote to Sol back in Flint that she has "acquired a new status in the Party now that I have remained married to you for nearly eight years. Comrades want to talk to me to obtain advice. I tell them I'm no father-figure."[90] She attended a citywide SWP meeting on Palestine and the future of the Jews there (several colleagues suggested that she convert to Judaism) and sat in on party seminars that discussed the nature of Stalinism and "Thermiodorian reactions"; she wrote to Sol that they must "get discussions like this in Flint."[91] Speaking to the New York Painters Union, which was contemplating a citywide strike at the time, she pointed out that there were 6,000 union painters in New York City but "40,000 scabs."[92] Women of the Chelsea and Harlem branches of the SWP invited Genora to speak, regarding her as "some kind of leader of the women in the Party . . . who should be sent on a National Tour."[93] Genora was flattered but frightened by the attention. Though she always spoke out on things that mattered to her, she had a residual inferiority complex—perhaps brought on by youth ful struggles with her father—that she covered up with bravado.

In leisure time in New York, she went to numerous movies, including *Panic, Les Enfants du Paradis,* and *Paisano,* many of which had to do with international themes of Socialism. She visited almost every museum and art gallery in the city and was thrilled at watching Jackie Robinson when the Brooklyn Dodgers confronted the Cincinnati Reds at Ebbets Field. Sol told her "to stay [in New York] until you have had your fill of intellectual atmosphere."[94] She wrote back, "Do you really know what you are saying?" She loved New York and showed a marked reluctance to leave. If she went back to Michigan, she was "so afraid that I'll never again get the chance to drink in New York as I have been doing this time." And then she remembered who she was, and said, "Oh, the lot of workers under Capitalism!"[95]

Genora Johnson Dollinger had come a long way since 1937: a new husband whom she adored, despite the long absences; vital roles in defense plants during World War II; personal family tragedies that would have destroyed many people; and, above all, the status of a rising luminary in the SWP throughout Michigan and New York and, indeed, the country. At the beginning of the 1950s, she gave every indication that she intended to continue her association with unionism and feminism. She kept assuring herself that she could handle any situation or crisis that might lie ahead. Only to a certain extent was she correct.

Five Trials and Tragedies

Genora Dollinger joined postwar critics of certain practices and institutions of American life. Why were blacks in the South and factory workers in the North deprived of compassion and benevolence, by both government and big corporations? Why were so many citizens without health care or even medical insurance? Why did the rich gain political power only because of their wealth, while millions of ordinary citizens had little or no voice in how government was run?

The political and social climate during the midpoint of the twentieth century caused these questions to be viewed suspiciously by much of the American populace. The Soviet Union was now our enemy, and criticisms of the United States were, in the minds of many citizens, tantamount to treason. An early sign of this feeling was the newsletter *Counterattack*, begun in May 1947 by a group of former FBI men.[1] This journal's purpose was to pinpoint—at least from its perspective—Communist infiltration into several retail, wholesale, and department store unions, as well as into numerous entertainment venues, such as radio, movies, and the newly developing one of television.[2]

The House Un-American Activities Committee (HUAC) of the late 1940s complemented *Counterattack*. This committee was inspired by the Great Depression, during which the Works Progress Administration (WPA) funded, among other things, authors and playwrights to keep them gainfully employed. Some members of Congress worried that the stories and plays might be too critical of the American way of life and wanted some oversight of the works produced. Congressman Martin Dies, of Texas, formed a committee to keep an eye on the writers and performers. In the immediate post–World War II onset of the Cold War between the United States and the Soviet Union, HUAC took up where the Dies Committee left off, except that its role was expanded to include not only literary works but also the activities of academics, labor unions, and civil rights workers as well as cinematic expressions. Over the years, HUAC sent many people to prison and ruined scores of professional careers. In June 1950, under the auspices of *Counterattack,* a group known as American Business Consultants published *Red Channels,* a book that listed numerous organizations, including labor unions and the SWP, as being affiliated with the Communist Party. These three entities—*Counterattack,* HUAC, and *Red Channels*—fueled the mood of suspicion during the postwar years. None, however, reached the levels of xenophobia expressed by Wisconsin's junior senator, Joseph McCarthy. He claimed to have found Communists in the State Department and other governmental agencies. How many did he personally find? None. This did not mean, however, that there was absolutely no influence of Communists in American government. It did mean that legitimate investigations were sidetracked and that serious assaults were made on the free speech provisions of the First Amendment and the due process guarantee of the Fifth Amendment. It also meant guilt by association. If one knew a real Communist, one was likewise tainted as treasonous.

With these newsletters and congressional committees and a sensationalist-seeking senator all looking for "Reds," Genora Dollinger had little chance of escaping scrutiny. She and Sol became the objects of FBI and even CIA investigations. Showing her disdain for the watchdogs of society, she seemed deliberately to gore the ox in expressing her opinions. She was even willing to run for government office to express them.

Her entry into politics was highly predictable. Unwittingly, perhaps, she had been preparing for a political debut since the 1937 sit-downs and her experiences as a shop steward during World War II. She had an alto voice that could, on occasion, become quite animated as she argued her points of view. Though she sometimes mistrusted her own abilities, she had never been never shy, even in grade school or the Methodist church. This combination of nerve and oratory produced a political savvy by the midpoint of the twentieth century. American voters, though, did not easily embrace Genora's message. Time and again the electorate hath shown its centrist characteristics, supporting neither the extreme left nor the radical right. Whatever else she might have been, Genora was a fire-eating leftist by the early 1950s.

In 1948 the SWP nominated her as a U.S. senatorial candidate for Michigan. When she became a senator, she told her followers, she would be a "thorn in the side" of big business corporations. She drew applause from her partisan audiences by asserting that, "as a representative of my class . . . the working class . . . one of the FIRST things I'll do is to draw up a bill . . . making it LAW . . . that ANY company or corporation FORCING ITS WORKERS OUT ON STRIKE . . . [presumably through shut-outs and failures to collectively bargain] WILL HAVE TO PAY LOST TIME TO THEIR WORKERS FOR EVERY HOUR, EVERY DAY, EVERY WEEK THAT THEY [corporations] DELAY [the settlement of] THE STRIKE." A "six hour day at eight hours pay," she believed, would reduce unemployment and the practice of "pitting one worker against another." After her election, she confidently claimed, she would be the "eyes and ears" of "her people." Her senatorial reports would show the *real* conditions of the country—that the entire government was a stooge of Wall Street—and she would print her reports in union publications. "And who knows . . . these actual . . . revelations may increase their circulations to such an extent that we have Union daily newspapers!"[3]

Even voters who disdained the ways of corporate management wanted to change the system through reform, not through the revolutionary tactics they came to believe Genora counseled. She came nowhere close to winning or, for that matter, even collecting any votes. Sol checked an area "where I was sure of the count from friends and family."[4] No votes for Dollinger were registered. The campaign was less important to her than the opportunity to publicize SWP philosophies and perhaps recruit new party members.

Genora told interviewer Sherna Gluck that after a time in the senatorial campaign, she did not really enjoy it. Michigan, she acknowledged, with its two large parts—the Lower and Upper peninsulas—was too big for the number of personnel she had campaigning for her and the amount of money in her treasury. She was "damn" tired by the time it all ended, and she had known all along that she did not have a chance of winning.[5] She did, however, greatly enjoy the shivaree, essentially a party with much food and drink, that a number of Irish voters staged for her in Lansing and that lasted all night and well into the next day. In fact, some celebrating groups went from one festivity to another in the capital city—exhausting but exhilarating.[6]

Politically undaunted, Genora forged ahead in 1950, running again on the SWP ticket for the U.S. House of Representatives from Michigan's Sixth District. The previous defeat, if anything, had emboldened her. She wrote to the *Flint Journal* that "the capitalist politician . . . is in a class by himself. He can lie, deceive . . . and is rewarded with honorary degrees and prestige. While he doesn't become a member of the Liar's Club of America, he can surpass them with his flights of calculated imagination."[7] She was running for Congress, she claimed, "to give organized labor an opportunity to vote for an . . . independent candidate." Both major parties, she asserted, used the "undeclared" war against Korea to create "colonial oppression" and placed the debt for it on the portion of American society least able to afford it: the working people. President Harry Truman, she exclaimed, had betrayed the country. He had supported injunctions against miners, broken a railroad strike on the eve of the Korean War, reneged on his promise to repeal the Taft-Hartley Law, and his and the Democratic Party's record on civil rights was "miserable."[8] The time was overdue, she claimed, for labor to "have its representative in Congress to defend [its] interests at all times."[9]

When Genora received official notification that her name was on the ballot, the mailman delivered it to Mrs. Sharpe, the Dollingers' landlady. He said to her, "You know, you got the biggest Communist in the city of Flint living in your house." Mrs. Sharpe replied, "No, she is not; she's the biggest Socialist," showing that at least one resident of the United States knew the difference between Communism and Socialism.[10] Again, Genora barely registered in the voting booths. It became clear that her radical message to Michigan and America would have to be sent through means other than governmental office.

She attended the 1950 New York meeting of the SWP, identified herself as a waitress, and claimed that her name was Jeanette Lane.[11] She explained that this was her Communist Party name, although she always avowed that she was not a Communist. She was, apparently, being facetious here. By the early 1950s, various Michigan state agencies and the FBI were scrutinizing the activities of the SWP, its personnel, and other groups that the U.S. attorney general had placed on its "subversive" list. To throw off the snoopers, both Genora and Sol (under the name Jerry Kirk, for example) used numerous aliases over the next several years.

She attended meetings of the predominately black Antioch Baptist Church in Flint and was elected to the executive board of the local National Association for the Advancement of Colored People (NAACP). These activities attracted the attention of government agencies because black activism in many instances was included in both state and national government's definition of subversive activity.

Several reform groups (including the NAACP) wanted to bring internationally famous actor and singer Paul Robeson to Flint to speak for the local and national Progressive Party, headed in 1952 by Vincent W. Hallinan. The city fathers and citizenry made it clear that Robeson would not be welcome because of his political ideologies. Genora angrily told a local newspaper that the drive to keep Robeson out resulted from a fear campaign. It was an escalation of the witch hunt going on at the national level with HUAC and McCarthy—a seeping down of political uniformity to the local levels. Genora wanted to know if this outrageous act would go unchallenged, charging that "union leaders, who should know by now that the ultimate recipient of the whiplash of the witch hunt will be themselves, participate in this disgraceful undemocratic orgy." Genora, acting as SWP spokesperson, wrote to the *Flint Journal* that the SWP supported the philosophies of neither Robeson nor Hallinan, but if the party had had enough space, it would welcome Robeson and his "progressive" ideas to Flint to "show how free speech is defended in practice." Both Robeson and the Progressive Party, she argued, were too capitalistic, as shown essentially by Robeson's success in movies, which reflected a "profit motive." The SWP, however, fought for the "new society of Socialism that [was] sweeping across half the world and [would] eventually, and not too long at that, embrace the entire world."[12] This was not the only prediction Genora ever got wrong.

The SWP in Flint and other industrial parts of Michigan decided to flood the ballots with candidates for local and statewide elections. Genora let it be known that she wanted to run in the November 1952 election for state superintendent of education and instruction. Before the ballots could be printed, let alone certified, the state legislature passed what became known as the Trucks Act. Taking its cue from the national level, Michigan (along with several other states) moved to curb the activities of subversive individuals and groups within its borders by requiring a loyalty oath to be taken by all political candidates and civil-service workers. As a result, SWP candidates, including Genora, were removed from the Michigan ballot. Both major parties, Democratic and Republican, she claimed, were responsible for the travesty of the Trucks Act. "The SWP will fight this police-state edict. We repudiate the infamous 'subversive' label." Who were the *real* subversives? They were the "state legislature which passed the law, the Governor who signed it and the Secretary of State who put it into practice." She threatened to sue "to regain our place on the November ballot in Michigan." And then she added, "It has become our duty to keep alive the best traditions of American democracy which are rapidly vanishing under the spur of the witch hunt."[13]

Genora's life fluctuated between heady political and union public appearances and health traumas and personal tragedy. In addition to tuberculosis, she developed high blood pressure, and a benign tumor was removed from her right breast.[14] In 1950, her father, Ray Albro, died. She and Ray had not always gotten along with one another, especially in earlier days when she thought of him as a capitalist and he thought of her as a revolutionary Trotskyist. As the years passed, however, their relationship had grown into mutual appreciation and love. Genora was closer to her mother, Lora, than anyone else. Losing her in 1949 was difficult (especially after Jody died in 1946), and now losing her father only added to her sadness. Ray Albro died on his way to work at the Buick plant. This was ironic because at one time he owned several photographic stores in Flint and elsewhere and had been relatively well off. Ruined by the Depression, he had gone to work for GM. He had just gotten off a bus when he suffered a fatal heart attack; the only identification on him was his Buick badge.[15] Genora, embittered by all the deaths in her family (three in the past four years), wrote a poignant letter to her deceased father:

> Next March you would have been 65, Dad, and you were planning to quit because you could get your GM pension. But you didn't live to receive that pittance because you were literally worked to death, as most workers are before their 65th birthday. . . .
>
> At the next quarter when GM's huge profits are announced we'll have the aching knowledge that this time it was our father's life—and death—that went into the greedy piling up of those profits. And all that GM left for the members of the family is to stand beside a white lined casket and whisper, "Goodbye Dad."[16]

Though Genora wrote this letter for the local press, it wound up in the files that the FBI had begun on her and Sol. The government apparently wanted to show how Genora was taking her fight against GM and other big corporations to a personal level. How this made her dangerous to the government, only the bureaucratic mindset of the FBI could explain. Genora seemed increasingly to embrace the thought that an individual's life was determined more by external forces than his or her own activities and character. She came close to saying that an unbridled, corporate-controlled society killed her father, just as it had her son, Jody, a few years before. But then she had suffered another bereavement, so one must make allowances.

Genora served as her father's executrix. Going through his effects, she found an old trunk full of books, including the Albro family Bible. The money in the estate provided his heirs (four children: Beatrice, Barbara, Jarvis, and Genora) seven hundred dollars each. Genora and Sol used their share of the inheritance as a down payment on their first house at 1507 Oak Street, in Flint.[17]

Genora's trials and tribulations did not stop with Ray's death. Her son, Denny, had always been a troubled child. Born in 1931, he was a teenager during the war and had lived in Detroit with Genora and his younger brother, Jody, during most of the conflict. Denny was difficult to discipline, getting into trouble with teachers at school and with the law. In 1949, at the age of nineteen, he was able to conceal his prior illnesses and disciplinary problems from recruiters and joined the United States Army. He was constantly AWOL, which resulted in frequent searches for him not only by military police but also by Genora, Sol, Kermit, and other friends and family members. Finally, Denny was judged to be seriously ill and was discharged from the military and sent home to Genora. Because his illness was not related to any part of his military service, he was ineligible for treatment at any Veterans' Administration hospitals. After numerous trips to civilian physicians and hospitals, doctors diagnosed Denny as suffering from multiple sclerosis, intensified, some health providers claimed, by Jody's death a few years before: Denny had been piloting the bike in the accident that took his brother's life. Genora and Sol could not afford private treatment for Denny. "It was a disheartening development," Sol recalls. "No author of a Greek tragedy could have conceived of a plot that could rival this real-life drama."[18]

The only hospital where Sol and Genora could take Denny was the Pontiac State Hospital, a facility primarily treating mentally ill individuals. They had no choice: it was either this hospital or none at all. Genora hitchhiked (although she worked for an auto factory, she didn't own a car) from Flint to Pontiac every weekend to see her firstborn but finally concluded that Denny's hospitalization had come to naught. He showed no improvement. In fact, Genora saw further deterioration each time she visited. She finally brought him home because she knew he was near death. When Denny passed away on December 26, 1950, Genora had now lost two sons, her mother, and her father within four years. Those who saw her in public and listened to her speeches had no idea of the inner turmoil she suffered. Her depression after Denny's loss took months of agonizing soul searching to conquer. As with her father's death, Genora lashed out at those events and institutions that she thought caused Denny's demise. She wrote angrily in *The Militant* that "this 19 year old boy didn't have half a chance under a decaying capitalistic system of wars and [economic and mental] depression and so fell its helpless victim just as thousands of his generation are now daily falling"[19] (this last reference was to the commitment of U.S. troops to South Korea). She and her friends began to view Denny as much a victim of World War II as any battlefield soldier. Sol wrote to Genora that her article on Denny in *The Militant* sounded bitter. It was as bitter, Genora wrote back, "as life has been to me and other working class fighters."[20]

She received numerous letters of condolence. One woman wrote that she was "sorry about Denny" and hoped her own son would "have a chance to live a full life, free of the privation and problems that faced Denny." Several survivors of the Holocaust who lived in Michigan sent Genora little red flags to put on Denny's grave, along with a quote from Rosa Luxembourg: "In spite of all." They also sent a dozen red roses to be placed on Denny's grave, with a note that read, "Goodbye to Dennis Robert."[21] She wrote to Sol that there had been "too many changes all at once—my job, my son, my husband, and I just can't put out the fire in the little house and let it get cold and dead too."[22] Nevertheless, always dedicated to labor and feminist causes, Genora went about her business. She gave a rousing speech to Local 659 in the middle of January 1951. Many present-day union members, she asserted, had no idea of the role women played in initially organizing the UAW. The GM corporation, particularly Chevrolet, of which Local 659 was a unit, "has never hired more than a handful of women and they think and speak only in terms of men," while present-day union members "never dream that if it hadn't been for the fighting wives, daughters, mothers and sweethearts," the "great victory of 1937 would not have been possible."

One old-timer said that Genora's speech brought "tears to his eyes" and caused some in the audience to want to "go out and bust some more GM windows, just like in the 'good old days.'"[23] She enjoyed the playing and singing on this occasion of the national anthem, which she referred to as the "Star Spanner Bangle," as well as the solemn and sincere invocation by the Reverend G. Curry. But only a couple of days later, she received a package that caught her up with reality: the package was from the hospital and contained Denny's belongings. She could not bring herself to unwrap it. Instead, she called Denny's father, Kermit, to her house to open it. The package had a book with marks in it, forty-eight cents in change, a pen and pencil, and letters that Genora had written to him. It was like a "knife in my heart," she said. "It made me cry," she told Sol, who was in New York. "I have weathered the sympathy cards, the friendly 'consolations,' representatives calling here [and] phoning about headstones, etc., but this box and its contents knocked me for a loop."[24] Genora Dollinger, the hard-bitten ideologist—at least to union, feminist, and philosophical audiences—proved vulnerable to the world's less positive events. This vulnerability manifested itself in her relations with Sol. It was clear that the two were dear to each other, but their mutual love did not prevent flare-ups concerning domestic issues, as well as ideological and philosophical ones. Genora was offered a job at the Checker Bar B Que restaurant, but she hesitated, waiting for the decision as to whether she was going to continue living apart from Sol. Briggs, in Detroit, was taking new applications, and she thought it would be wonderful to be back there, perhaps momentarily forgetting that she had been blacklisted. Sol went to New York in early 1951, taking leave from his job at GM in Flint. He attended the SWP-sponsored Trotsky school to read and study books that explained Socialist positions, particularly those of Karl Marx and Leon Trotsky. He wrote to Genora on January 24, 1951, and asked, perhaps too nonchalantly, "Why are you staying in Flint? There is no reason wondering about the future 'til you have had a chance to relax."[25] This question was ironic as he had tried so long to get her to leave Detroit and return to Flint. When she did because of her 1950 congressional race, Sol then spent much time trying to get her to leave Flint, primarily to join him in New York or wherever he happened to be. He regaled her with descriptions of the books he was reading, including some by noted American historians Charles Beard, Samuel Eliot Morrison, and Henry Steele Commager, and how enthused he was with all his learning. Genora told him that she dreaded being around a lot of people for long periods of time. "I get dizzy and this is not a figure of speech." She was afraid she would stutter in front of groups or in the presence of others. "On the surface," she said, she coped with Denny's death and other problems "the best I know how."[26] Perhaps it was that mood that caused her to explode upon receiving Sol's letter of the 24th. "Don't write me any more letters! For God's sake there is no one here to help me with my problems and you tell me how 'little' they are—constantly." His letter only showed her that "you never knew how to write, to think, to analyze, to appreciate, to understand, to compare, to reason, to detect—or anything else—on advising me." She informed Sol that she was planning to visit New York in the near future as the guest of James P. Cannon, national secretary of the SWP, and she did not "want to see [Sol] for a couple of weeks."[27] The next day she wrote another letter to Sol, full of remorse for her previous statements. Such letters became standard procedure between the two: writing hastily one day and regretting it the next. Sol wrote back that "while I am a long way from Flint, your letter reads like I am on another planet. I thought that writing on these things [described in his letter of January 24] would give you a chance to place them in perspective . . . and I know you can."[28]

She stayed in New York a few weeks and then she and Sol, together in Flint, at least for a time, threw themselves into the activities of the Michigan SWP. Despite her recent protestations to the contrary, Genora always wanted to be the center of attention, but during these accelerated actions in the SWP, she found—to her bemusement, even amusement, and some chagrin—that the FBI had begun to take an interest in her. She told Sol that apparently some of his New York letters to her had been opened, and she immediately suspected the FBI. They needed, she said, a "foolproof" way of sealing envelopes because she didn't believe in "making it easy" for "our friends in the FBI."[29] Genora was aware that the FBI knew of her letter to Sol that lauded India's prime minister Jawharwal Nehru for his attack on Western powers for their "imperialist" practices against Asia, particularly China. "From the depths of Asia comes this powerful roar," she told her husband. "The British Commonwealth knows what this means," she proclaimed, "and so does Wall Street, even tho [*sic*] they must be a little dazed at the audacity [of India's attack on Western policy toward China]."[30] She also knew that the FBI had gotten wind of a speech in which she asserted that the world would eventually come under Communist domination and that there was unrest among workingpeople, who would be in control of the world in the near future. The example of the British government in the postwar period, Genora thought, showed the futility of the Stalinist approach to Socialism. "Gradual socialism was impossible," she believed. Only immediate worldwide revolutions would bring the political results she and her colleagues wanted.[31]

In the summer of 1951, Genora attended a SWP rally at the New Kensington Recreation area in Milford, Michigan, dutifully reported on by an FBI informant. She joined her colleagues in celebrating the successful subscription drive for *The Militant,* the official newspaper of the SWP. Genora asked her followers to compare themselves to the leaders of the first American Revolution. It had not been a "mass uprising of all people wanting the same thing," she argued, "but was led by a group of prepared leaders." SWP members must prepare themselves for upcoming ordeals that would "lead the workers in a successful fight against capitalism."[32]

The strength and vitality of the SWP in Michigan remained minimal throughout the early 1950s, as demonstrated by Genora's failed campaigns in the Senate and House races. Then, in early 1952, the SWP's executive committee of the Flint branch dissolved, presumably because of widespread inactivity, and Sol and Genora resurrected it. They became the executive board and made all the decisions affecting the party in Flint. The couple was to issue all public statements "without the consent of the general membership." The FBI gleefully pointed out that Genora was "one of three publicly acknowledged members of the SWP in Michigan," as was Sol, while the third was unnamed.[33] (It must be kept in mind that although Genora and Sol were aware of FBI surveillance in the 1950s, it was not until much later, through the Freedom of Information Act, that they secured and reviewed their records.)

Another troublesome event occurred in 1952 when Sol himself contracted tuberculosis and was admitted to Genesee County Sanitorium, where he stayed for nine months. He was home, however, for an event that elated them both and helped to ease the depression Genora had suffered since Denny's death: their son, Ronald, was born on April 24, 1952, and he quickly became their pride and joy. They affectionately called him "Ronnie Hossenfeffer" (slang for "Bunny"?) presumably after a German fairy tale character.

When Sol returned to the sanitorium, Genora wrote to him, describing Ronnie's progress (by his first year, he had a vocabulary of forty-nine words).[34] At about four years, Ronnie cheered his doting father by writing to him, "Dear Dad. I love you. I know you are in the hospital and I know you can't help it. . . . You are a sweetheart. Goodbye. Ronnie."[35] Genora comforted Sol as well, telling him that she knew what it was like to be in a sanitorium, with its "country-charity attitude of 'be grateful for your physical care and to hell with your psychological problems.'"[36]

In late 1953 Genora wrote to Sol that he was, once again, going to be a father. "I am sure you have given me a little daughter this time because she has been so cooperative and hasn't bothered me at all in any way."[37] She was elated to be pregnant again—rebuilding a family, with a considerable amount of nostalgia here—and it helped to lessen the flare-ups between them. Their slogan in earlier times had been "we'll find a way or make one," and now they seemed to be on track again. Sadly, however, Genora suffered a miscarriage, which plunged her into another deep depression. Her fragile health contributed to this unfortunate incident. In fact, the miscarriage almost cost Genora her life. The hospital attendants shunted her off to a small room, where Sol found her in a state of disarray. She quietly told him, "For God's sake, get my doctor. I'm dying." Sol brought in Genora's longtime physician, Dr. Maxwell Golden, and he found that she had septicemia of the blood. He and his colleague, Dr. Englemann, a chest specialist, used heroic measures to save Genora, filling her with the latest antibiotics, including penicillin.

Even with health and personal problems, Genora and Sol tried to stay active in the SWP. They attended most of the local meetings and some of the national ones; remained active in recruiting; gained subscriptions for their magazine, *The Militant;* and sponsored numerous social activities. On the surface, at least, all was well between the Dollingers in Flint and the national headquarters in New York. But unbeknownst to Genora and Sol, a fight had been brewing in the SWP for some time over ideological disputes. One of the first signs of trouble occurred when Walter Reuther, president of the International UAW, stated that he would brook no political interference in the performance of his duties. His caveat extended not only to Socialists and Communists but to Trotskyists as well. "This was the first time in the UAW," Sol Dollinger said, "that one was to be excluded because of political beliefs."[38] A large minority of the UAW who followed the SWP disagreed with Reuther's growing despotism, including his opposition to a sliding-scale wage to offset inflation, and defeated him on a number of critical occasions. Such actions by the SWP minority group, to which Genora and Sol belonged, angered national SWP leader James P. Cannon; he thought the minority group wanted a party of "mass action" and predicted an economic depression that would lead to a Trotskyist-dominated American revolution. Such panaceas were idyllic, never coming close to fulfillment. Instead of the American worker engaging in "mortal combat" with capitalism, the movement to get rid of Stalinist influence in the trade unions became paramount.[39] The Communists and the Trotskyists turned on each other, "letting loose a paroxysm of name-calling . . . that soon poisoned the atmosphere in the unions." One independent Socialist remarked, "It's fantastic the way the Communists and the Trotskyists hated each other."[40] A quarrel also developed between much of the SWP membership and Cannon over affairs in Europe and "fears of Stalinism," which became a determining consideration. Two examples of this erudite ideological struggle included the Shachtmanites, led by Max Shachtman, who did not "view Russia as a workers' state to be defended," and the Lovestoneites, led by Jay Lovestone, who believed that "American capitalism was unripe for revolution."[41]

Was Europe going in a Marxist direction? If so, was the emphasis going to be on Stalinism or Trotskyism? Another question was how to categorize several Eastern European countries. The SWP minority faction wanted to declare countries like Yugoslavia as "deformed workers'" states—not capitalistic but not full workers' states, either—"because they had already been absorbed into the USSR." They were, however, eligible to be defended from "imperialist attacks."[42] Yugoslavia's revolution gave it a deformed worker status because it did not side with the West or kowtow to the Stalinist regime, although it possessed some economic and social characteristics of each system. Yugoslavia was special in Europe because it produced a genuine revolution and showed the world, including the USSR, that it could and would fight to maintain its independence. Hungary, Czechoslovakia, Poland, Bulgaria, and the Baltic States remained under the bayonets of the Red Army and should be considered the same as the Stalinist-dominated USSR. Events in China also deepened the developing schisms within the SWP. These fierce and angry ideological disputes threatened to destroy the SWP in the United States. Its leader, James P. Cannon, realized that the SWP minority constituted a third of the party and was growing rapidly. The Dollingers stated, "Fearing that we would soon become a majority, he expelled us in 1953."[43]

An increasing number of SWP members, led by Bert Cochran, worried that their party had become a sect with "narrow ideological doctrines" that the faithful were required to believe; dogmatism had set in. While such an organization might have been appropriate in the context of Russian centrism, it was "out of place" in the democratic atmosphere of the United States. Cochran's followers, including the Dollingers, wanted an open party to "study the real situation in [the United States] and the world."[44] This meant, among other things, that the SWP should educate its members and workers in the broad aspects of Trotskyism, without always trying to start and lead a revolution for which few, if any—at least in the United States—were ready.

Although a dedicated member of the SWP—even serving as its statewide Michigan treasurer for some time—Genora joined Sol, Bert Cochran, and others, in creating the Socialist Union of America (SUA) as a replacement for the SWP. On November 21, 1953, in Detroit, the Midwest founding conference of the SUA outlined its principal programs. Its chief intention was to encourage members to join educational, political, and social organizations to convert people to the Trotskyist persuasion, thereby hastening the revolution. Their ambitions extended to religion, as Genora was quoted by the FBI as saying, "When we take power, we will educate people against God."[45] If true, this statement alone would have alienated most Americans from the SUA. There is, however, no evidence, either before this time or afterward, that she made this assertion. FBI agents were not going to say anything positive about Genora Dollinger, so it is entirely likely that they engaged in slanderous activities on more than one occasion.[46] In retaliation, she railed publicly against "stool pigeons" hired by the FBI to infiltrate industrial plants and report subversive elements and activities, and these public appearances and pronouncements did not go unnoticed by the federal agency. The proletarian revolution, Genora exclaimed, was "the only means of salvation to the chaotic conditions of the world today,"[47] and such statements led the FBI and other government agencies to think she meant force. Her party, first the SWP, and then the SUA, Genora thought, must be prepared to lead the way through mobilization of the disaffected social and industrial units in the United States and, indeed, the world.

Few U.S. workers embraced any kind of firebrand Socialist solutions to whatever problems they had. The last person an American worker might contemplate as he drove his car to work was his laboring brethren in other parts of the world. He was thinking of owning a home in addition to, perhaps, another automobile and obtaining what he considered the finer things in life. He was too concerned and tied up with his own personal household to worry about workers of the world uniting. The post–World War II American worker vowed to fight any system that might drastically challenge his way of life. To his mind, and to millions like him, the greatest threat to his well-being was Communism, whether it be Stalinist or Trotskyist. For these and other reasons Socialism became an ugly word in the American vocabulary.[48]

Such thoughts, however, did not deter Genora and Sol and their SUA colleagues in their socialist endeavors. They did begin to wonder—as it turned out, most rightly so—if their organization reflected ivory-tower philosophical musings rather than realistic concerns in an industrial world. While sincere in their beliefs of a proletarian-dominated society in the United States at least, the ingredients and motivation for the revolution for which they hoped and expected did not exist. The SUA membership expressed the futility of its proclamations, bulletins, and appeals in its official journal, *The American Socialist,* and at a Chicago conference in the summer of 1957 the SUA dissolved itself and was replaced by the newly created New York–based American Socialist Club (ASC). Its members dropped the appeal for a proletarian revolution and worked toward the "education and organization of new socialist forces in order to prepare the way for the building of a new movement of democratic socialism in the United States."[49] The ASC was reformist, intending to work within the system, rather than revolutionary, proposing to destroy the system.

In the late 1950s the cause of Socialism as it related to unions in the United States had fallen on hard times. For one thing, industries steadily moved into the American South, where unionism had never been as pervasive as in the North. Second, economic conditions dictated against a workers' uprising, and third, American workers were loath to support a system they had always viewed with suspicion. Nevertheless, the SWA, SUA, and ASC had validity. They constantly petitioned national, state, and local lawmakers for improvements in worker compensation laws and, in particular, for increased worker safety. In one speech after another, Genora hammered away at the inequities suffered by many workers. She and hundreds of others with a Socialist bent helped ultimately to set laws in place, such as the Occupational Safety and Health Organization (OSHA—a federal organization for monitoring factory safety), which have been beneficial to both industrial and agricultural workers around the country. These Socialist groups had an intense concern for the environment, and Genora, later in life, joined forces with nationally active environmentalist Barry Commoner to protect generations not yet born from the impact of industrial and automotive pollution.

These groups condemned U.S. military involvement in Korea and, later, in Vietnam. These were capitalist ventures, they argued, against people too weak to fight back and ultimately win. These initiatives and others justify some of the Socialist activities in post–World War II America. These Socialist groups were stronger and more effective as reformers than as revolutionaries. Most workers in the United States belonged to the reform-minded Democratic Party. One Socialist, Harry Braverman, wanted his followers to be ready to fill the breach in the future when it became clear that the Democrats were not really helping the working classes. If the Socialists have done their jobs, Braverman asserted, the Democratic Party "will turn to us to lead them in a fight against the imperialist wars, depressions and recurrent crises in the capitalistic government."[50] In the long run, however, workers continued to shy away from Socialist programs.

Genora and Sol grew aloof from the Trotskyist splinter groups that developed in the late 1950s and early 1960s. If any of these Trotsky sects asked for help, Genora contributed her thoughts. The Trotskyist organizations, however, remained isolated from the broad working-class movement, causing members to behave "like the Christian sects of old Rome. They all sought salvation in the scriptures of Trotsky [and] were treated like the students at a Bible School."[51] The various Trotsky groups thought of themselves as martyrs to an overwhelming capitalistic, antisocialist society. The Dollingers, in a way, became the mother and father confessors of the Socialist movement in the United States. But their message increasingly focused on reform within the system rather than overthrowing it through revolution. Genora supported Fidel Castro, joining the Fair Play for Cuba Committee and then, later, Medical Aid for El Salvador. Only much later (1991) did Genora and Sol formally join another political party.

Ideology notwithstanding, the Dollingers found themselves in the company of tens of thousands of other people in the United States who were trying to find and maintain gainful employment. Political, economic, and social philosophies are fine and dandy, but they don't put food on the table. Throughout the 1950s, after her forays into politics, Genora was usually listed in FBI files and other documents as a housewife. She was blacklisted both in Flint (GM) and in Detroit (Briggs). Furthermore, her name had been given to most other employers in these two cities, so her chance of finding sustained employment was practically nil. This condition deepened her radicalism. She personalized things, and her continued unemployment only encouraged her to blame government officials.

The FBI file reference to her livelihood was misleading. She worked, in fact, as a typist, bookkeeper, and stenographer for AFL-CIO Local 21 in Flint for much of the late 1950s. A board member of this union, Jack Johnson, identified her as a Communist and asserted that he would abstain from future meetings of the union if she remained employed. Such an assertion caught Genora's attention. She wrote a heated letter to Johnson on April 23, 1958, and recounted her activities in 1937, particularly those having to do with creating the Women's Emergency Brigade and being shot at and tear gassed. Having done her part for organized labor, she felt she did not have to apologize to the likes of Jack Johnson. She also mentioned her work with the Death Watch at Oak Park and the brutal beatings that both she and Sol had suffered in 1945 at the hands of alleged corporate thugs. As for Genora's Communist affiliation, she said, "Of course, this is the Pandora's box of smears, when once opened is supposed to shut off all defense. The only thing wrong with it is that it is common knowledge that I have never been associated with the Communist Party [a statement that raised doubts in many circles]. . . . My political beliefs are a matter of public record. . . . For five years [prior to 1958] I have not belonged to any political party." She was, however, a member of the ASC, which, by proclamation of its membership, was not considered a political party. She stated in this letter that she was still an "Independent Socialist" without specific political affiliation. She hardly expected, she told Johnson, a union official to use the same blacklisting tactics used by GM and Briggs—she considered it child's play, in fact. "After all these years of being shot at, clubbed, and beaten for the building of the union movement, you could hardly expect me to maintain silence while these vicious tactics are employed by you." Brother Johnson had the right to his own opinions, but she questioned his tactics to deprive her of a job, the same prejudices employed so long by the corporations. "I have learned how to fight for principle," she told Johnson.[52] Within the context of her social, economic, religious, and moral definitions, she did just that—fight for principle.

Still another critic, Charles Wilderspin, at a Greater Flint Industrial Union Council meeting on June 31, 1958, repeated Johnson's charges that Genora was a Communist and that unions should have nothing to do with her. If Genora was angered by Johnson, she was enraged by Wilderspin. "As much as I dislike taking court action against union people," she told him, "I feel you have left me little alternative this time."[53] Although some of her public statements were confusing on the matter, she denied that she was a Communist and stood ready to sue anyone who claimed otherwise. She gave Wilderspin a way out: "I prefer to ask you first for a retraction of your charges against me of being a communist." Apparently he retracted and apologized, for nothing more came of the matter.

While Genora defended herself against what she considered to be unfounded attacks, Sol, after his release from the TB sanitarium, found that he had been transferred to the toughest jobs (speedups, for one) at the Chevrolet Assembly plant to "build a case to eventually lead to a firing."[54] He filed a grievance, but nothing ever came of it. Because of his physical condition, he finally stopped going to work, and GM removed him from its employment rolls once and for all. Sol gained employment of thirty dollars a week by selling televisions for Ralph and George Hamann, both well-known Flint Socialists.[55] Sol and Genora tried to sell real estate for Coburn S. Walker Company in Flint with limited success. Sol became convinced that his chances for permanent employment were better in California than Michigan. He started out for the Golden State, but on reaching St. Louis he found that he had forgotten his packed bag (a Freudian slip, perhaps?) and returned to Flint.[56] In the fall of 1957, he enrolled in Flint Junior College because he believed the "soft economy" of the future would hinder his economic capabilities unless he had some kind of higher education.[57] Economic strictures prevented him from completing his education, so he tried to sell encyclopedias for the Britannica company and was a "hot shot salesman" for a while. The recession of 1958 brought his salesmanship to an end; in fact, the commissions he had previously earned were rescinded when buyers defaulted on their payments.[58]

Paraphrasing Abraham Lincoln (greatly admired by Genora, who considered him our greatest president), when you don't have a solution to a basic problem, do nothing, and it will solve itself. Leaving their political and economic problems behind them—at least for a time—the Dollingers traveled to Mexico. In 1959, the three of them—Genora, Sol, and Ronnie—started out with five hundred dollars in a "reliable" Lincoln and headed South, without any specific Mexican destination in mind. Sol recalled that "the FBI was in a tizzy trying to find out why we were going to a foreign country. . . . [T]hey . . . called on the CIA to track us down. They couldn't find us. It is not surprising since we did not know where we were going nor where we would find sleeping accommodations for the night."[59] They were not the first nor the last Americans to find enchantment in Mexico. The Dollingers spent a fortnight there and then drove leisurely back home to Michigan.

As the decade drew to a close, Sol and his family got the break they had been waiting for. He was hired by the Development Corporation for Israel, better known as State of Israel Bonds (raising funds to build an Israeli infrastructure for industry and commerce), and in this employment he initially worked out of Detroit. The family prepared to leave Flint and again take up residence in the Motor City. His job ultimately took them to California; this was definitely a life change for Sol, but wherever she went, Detroit or otherwise, Genora instantly looked for the first radical cause to become involved in. She found plenty. And in doing so, she became a living contradiction to descriptions of American women of the 1950s by feminist leader Betty Friedan. In her book *The Feminine Mystique* Friedan argued that female magazines had created an image of the American woman as "young and frivolous, almost childlike, fluffy and feminine, passive, gaily content in a world of bedroom and kitchen, sex, babies, and home."[60] Friedan's book inspired thousands of women, in what became known as the second wave of the women's movement (1960s–1980s), to leave home and seek outside employment. Such moves, she assured them, would fulfill their lives. Genora was an unwitting second-waver long before the concept became fashionable. From 1937 onward, her life was geared to serious purposes; from 1953 on, she was a freelance Socialist, and she spent most of her working career away from home. Indeed, since grade school, she had railed against what she perceived to be capitalist injustice to both men and women. Friedan wrote about whom she considered to be the average woman in America. Nothing about Genora Dollinger, however, was average.

Six **California Girl**

In 1960 Genora Dollinger celebrated her forty-seventh birthday, still young enough to be vigorous despite continuing health problems but old enough to have gained some wisdom. National and international labor organizations called upon her for advice and counsel. She had become the grande dame of the labor and Socialist movements in the United States. Many organizations—labor, capital, and otherwise—asked her to speak for their special occasions. She spoke to UAW Local 659 each year on the anniversary (February 11) of the 1937 union contract with GM.

Genora considered the advent of the 1960s as a time of promise for American women and looked optimistically to future developments. She welcomed John F. Kennedy's election in 1960 (though she did not vote for him—or anyone else for that matter) because she sensed a liberal upsurge that would include rights for women. Kennedy's presidency, together with Title VII of the Civil Rights Act of 1964 under President Lyndon B. Johnson (prohibiting discrimination by employers and unions on the basis of sex, race, color, religion, or national origin) helped women in terms of hiring and promotion.[1] Genora supported the equal rights amendment (ERA) and worked for its passage. She also joined the National Organization of Women (NOW) when it was formed in 1965 under the leadership of Betty Friedan and others. NOW quickly became known as an organization that sought equality in the public rather than the private sphere. Genora was of a mixed mind on this question. She always believed that the woman who chose to be a homemaker was as worthy of attention as the one who worked outside of her home. Another misgiving Genora had about NOW was that in its formative years it largely excluded women of color, presumably because at that time so few of them worked outside the home. Genora disagreed with this practice of exclusion but joined NOW anyway in the hope and expectation of changing the system from within.

Increasingly, she became strident in her opinion that labor historians had ignored the role of women in the 1936–37 sit-downs. These labor historians, she charged, were animated by male machismo and did not actually want to acknowledge the work of the Women's Emergency Brigade of 1937 and its significant influences not only on the strike but also on its successful conclusion. One story making the rounds over the years that thoroughly infuriated Genora was that Mrs. Henry Ford had been responsible for the UAW victory in 1937. Henry Ford was supposed to have told his wife that "he would close every auto plant in the world before he would permit unions." Mrs. Ford supposedly replied, "Well, if you do that, I shall have to leave you."[2] Mr. Ford wanted to keep his wife so he ameliorated his views on unionism. Thus the UAW victory in 1937. Such stories were typical, Genora argued, of the historical distortion that had accumulated in reference to the sit-downs of 1936–37. The truth of the matter, she and fellow pioneers kept hoping, would one day be realized. She continued to maintain that no male could ever possibly understand the female psyche. You have to be a woman to understand a woman was the message she projected. Women had special "vibrations" (unfortunately, she did not identify these "vibrations") that no male could ever understand. She reluctantly acknowledged that some male historians (Sidney Fine, for example) had "hit the spot," but most, such as Henry Kraus, writing about the labor movement were, in her judgment, far afield from reality.

These thoughts and progressions were interlaced with the Dollinger family's preparations for residence in Detroit. Genora and Ronnie stayed behind in Flint while Sol took care of numerous technicalities relating to his new job. He had to go through a training program for several weeks and was put up in a Detroit hotel room, with his new employer footing the bill. Sol's starting salary was $6,500, more money than he had ever made before. Remaining in Flint, Genora maintained her activities in the worlds of justice and reform. She and her NAACP colleagues responded to numerous complaints from the black community. Some teachers at the Martin School in Flint played phonograph records of the "Little Black Sambo" stories to their pupils. The offending records were removed. At Franklin D. Roosevelt High School, a teacher referred to the head of the school as a "nigger principal."[3] The teacher was reprimanded. A dance studio in Flint segregated a four-year-old African American student from her white classmates. The NAACP, through the city attorney's office, forced the studio to change its practices. A bar at the corner of Cornelia and North Saginaw refused to serve African Americans until the NAACP, led by Genora, stepped in. A grocery store owner on St. John's Street was chastised when he fired all the African Americans working there because he "could not trust colored people." Racial matters even got into the death business in a case known as *Spencer v. Flint Memorial Park Cemetery.* A black man, J. M. Spencer, bought lots from George Hamann, and at first the cemetery officials refused to make the necessary transfers of ownership titles. In another incident, a black citizen of Flint, Edward Hall (alias Calvin Williams), was found to be a fugitive from a Georgia court (for unspecified offenses). He was placed in the Flint jail to await extradition to Georgia. Genora and NAACP colleagues, determined that Hall not be sent back to a "Georgia Chain Gang," spent much time and money fighting his extradition. Because there had been no black jurors in this case, extradition was not granted and Hall stayed in Michigan.[4]

Genora savored a letter from Dr. Martin Luther King Jr. expressing his gratitude for the work of the Flint NAACP. In a NAACP newsletter she announced plans for a statewide boycott of the Woolworth stores, "in solidarity with our brave and courageous brothers in Dixie." If blacks could not sit at lunch counters in North Carolina's Woolworth stores, reform-minded people should protest at every Woolworth outlet in the country. Organized demonstrations against Woolworth took place in Flint, Detroit, Grand Rapids, and Lansing. Genora and her coworkers called for "sympathy marches" throughout the country, and there were several of these, all the way from New York to Chicago to Los Angeles. Genora forcefully told her followers that "if Woolworth practices Jim Crow in the South, we can buy dime store items elsewhere."[5]

"Genora and activity went hand in hand," an admiring Sol said of her. "There was a restlessness that I attributed to an inheritance from her Puritan ancestors. The idea of staying home, cooking, sewing, washing and ironing were alien to her nature, although she was a good cook and could sew her own stylish clothes." She was a natural organizer. "If a project she was engaged in ended," Sol said, "she sought out a new one.

The word 'defeat' did not exist in her vocabulary. She had enlisted in the cause to . . . change the capitalistic system. Genora was prepared to make any sacrifice to accomplish that goal." Despite Socialist commitment, Genora maintained an affiliation with the Unitarian Church. She had joined, not particularly for religious reasons—although her membership did show the FBI's statement about her and God to be libel—but because of the intellectual content of its services and public-forum meetings.[6] Anything and everything that furthered the cause to which she had dedicated her life was fair game for Genora Dollinger.

The greatest activity in the early 1960s that the Flint NAACP and, to some extent, the national organization engaged in took place in Monroe, North Carolina, one of the flashpoints of the early civil rights movement. The first event involved a black veteran of the Marine Corps, Robert Williams, who had worked for Ford in Michigan; he formed a chapter of the NAACP in Monroe, North Carolina, with a local physician, Dr. Albert Perry, as its vice president. One of their first endeavors was to get swimming privileges for black children at the municipal pool. Not wishing to integrate, they just wanted to have one day a week set aside for black swimmers. They were told that the pool "would have to be drained" after each black use and filled up again with fresh water, a procedure that was too costly. Another event was the "kissing case," which involved a young white girl kissing a young black boy on the cheek. The boy, nine, and his friend, seven, were brought up on rape charges by authorities. They were not allowed to see their mothers for several weeks and were given lengthy sentences. A British photographer sneaked a camera inside the jail and printed the two young boys' photographs in a London newspaper. The story exposed the North Carolina incident to worldwide scrutiny and notoriety. Protest demonstrations occurred at numerous U.S. embassies in Europe, and subsequently Eleanor Roosevelt asked President Eisenhower to end this farce. Ike, in turn, told North Carolina governor, Luther Hodges, to "deal with it."[7] He did. The children were released to their parents, and the white bigots of Monroe (headquarters for the southeastern division of the Ku Klux Klan) were thoroughly and justifiably ridiculed for their backwardness. Then came the Freedom Riders. Mr. Williams was asked to join them, but he let it be known that, while he admired Dr. King, he would not countenance passive resistance. He formed a rifle club in Monroe with the blessings of the Washington, D.C.–based National Rifle Association (NRA). In late summer 1961 (by now, Genora was working with the Detroit ACLU), a serious altercation occurred between the Freedom Riders and residents of Newtown, the major black district of Monroe, and the white residents. The upshot was that several Freedom Riders were jailed, and Williams was indicted for kidnapping a white couple who strayed into the black community; according to black opinion, he had put them up in his house for safety, and according to white opinion, he had detained them against their will. Williams fled to Cuba to seek the protection of Fidel Castro, whom he had met on previous occasions.

The Monroe defendants activated the Flint chapter of the NAACP. Why the Flint chapter? Apparently "pecksniffian liberals" in the North would not touch any of this stuff, especially the one about "kissing" and "rape."[8] Most important was Genora's drive to enlist working-class blacks—and even working-class whites, for that matter—into the NAACP.

Nationwide, the NAACP appealed to middle-class black citizens: the small business owners, entrepreneurs, and what is commonly called the white-collar segment. At this time, neither Monroe, North Carolina, nor Flint, Michigan, had a large population of middle-class citizens, black or white; the working class outnumbered them considerably. Genora's work in bringing the working class to the NAACP was ready-made for her, although she had been born and raised (at least for about sixteen years) in a middle-class atmosphere. Her youthful reactions against a bigoted father who joined the Ku Klux Klan could very well have been one of the subconscious reasons why Genora so constantly favored poor and working classes.

Little news of Monroe filtered down to interested agencies in the North. ACLU attorney Conrad Lynn visited Michigan in December 1960, and, at Genora's instigation, a meeting in Flint was held and Lynn told all interested parties what was happening in Monroe, North Carolina.[9] Genora received a letter from Berta Green, a former SWP activist and secretary of the Committee to Aid the Monroe Defendants (some fifteen of them), asking for help in Monroe.[10] In a letter to attorney Sam Duncan on the same day she wrote to Genora, Mrs. Green said that unless attorneys of goodwill "immediately" undertook a publicity campaign aimed at getting "federal intervention" and conducted "exhaustive research" of all the constitutional points involved, "any and all black defendants will surely be found guilty" of a felony that would get them at least twenty years in the state penitentiary.[11]

The Aid the Monroe Defendants Committee learned that in late 1961, counselor Lynn got permission from the State Department to go to Havana and interview Robert Williams about the affairs in Monroe. They also learned that Dr. Perry's credit had been cut off and that he had been banned from the practice of medicine in Union County, of which Monroe was the seat. And they heard of one of the more incredibly ugly incidents carried out by the FBI (since Williams was an international fugitive and accused of kidnapping, the federal agency entered the case) and local law enforcement officials: Robert Williams's aunt died, and the lawmen came into the funeral chapel and pasted a "Wanted" poster, with a photo of Robert, on the casket.[12] This utterly outrageous behavior became the subject of jokes and guffaws in this hateful community for several weeks to come.

Genora's committee publicized Monroe, North Carolina, pointing out the constitutional deprivations that blacks suffered at the hands of white tormenters. The committee wanted the U.S. Justice Department to intervene in the matter, but both Attorney General Robert Kennedy and his chief assistant, Burke Marshall, declined involvement. "The entire civil rights movement will be struck a severe blow," Genora reported, "if the Monroe racists are successful in victimizing these young people because they dared protest the Jim Crow laws."[13] The Monroe defendants were ultimately released on bail with money Genora helped to raise. Their cases were postponed from one month to another and then from one year to another. Their status remained in limbo throughout the civil rights years and then, as in so many instances, most were quietly dropped.

After Monroe, Genora soon experienced another dose of racism. Sol's new employment enabled them to take more vacations than before, and as the sixties progressed, Mexico increasingly became their haven, particularly Acapulco. On one trip, Genora had a firsthand experience with the "demented minds" of the Ku Klux Klan as it existed at the time in southern states. (She had met the mother of Mississippi murder victim Emmet Till at the NAACP Flint office.) As they drove through Kentucky, Tennessee, and Alabama, they "saw all the expected signs of white supremacy." Nonetheless, Mississippi shocked her the most. They stopped at a roadside eatery for coffee, and even before being served, someone had told the owner their Michigan state tag number. The Michiganders noted a revolver on a shelf and innocently asked if it were real. This started the Mississippian on a tirade. "Yes, it's real," he asserted, and then added ominously, "and loaded." He told the Dollingers a story, a "tale of terror" that made Genora's "blood run cold," about the "vile and blind hatreds of the KKK for anyone wanting citizenship for the Negro." It seems, as the white proprietor told it, that a black man, his wife, and their six children had stopped at another greasy spoon a few days before and tried to order food. The restaurant owner ordered them out of his establishment because of strict segregation laws and then called the police. The local constable found the black man a few miles down the road, once again trying to feed his family. The constable shot the black man in the stomach and he died the next day. The man telling the story to Genora and Sol expressed support for what the police had done, saying repeatedly that he wished he had been the one to pull the trigger. Leaving, "with our coffee turning bitter-poison in our stomachs," Genora vented her emotions to Sol. "A father comes for food and his little ones wind up without a father? Why isn't the NAACP ten times stronger than it is? Why isn't every Negro and every white liberal a member? Why are so many Americans lethargic on this terrible situation?"[14] She could not put the incident out of her mind as they sped south, toward Mexico. (While it is entirely possible that these events as described by the racist restaurateur actually occurred, given the racial inflammations of the time in Mississippi, it is also plausible to conjecture that the man was having a bit of sport with a couple of "Yankees.")

After their vacation, the family made plans for their move to Detroit. Genora regretted leaving Flint again, for she had so many causes to pursue, loyal friends, and significant connections. But Detroit had been her wartime home, and it was not exactly as though she were a total stranger to the area. The first thing Genora did upon arriving in Detroit was to work full-time for the ACLU, which, in its quest to preserve First Amendment rights, frequently called itself the "most conservative organization in the country." The Michigan state chairman of ACLU was Ernest Mazey (brother of Emil, an official in the UAW and a longtime friend of the Dollingers). Genora was development director; her chief function was to travel around the state, set up new chapters, and advise them on financial matters and how best to carry out the functions of the organization, making the Michigan ACLU one of the most active and successful organizations in the country. In addition to recruiting new members for the Michigan ACLU, Genora spoke her mind about the United States' growing involvement in Southeast Asia, becoming an anti-Vietnam activist before it was fashionable. The entire world should have learned a lesson in 1954, she believed, when the Vietnamese ousted the French at the battle of Dien Bien Phu. It was economic and imperialistic interests that caused the United States to take France's place in this outdated struggle that was not so much for the creation of colonies as for new markets.

On a local level, Genora acted on behalf of a young wife whose military husband had been shipped to Vietnam during the early years of U.S. involvement in the war. Pregnant with their second child, the lady suffered extreme nervous problems as newspaper, radio, and television accounts of the fighting in Vietnam "terrified her." Genora and her colleagues hoped, for the future health of this family, that the U.S. Army would release the young soldier so he could return to Detroit and run his household.[15] Her efforts were unsuccessful.

In 1962, she was elected president of Women for Peace. In this capacity, as well as in her ACLU role, Genora and her followers met every Saturday in downtown Detroit to display antiwar banners. On occasion, Genora invited public officials and other well-known individuals to speak, and these events usually drew large audiences.[16] At one gathering, invited guest speakers Gus Scholle, president of the Michigan CIO Council; Emil Mazey of the UAW; and Al Barbour, president of the Wayne County Council, made numerous antiwar remarks. The biggest demonstration that Genora organized was down Woodward Avenue, a leading Detroit thoroughfare. Included in the huge crowd were a Methodist minister, a Jewish rabbi, and a Catholic priest. All three, dressed in their respective vestments, carried maces with the seals of their faith upon them. Occasionally, the Detroit protesters joined thousands of others from around the country in Washington, D.C., where they demonstrated in front of the White House. The saddest anti-Vietnam event that occurred while Genora was president of Women for Peace was when one of its members, Alice Hertz, immolated herself for the cause. "She was a kindly old lady," eighty years old. She doused herself with gasoline and set herself on fire. Her death, said Sol, helped to harden "the country in opposing the undeclared war."[17]

Genora and Sol participated in a "teach-in" at the University of Michigan, well attended because the famous playwright, Arthur Miller, was to be present. He spoke to the group about protest groups when he had been a student at Michigan, including the fascist invasion of Spain in the 1930s. Miller invited Emil Mazey to the podium. The highlight of

Mazey's speech, picked up by the national press, was, "I don't like my President lying to me,"[18] a reference to President Lyndon B. Johnson, who had won in 1964 on a nonescalation platform. According to Sol Dollinger, President Johnson got wind of this statement and contacted Walter Reuther, head of the international UAW, telling him that "you better get your guy [Mazey] under control."[19] Reuther called a meeting of the UAW executive board and pushed through a motion that "effectively silenced board members [including Mazey] from speaking out publicly against the war."[20] The Dollingers had not particularly respected Walter Reuther since the sit-downs of 1937, quarrels over sliding wage scales, and other matters, but this turn of events solidified their antagonisms. "Of all the treacherous acts of Reuther," Sol maintained, "this has to be put at the head of the list." This was "democracy" Walter Reuther style.[21] Genora thought it was Reuther's hobnobbing with U.S. presidents that caused his union militancy to be compromised. His visits with presidents "changed this man completely. Completely. Then he wanted to control." He began to develop as a bureaucrat instead of a labor leader because of "the pressure of capitalist society."[22] Reuther's direction here, Genora believed, led later to what she called tuxedo unionism, a condition in which labor and capital became cooperative rather than confrontational.

Genora put her heart and soul into reform work, fighting for social justice wherever she saw the need for it. In the mid-1960s, one of her admirers, David Herreshoff, summed up her value: "Her name reminds me of an essential part of every vehicle which rolls from Flint. . . . Just so Genora crackles and sparkles through human vehicles. . . . She is what [Walt] Whitman means by the 'body electric.' No room she is in is inadequately lit. No cause she is in is hopeless."[23] All the while she fought for the causes she believed in, health problems continued to plague her. She developed chronic arthritis, aggravated by Detroit winters. On a blustery winter day in 1966, Sol telephoned Genora at her ACLU office and told her there was a chance of a transfer within his company to Los Angeles. The union representing workers for Israel Bonds required that job openings always be posted. Sol considered himself a good salesman, though he had not been successful when trying to peddle *Encyclopedia Britannica,* so he felt his chances of getting the Los Angeles appointment to be good.[24] Would Genora be interested in Los Angeles? Sol wanted to know. Yes, she quickly replied. A change in geography and climate might have an ameliorating effect on her arthritis. With all the things happening in California at that time, it might be a mecca for Genora's talents. The antiwar campaigns and growing interest in women's rights, racial justice, educational reforms, and environmental issues seemed tailor-made for Genora. Besides, at the time she thought it was closer to Mexico than was Michigan (paradoxically, Detroit and Los Angeles are almost equidistant from Mexico City).

Again, there was to be another move. When Genora figured up how many times she had moved, it was unsettling. Flint to Detroit and back to Flint and then back to Detroit—how many times? But, all things considered for the Dollingers in the mid-1960s, California was the place to be. Once again Sol went ahead of Genora and Ronnie. She had to wait until Ronnie's school year ended to sell their Detroit house and allow Sol time to find a suitable residence for them. She signed her letters to him "Shalom Alacheim!"[25]

She wrote to Helen Travis (wife of Robert Travis, an early UAW leader), "Have you heard? We're moving to L.A." She would not miss Detroit as a city, "but it is hard, after all those years in Michigan, leaving the wealth of friends I have accumulated. The farewells are hard." She expected, she told Helen, to get work as soon as she arrived in the western city. She was proud that the Michigan ACLU beat southern California and every other affiliate in the country in recruiting new members. And then she paid a tribute to her organization: "We started out from scratch here to build ACLU of Michigan and worked so many long hours before we were paid for it. Two months ago I was given the first decent wages in relation to the work performed. Well, at least it will not make it difficult to find a replacement."[26]

Her boss, Ernest Mazey, sorry to see her go, nonetheless gave his blessings and congratulations. He even wrote a strong letter of recommendation for both Dollingers to Eason Monroe, director of the Los Angeles branch of the ACLU. He was so certain that they would be of inestimable worth to Monroe that "the only fair and reasonable thing for you would be to send ACLU Michigan a check for $5,000 as a token in advance of appreciation for the value . . . they will be to you." On a serious note, Mazey pointed out that Genora had instituted new record-keeping procedures in Michigan that easily kept track of cases; worked constantly with lawyers, college professors, and psychiatrists; and had recently been awarded a plaque for her good work from the state organization.[27] In the year she left, 1966, the Michigan ACLU boasted 5,029 members.[28] Some of her innovations in Detroit were copied by other branches of ACLU around the country. A few months after the Dollingers left for California, Ernest Mazey sent an "invoice" to them in the amount of $10,000 "for the disasterous [*sic*] decline of ACLU in Michigan income" following the "unreasonable, arbitrary, and unfaithful change of residence to California."[29] This couple was missed back east both personally and professionally.

Another official in the Michigan ACLU, Ed Galligan, wrote to Genora, "Damn it, why does [Sol] have to go barging out to L.A.? What's the matter with good old Michigan?" Sol's taking Genora away from them was a "profoundly dirty trick." Perhaps, Galligan said, he could urge divorce upon Genora and keep her in the Wolverine State. Undoubtedly, she and Sol and Ronnie would be miserable in all that smog. Finally, "Gritting my teeth, muttering imprecations against Los Angeles and all the people who drag other people out there, I wish you and your husband the best."[30]

Walter Bergman, a longtime civil rights activist, college professor, and close friend of the Dollingers, wrote in a general letter of recommendation that Genora would not be as much looking for a job as "for a cause in which she can have faith, pride, and devotion." Whoever hired her, Bergman asserted, would be fortunate, for she would invest "organizational ability and social conscience" into her work. On a personal note he told her, "We hate to see you go, drat your husband, anyway."[31]

The letters between Genora and Sol, while she stayed in Detroit and he looked for a house in Los Angeles, were a mixture of personal and public observances. Sol worried about Genora's health. She had begun to experience heart problems (which ultimately led to a pacemaker). She underwent a series of tests, and Sol did not "like for a moment being out here" while Genora was back there.[32] She assured him that everything was fine with her: she was sleeping well, without nightmares. Sol, good-naturedly "offended" by this last statement, asked, "What are you suggesting? Are you allergic to me?"[33] In public matters—because they intensely interested both Dollingers—Sol wrote about the antiwar demonstrations or intimated the lack of them.[34] The "peace movement," in the minds of reformers like Genora and Sol, did not "catch on" until the Tet Offensive in 1968. Sol told Genora that President Johnson "is over his head" in the matter of Vietnam. Even a large portion of the capitalist class "wishes us out of the war" because rising inflation was beginning to frighten them.[35] How then,

Sol wanted to know, do we get out of this predicament without a complete capitulation? On domestic matters, Sol's analyses of Los Angeles were foretelling. "There is little association" here between blacks and whites. The NAACP, with its message of reform—one of its meetings attracted only one hundred people—continued to be outmaneuvered by thousands of Black Muslims. It seemed clear that the message of African Americans in Los Angeles was revolution rather than reform. "Negroes moved here from the southern states," Sol said, "with a normal amount of hatred for whites and the police." Watts did not look like a normal slum, but "the Negroes were packed together like sardines, and they just can't find any jobs." The mayor, Sol noted, campaigned on a "rather open anti-Negro position."[36] These conditions, he believed, did not bode well for the future.

Genora and Ronnie got to California in midsummer 1966 and moved into the house on South Hudson that Sol had acquired. It was of Spanish decor and, at Sol and Genora's insistence, in a fully integrated African American–Latino community. Not long after they moved in, a fire destroyed much of their house. Their old friend, Larry Jones, wrote to say he wished there was something he could do to lessen Genora and Sol's hardships. If he and his Local 659 could aid them financially, "we would be very pleased to provide an interest free loan."[37] Touched by the offer, the two turned down any loans.

Genora did not get the ACLU job she had expected. Easton Monroe informed her that the position was filled. It did not take long, however, for her to become an active volunteer in the Los Angeles branch, later being appointed to its board of directors. Not finding immediate employment turned out to be to Genora's advantage, for she had time to read and study reform movements within the context of Trotskyism. For a time, she became a secretary for the law firm of Wirin, Rissman, and Posner, which handled ACLU matters in Los Angeles. Then she worked as Sol's unpaid assistant at Technion Society of America, where Sol was employed after a short stint with Israel Bonds. This enabled the two to travel together—which they had rarely done in the past—to various fund-raising events, sometime mixing business with pleasure. They especially liked Mexico, where Sol opened numerous drives for funds from wealthy businessmen. Genora began to refer to that country as her beloved Mexico.

She was saddened, along with thousands of other people, to learn shortly after arriving in the West that her first husband, Kermit Johnson, had died on May 7, 1967, in Humboldt, South Dakota, at the age of fifty-five; it was widely claimed that the cause was cirrhosis of the liver. Many editors of journals dedicated to spreading the word about labor unions in the 1960s had never even heard of Kermit Johnson. This lack of knowledge caused some reactions. Even the editors of *Searchlight,* the journal founded by some 1937 sit-downers, seemed reluctant to give any publicity to Kermit's demise. Larry Jones, a former editor of *Searchlight,* wrote a eulogy for Kermit but informed Genora that he was shocked at the "crude, miasmatic, and revolting actions of this local [659] in the matter of publication of the eulogy to Kermit." He had learned of Kermit's death in early May and presented his eulogy on the twenty-first. Nothing happened, despite Jones's pushing through a resolution at Local 659 to print a commemorative issue of *Searchlight* for Kermit. After all, Kermit had engineered much of the sit-down and had gone on to become a paragon in the labor movement. Surely his memory deserved such an issue. Jones contacted *Searchlight* editors for an explanation "but met only evasive and idiotic double talk." Jones told Genora that he thought of her often. He respected her for her "keen sense of social justice and fair play."[38] In another letter to Genora a fortnight later, Jones asked Genora if perhaps they were living too much in the past. "I know that I find myself out of step with our younger workers—could it be that I am simply dogmatic and they the *avant-garde*?"[39]

Jones's melancholy question only intensified Genora's sadness at Kermit's passing. After all, he was the father of her two deceased sons, and his departure closed once and for all an important phase of her life. Though she was happy now with Sol and Ronnie in California, she nevertheless cherished poignant memories of Kermit. She was not surprised by Jones's descriptions of how difficult it had been to get Kermit's eulogy printed (the eulogy to this unsung hero of the labor movement was finally printed on September 14, 1967, some four months after his death). It was clear that a generation gap existed between the veterans of 1937 and the labor leaders of the 1960s. Things had changed, and they were not to Genora's liking. This new generation, while reaping benefits from past actions, did not appreciate the hardships the sit-downers had suffered or the sacrifices they had made. To make matters worse, union leaders and their publicists in journals like *Searchlight* were getting increasingly close to creating a "company union," one that almost always agreed with those in the executive suites. She predicted hard times ahead for organized labor in the United States.

Genora threw herself into a frenzy of causes, telling a friend that "I used to wish when I was a kid that I was a twin; now, I wish I had been born a twin million [because] it would be a little easier!"[40] She operated within the context of California's ferment of great issues: the environment, education (Genora organized numerous advisory councils and appeared before school boards with suggestions for pedagogical improvements), civil liberties, the feminist movement, and the race question. On this latter point, Genora and Sol both opposed the "fawning manner" of white reformers toward the "lumpen proletarian," or Black Panthers. "These were people," Sol asserted, "who had guilty consciences over their relations with blacks." Neither Genora nor Sol had such guilt, for they had spent many years of their lives "advancing the cause of integration," citing their work with the NAACP and ACLU in Flint and Detroit.[41] Genora joined the Peace and Freedom movement, and for a time she and Sol served on its steering committee.[42] Peace and Freedom, made up of thousands of young people, opposed U.S. involvement in Vietnam. The "ultra-leftists" in the party, however, hinged their program to the fate of the "undisciplined, nationalist, obscurantist, Black Panther party."[43] Genora and Sol, while respecting some of the tactics of the Black Panthers, viewed them as an "anarchistic group unable to engage the system over a long period of time."[44] Genora became active in the People's Lobby, a grassroots movement indigenous to California. With the People's Lobby, she fought to raise political and environmental awareness about the steady erosion of the country's natural resources. She involved numerous high school clubs, including one to which her son, Ronnie, belonged, to try to save the palm trees on Highland Avenue and prevent the development of the Pan-Pacific Park for the simple reason that too many trees would have to be destroyed. Sol modestly said later, "They won small victories."[45]

During these activities, Genora coped with continuing health problems. She already had arthritis (although she continued to take painting and sculpture classes sponsored by the city's Adult Educational Program), heart problems, periodic spells of TB, and now she had gall bladder problems. In 1968 her gall bladder was removed, and for several weeks afterward she suffered a weakened and depressed condition. Sol suggested that she go to Acapulco and lie in the sun to regain her strength. She thought this an admirable idea, so she and a friend, fellow ACLU volunteer Susan Stein, headed south. It proved to be a memorable trip, raising questions about "ugly Americans." Stein, a widow, was a "knowledgeable world traveler," at least in her own mind.[46] Genora discovered, to her dismay, that Susan did not like Mexicans and was not bashful about showing it. She was too direct and abrupt for Mexican personalities and lifestyles. She got "told off" by a waiter serving drinks, and, Genora reported, "she richly deserved it." Genora apologized for Stein's brusque ways in the Spanish that she had picked up over the years. "I don't think she [Stein] was ever conscious of national customs or common courtesies in any of the countries she visited," Genora wrote to Sol. One thing that both amused and disturbed Genora on this trip was when she took a bus to various destinations and was constantly asked if she were French, Italian, or Australian. When she told her inquisitors that she was American, they didn't believe her because "no American would be waiting for a bus."[47] The stereotype was clear: every American was ultrawealthy. Genora and Susan stayed in Acapulco for a while and then went to Mexico City, where they separated. Just as well, Genora must have thought, because of the constant confrontations between the Austrian widow and the local populace. Genora had a temper and could always show it when provoked, but she was also blessed with good manners and decent behavior.

On their numerous trips to Mexico, Sol and Genora had made many new friends and constantly received invitations to stay with them for extended periods. One person was Stanyo Kaminski, an up-and-coming sculptor and social activist. He had written to Genora in May 1968 that he was trying to produce a radical magazine, and Genora suggested ideas for its content. "Should the magazine *Hora Cero* ever see the light, I shall send you some copies. But HUSH! We *also* suffer bullies,"[48] Kaminski wrote, referring to the FBI surveillance to which Genora and Sol had recently been subjected. For all practical purposes, however, the FBI had taken both of them off its list by 1964.

In Mexico City, Genora was the guest of Amelia Ramirez, whose deceased husband had once been a justice on the Mexican Supreme Court, and her family. The Dollingers had known the Ramirezes since 1960, when they made their second trip to Mexico. For breakfast one morning their hotel served them papaya, and neither Genora nor Sol had ever seen such a fruit. "How do you eat this thing?" Genora asked, perhaps too loudly, to no one in particular. Amelia, sitting at another table, overheard the question and said "with sugar and lime on it." She had used "limon" for "lime," so Genora drenched her fruit with lemon juice—still delicious, but funny to the Mexicans.[49] Genora and Amelia remained friends for the rest of Genora's life.

The Ramirez family nursed Genora back to health after her gall bladder operation. They heated packs for her chest and put hot water bottles in her bed. Genora flourished under such tender loving care. A son, Homero, an accountant by trade, took Genora out to see the sights of Mexico City. They stopped at a restaurant for a Mexican chocolate drink spiced with cinnamon and nutmeg. When the bill came, Genora wanted to pay for the drinks. "Senora, I am a Mexican," Homero told her imperiously. Genora immediately countered with, "Senor, I am an American."[50] On this occasion Mexican machismo met its match with American independence, and they went dutch treat. It was really all in jest, but still the stereotypes were painfully present.

Genora came back to southern California fully refreshed, proclaiming that her health had been restored and she was ready for just about anything. When 1969 opened, she came out swinging. There was much to be done in Los Angeles to recuperate from the Watts riots in the summer of the previous year, and there were rumors of school teachers' strikes all over the state, to say nothing of environmental issues that needed attention. Through all these flurries, Genora maintained a closer relation with Sol than perhaps she ever had in the past. But she was even closer to Ronnie. (Was it because she remembered her first two sons, with whom, she frequently lamented, she had not spent enough time?) She admired her young son's versatility; he belonged to six clubs in high school yet always made A's and B's—he was so busy he even limited his telephone conversations to ten minutes.[51] She was pleased with his independence of thought. Neither she nor Sol tried to lead him into any specific kind of political, economic, or social theory: they let him make up his own mind. They never even knew, for example, which political candidates Ron supported and voted for.[52] Although Ron shared many of Genora and Sol's beliefs, it would have been out of character for either parent to indoctrinate him, after spending many years of their own lives supporting freedom of choice, though years after Ron married and become the father of a little daughter, Genora "signed up her five month old granddaughter in the National Organization for Women."[53] "He's busy on his own terms," Sol said of Ron. "He's very busy."[54] It is undeniable that some of Genora rubbed off on Ron. In a sociology class at the University of California, Santa Cruz, he wrote a term paper on "womanhood" and complained that in higher education, one had to produce the "junk" his professors demanded.[55] One could see shades of Genora when a professor told Ron that he had "a unique way of looking at things. Your ordering is practically the reverse of everyone else's. Who's out of step?" (Genora thrilled at this assertion because it had been said of her so many times.) Ron (getting too old now for "Ronnie") scoffed at the teacher, saying, "And he represents the hope for Progressive teachers in the future?" Sol, calling himself the "Huffer and Puffer" of the Dollinger Company, frequently challenged Ron, most always to his disadvantage, to tennis matches. (Ron was on the varsity tennis team in high school.) Ron wrote in jest to Genora that "I hope this is no shock to you, but it is very difficult to not make him [Sol] feel like an invalid on the tennis court." He claimed that he had "been going easy on the old man for nearly 20 years."[56] Genora relished these encounters between father and son. The admirable family life that the Dollingers had created remained full of love and respect for one another.

Privately, they were a loving family, but publicly Genora and Sol were never far away from one cause or another. The war in Vietnam demanded their attention, the threat the world faced from atomic power was worrisome, and the seemingly unabated proliferation of smog and other pollutants endangered people's health. When one puts civil rights and liberties into this mix, one can see that the Dollingers continued to be an extremely busy couple. One of the most pleasing events in the early 1970s for Genora and Sol and Socialists everywhere was the unprecedented assumption of power—in October 1970—of Salvador Allende as president of Chile. He became the first Marxist ever chosen in a free election, and it was significant to Genora that Allende's ascension should have been in the Western Hemisphere because she had always believed the Socialist revolution that would ultimately spread to the United States would start somewhere in Latin America.

Genora was attending a UAW convention in Detroit on the very day the Chilean Congress (after an election the previous month by the public) swept Allende into office. She had not been back to the Motor City since her 1966 move to California. To honor her homecoming, about seventy-five people greeted her at a party hosted by old friends, Wayne State University professor Harry Becker and his wife, Frieda. After eating a huge cake decorated with roses and emblazoned "Welcome Home Genora" and imbibing a few spirits, the assembled guests decided to make a tape for Sol and Ron back in Los Angeles. The main topic of discussion was President Allende of Chile. "I feel that we can learn quite a bit from Allende," Frieda Becker told Sol, "who as a Marxist has been one of the founding fathers of the Socialist party." Allende, the group believed, would unify and solidify the disparate forces in Chile and mold them into one entity. "Perhaps we can learn from him here in this country," said one of Sol's correspondents. Many who spoke on the tape expressed fears that the CIA would spend "hundreds of millions" of U.S. tax dollars to overthrow Allende. They were convinced that the Nixon administration was not going to allow another Socialist government (after Cuba) in the Western Hemisphere. (And, as is well-known, Allende was overthrown in 1973 by Auguste Pinochet.) As the night wore on, those taping the gathering for Sol and Ron included subjects other than Allende. On the tape, "Gladstone," a professor at Highland Park College, strongly recommended that Genora write a book. There was a need for such a project, Gladstone asserted, "because of the role that the women's liberation movement is playing, and the need for . . . clarity on the history of the labor movement in relation" to feminist reforms. Genora must surely have balked at Gladstone's suggestion that the proposed book was "not only a job for your [Sol's] wife, but [one] that would call for a great deal of collaboration and possible direction from you."[57] Genora had long scoffed at male historians who had not done right—at least in her opinion—by the labor and feminist movements and the relationship between the two.

All things considered, the Detroit party was a tiring but wonderfully uplifting event for Genora. She relished listening to one taped correspondent after another tell Sol that "we are here having a good time organizing the revolution." It was well after 3 A.M. when the party ended. Even then Genora had some strength left. She taped a message to "her boys," describing the happy but "emotionally draining" experiences of the day. She and her old friends had had tears in their eyes as they met again for the first time in nearly five years. Even friends who were not there knew of her presence. She received telephone greetings from Florida (where many past labor leaders had retired). And then there were more tears when it was time to depart, because Genora added to the tape, "I think they knew and I knew that it might be a long time again before we met again."[58]

Her trip to Detroit was challenging (she had been scheduled to sit in on a sculpture class at a local college but at the last moment was invited to speak to pupils at an elementary school—she thought this more important than sculpturing), tiring—after all, she was now fifty-seven years old and not at all accustomed to parties that broke up only in the wee hours—and rejuvenating; she experienced no health problems on this trip, around all her old friends. But, like all parties, when this one ended she had to come back to reality. Many things back in California demanded her attention: the continuing school crisis in Los Angeles, for one thing, and some plans for trips abroad. So she made her way back to the West.

Seven "It Makes My Heart Sing"

The status of education in America worried Genora and other reform-minded people throughout the country. Some Los Angeles schools were graduating students who could not read and write in any language or even do elementary arithmetic. Here was a ready-made crusade, and in only a short time the lady from Michigan was fully involved in it, adding education to her lengthy list of causes. She feared the situation in Los Angles might reflect—in a sort of microcosm—the rest of the state and country. She spearheaded the founding of the Los Angeles High School Community Advisory Committee (becoming its vice president) that ultimately represented 362 schools and had such notables as Ralph Nader and Paul Erlich on its board of directors. She and her colleagues wanted to involve the entire community in educating children. Parents should visit schools on a regular basis. There should be improved counseling services, a special school for incorrigibles (except Genora wanted to know how to define "incorrigible"— perhaps because she herself had been called incorrigible in her early life?), and opportunity classes where students could learn productive skills and become future tax-paying citizens. Parents and teachers should enlarge social contacts by inviting each other to functions at their homes. Efforts should be made to retain black faculty in the Los Angeles schools, and student-teacher committees should strive for good teaching and learning conditions.[1] As the old adage tells us, easier said than done.

This council had its work cut out for it. Some of the schools were so bad, Genora claimed, that they should be closed outright. "They are unsafe," and their educational programs reflect a "sham and waste of money." Class sizes were too large, there were not enough textbooks, and a third of the students dropped out of school before graduation. Los Angeles city schools, she said, "had the worst reading scores" in the entire country and were not educating children for life in a complex industrial society. Members of school boards, however, seemed not to care. Made up primarily of "capitalists," she declared, they have "made us pawns in this struggle."[2]

With an affiliate of the council called the "People's Lobby," Genora set up petition drives to get citizens behind antismog laws after a young student died, presumably from pollution. "How many other children who are developing asthma and cancer and heart conditions are dying—really of the smog and pollutants to their young bodies?" she asked. Nearly 10,000 signatures were obtained in one day. They set up petition booths at shopping centers throughout the city. Genora reported that "we are witnesses to a number of older people who come up to our petition tables with tears in their eyes and tell us they are dying of emphysema."[3] Some shopping center directors tried to block the tables, and the group, represented by lawyers known as "Nader's Raiders," went to court against them. The People's Lobby won as the court decreed that "owners [of shopping centers] may not rely on their private ownership to justify blanket prohibitions on First Amendment activities."[4] The collection of these signatures helped pave the way for the ultimate passage of California's strict antismog and pollution laws.

Genora lamented a lack of sensitivity by school administrators and police departments. The former acted too quickly to send troublesome students (she herself had been a "troublesome" student) to special classes or even camps until they straightened out. Genora believed it better for delinquent students to stay within the community, where they would have a better chance at rehabilitation. A group of fourteen students peacefully demonstrated at a high school. The principal called the police, who arrested, booked, and fingerprinted the students. This action was outrageous, according to Genora and her colleagues on the Los Angeles Advisory Council. Another time a principal had the police round up 109 "incorrigible" students for offenses ranging all the way from "sassing a teacher to being tardy." The obviously ineffective principal got the police to do his job for him. Little wonder, then, that for several weeks in 1970, starting in mid-April and ending in late May, a majority of teachers were on strike in Los Angeles. Genora and Sol strongly supported them: "We commend the striking teachers . . . for their courageous actions in refusing to allow the deterioration of our schools to continue."[5]

Genora stood picket duty during the strike—as did Sol and a large number of students in the system—and opened her home on Queen Anne Place as a place for the striking teachers to hold daily union meetings. The Dollinger house became striking teachers' headquarters, with Genora serving sandwiches and cold drinks, and offering a "comfort station." Students, as well, flocked to the standard. Genora and Sol's son, Ronald, thoroughly favored the strike and helped to further its interests any way he could. This was heady stuff; it was wonderful, Genora thought, to be back in the midst of a strike and walking picket lines again.[6] She thrived on controversy.

Her work with the Los Angeles school systems made her publicly known in the city—through television and newspapers—which in turn led to additional reform activities. Genora now frequently responded to questions from various authors on the role of women in the 1937 sit-down strike. As the women's liberation movement intensified, the requests grew almost too numerous for Genora to handle. She was affronted by queries over the telephone but did make many personal appearances. One such occurred at the 1970 meeting of the Organization of American Historians in Los Angeles. Stanford professor Staughton Lynd invited Genora to speak at a session called "What Is Radical History?" Introducing Genora, Lynd said that most history is written from the top down, and it is time to do it from the bottom up. "Top down" meant "divine right of kings"; bottom up meant "equality for all," as expressed in the Declaration of Independence. Lynd could think of no better person than Genora Dollinger to lead the way in the promises and hopes of equality. Genora had expected only a dozen or so to be at this meeting; more than 200 attended.

She thanked the group for inviting her, exuberantly telling them that she had just left a picket line in the ongoing teachers' strike. She was glad when those "predisposed to make history with [their] physical bodies" were able to speak before "writers of history." She gave an account of the 1937 sit-downs, with an emphasis on the role played by women. The Emergency Brigade, she argued, had helped to save the day for the union. She knew the truth, she said, about the taking of Chevrolet Plant Four. With her help, her husband, Kermit Johnson, had devised the strategy of using their bodies to make history, only to be left out by those who wrote about it. Subsequent history books, such as Henry Kraus's *The Many and the Few: A Chronicle of the Dynamic Auto Workers* (1947) and Sidney Fine's *Sit-Down: The General Motors Strike of 1936–1937* (1969) she believed, grievously overlooked Kermit's role. These were examples of what Lynd and his "radical" colleagues meant by history from the top down.

Her audience listened carefully; they had never met a woman quite like this. Many of them learned for the first time that the modern women's liberation movement in this country started, according to Genora, with the Flint sit-downs of 1937. With that initial experience, and then with World War II, there was no turning back. Genora was asked, "How did you go about educating the people of Flint and Michigan in general as to what was happening [in the sit-downs]?" Genora answered that the people of Flint "had been educated by General Motors." But by distributing their own mimeograph sheets, holding rallies, and challenging the police, the union had finally caused many citizens of Flint to question the methods of GM. Another question elicited from Genora the rather painful way in which she became one of the original members of the women's liberation movement in Flint. She related the story of how her father, Ray, had kept the women in his household "in their place" and had brooked no criticisms from them. She despised the way Ray had treated her mother, Lora, a distinguished woman with a musical degree. This attitude toward her father and then the events at the Flint sit-downs in the context of the Great Depression had molded Genora's life. For a woman who had once argued that she couldn't give a public speech, Genora was doing all right.[7] She was immensely pleased to be spreading the word about the contributions women made not only in the sit-downs but also in helping to shape the UAW itself. She was piqued, however, when the *Los Angeles Times* and other newspapers around the country failed to give her presentation any coverage. Without publicity, she argued, "young women" could not know "about their past history."[8]

She spoke to several classes, mostly those of history and sociology, at the University of California, Los Angeles (UCLA). "These students were unbelievable," Genora exclaimed.[9] Initially expressing incredulity at what Genora told them, some, she exulted, were teary-eyed by the time she finished. She was not trying to convert them to any political, economic, or social ideologies; all she wanted to do was tell them the truth as she perceived it about the women's movement and the

Flint sit-downs. Her argument that women's liberation started with the sit-downs of 1937 is, to be sure, controversial. There is, however, some justification for her beliefs here. She associated women's liberation with getting out of the house and having a career, as did all the other women's movements. Even at the point where the United States entered World War II, one citizen was quoted as saying, "Industry is not yet ready for women." There were enough men, "either too young or too old" to be drafted, to fill any industrial gaps.[10]

By 1930, still only one in nine married women was a wage earner, and by the end of the 1930s, 15.5 percent of all married women were employed, "with public opinion lined up against them."[11] The 1937 sit-downs in Flint and the work of the WEB, led by Genora Johnson, was a turning point for women in the work force: unionism and feminist activism were synonymous, at least in Genora's mind. Just after the "Battle of Bull's Run," thousands of workers—including women—lined up to join the UAW. When the strike ended (some referred to it as the "Battle of the Century), a "new type of woman had been born."[12] As Karen Johnson writes, World War II accentuated and intensified the feminist gains that came of the sit-downs: "Because it greatly accelerated the tendency of women to seek paid employment, especially including those with family responsibilities, World War II was a profoundly important event in American social history. The influx of large numbers of married women into the labor force marked an important turning point for women, involving as it did the implicit rejection of the idea that a woman's household responsibilities could not be reconciled with employment."[13]

In the 1950s and 1960s, second wave feminism became pervasive. It was based on the idea of married women entering the workforce and support for Title VII of the Civil Rights Act of 1964 and the National Organization of Women. Historians such as Sara Evans maintain that the second wave started with the civil rights movement of the 1960s in the American South. Important, too, in the second wave was the idea of sisterhood, with the movement focusing primarily on middle-class white women. In the second wave and then, ultimately, the third wave of feminist activity, the labor movement was fairly well abandoned. This is where Genora parted company with both waves of the feminist movement. She deemed unionism and feminism to be two sides of the same coin, and though later "libbers" did not agree with this assessment, Genora's dating the modern women's movement to the 1937 sit-down strike in Flint and the work of WEB is as credible as any of the other multitudinous explanations of this phenomenon.

On a trip back to Flint in February 1974, the anniversary month of GM's capitulation to the union, Genora spoke at five different colleges and universities. "All of my life," she told her audiences, "I have fought for equal opportunities and pay for women, so I am happy at the growth of what has been called 'the women's liberation movement.' And I am happy that there are women historians coming out of the universities who are probing into all phases of history and coming up with some very interesting contributions made by women." She singled out Patricia Yeghissian, who had written her honors thesis on the WEB. Yeghissian's professor at the University of Michigan had discouraged her in this, saying that Yeghissian was attributing her 1974 "liberation" views to the women of 1937 and that the topic was "not legitimate material for history."[14] Yeghissian won a prize for her work, and Genora thought it captured the spirit of 1937 and showed the revolutionary beginnings of the women's rights movement.[15]

Genora regretted the tall tales that crept into the Flint sit-down story. One woman claimed that two bullets penetrated the fur coat she was wearing on the fateful night of the Battle of Bull's Run (January 11, 1937). Genora scoffed at such claims and implied that a woman wealthy enough for a fur coat would not have been there in the first place. Several "brave" men as well, Genora said, had embellished their roles in the affair. In the succeeding years some of the older workers liked to brag to younger factory men of their "daring exploits."[16]

On another trip back east she addressed a luncheon meeting of the Women's Studies Department at the University of Michigan. Chairing the meeting was professor Sidney Fine, author of *Sit-Down.* After her speech, the assembled professors asked Fine more questions than they did Genora. Why had he not fully documented the role of women in the strike? Why had the "unique contributions" of women been "overlooked by one labor historian after another?" "Looking back," Genora said, "it can be seen that most of the male historians seem to have found it incomprehensible that women could have played a most significant and valiant role" in winning the strike against GM. "Some writers who knew better slighted our role out of a callous and deliberate disregard for the truth because of deep-seated political differences. There were some who wrote out of ignorance and a slothful failure to do the necessary research."[17] Genora was increasingly pleased throughout the 1970s that history was catching up with her and her feminist colleagues; they were being transferred from a footnote to the main text.

Genora came to believe that Socialism could and perhaps would be the order of the day in the context of equal rights for all. "Not the worst people," she claimed, "are now saying publicly that they are socialists." For "millions" of their followers, "it should remove some of the fear of that word [Socialism] and stimulate . . . discussions on a large scale."[18] But the American public would not agree with her on this question, and neither did many of her closest friends and correspondents. Joe Rosenthal, from Canada, told her that the feminist movement was on a downward trend. The Women's March in New York in 1970 contained, he claimed, more than 30,000 women. Just a scant two years later, it was down to 3,000. The influx of "radical lesbianism" harmed the movement, and the National Organization of Women did not, in the name of Socialism or any other "ism," threaten capitalism. On the contrary, "This movement is to bring women into the system and so give them a stake in capitalism." The declining influence of feminism, he argued, was one indication that its movement had been successful, with increasingly large numbers of women getting into the workforce, sometimes in high-managerial positions, and even becoming paragons of capitalism.[19] Genora would have preferred a Socialist settlement in the matter of feminism, but she was pragmatic enough to realize that, given the history and nature of this country, reform movements were apt, ultimately, to benefit capitalism. Nevertheless, she told a friend, she was glad that women, the "first slaves," had finally obtained some rights and recognition.[20]

There was still a ways to go, however, and much to be done. Genora became an ardent supporter of the ERA, which worked its way through Congress and then thirty-five states, three short of ratification, in the 1970s. Sent by Congress to the states in 1972, it was inexplicably "encumbered with an arbitrary seven-year deadline for ratification."[21] Genora told audiences and wrote in magazines that the best way to honor those valiant women of the sit-downs and remember their contributions and sacrifices was to stand "beside us still living—and all womanhood—as we now fight for the Equal Rights Amendment." She beseeched her audiences and readers to "help us to end the world's first and oldest form of exploitation—exploitation because of sex" and maintained that the ERA "will mean that every individual has the right to full participation in American life. This should be the spirit of '76."[22]

The ERA had first been introduced in 1923 by Alice Paul's National Women's Party. Its message, said Genora and her friends, was simple and fair: "Equality of rights under the law shall not be denied by the United States or any state on account of sex." They believed the ERA to be "the culmination of long years of struggle by women who had come before them."[23]

Phyllis Schlafly, an attorney with a master's degree from Harvard, strongly opposed the ERA and founded an organization called "Stop ERA." The ERA, she feared, would "destroy the right to be a woman" and "deprive the American woman of many of the fundamental privileges we now enjoy." The greatest right of all women is *not* "to take a job," but to tend to her babies at home and be "supported in these endeavors by her husband." Schlafly railed at "selfish and misguided women on TV talk shows" who argued otherwise.[24] Moreover, there was a widespread perception among poor and working-class women that the women's movement was interested only in gay rights and abortion when it should be stressing educational equity and economic opportunities.[25]

Genora realized that the ERA was too controversial for any consensus among varied interest groups in America and that it was not going to pass. Although the UAW was the first major union to endorse the ERA, the labor movement was not entirely behind it.[26] Historian Dorothy Sue Cobble notes that waitress unions argued that the ERA would weaken sex-based laws, "in particular those mandating limits on overtime and those requiring maternity benefits, rest breaks . . . and other amenities." There were age and class differences as well when considering the ERA. Betty Friedan, a leading feminist activist of the day and strong supporter of the ERA, was viewed as a "middle class college intellectual who knew nothing about working women's real problems."[27] Though Genora was not a college intellectual, many younger union members placed her into the same category as Betty Friedan. Still others, both in and out of the labor movement, called the ERA a "lesbian plot" and postulated the "destruction of the patriotic, godfearing, male-dominated nuclear family."[28] The hostility toward the ERA gathered strength as the Congress of American Women (formed in 1946 to represent the rights of women throughout the nation) came down against it. The Congress "supported a more ambitious approach [than the ERA] embodied in its Women's Status Bill, which combined protective legislation and the elimination of discrimination."[29]

Genora and friends believed these objections to the ERA represented the opinions of younger union members, both men and women, who knew little or nothing of the travails of 1937. In the late 1960s and into the early 1970s, much of organized labor fell on hard times. Genora warned that "women would remember labor's stance [on the ERA] when the anti-labor sentiment . . . caused labor to cast around for friends."[30] While speaking and writing for ERA and other causes, Genora kept up a steady stream of correspondence with public officials and editors of news magazines on issues of concern to her. She complimented Senator Edward W. Brooke, of Massachusetts, for his resolution for a joint U.S.–USSR suspension of the Multiple Independent Re-entry Vehicle (MIRV), from which nuclear warheads could be sent in different directions and at different speeds. "The consequences of MIRV," she wrote to Brooke, "must be understood by the government as by individual citizens."[31] To Senator Edward Kennedy, also of Massachusetts, she said that the tide seemed to be turning away from the Nixon administration on the matter of the "illegal war" in Vietnam.[32]

Amid her crusades, Genora found an opportunity to discover Europe for the first time. Sol's job with Technion took him to numerous parts of that continent, and in the summer of 1971, Genora accompanied him. Landing in London in the middle of June, and quickly picking up a few English swearwords, she found the city to be "bloody chilly" but "quaint."[33] In Italy, she was the perfect tourist: the Italians loved her. She wrote to Ron from Florence, "You must see this most beautiful city in the world."[34] Sol said, rather wistfully, that Genora had to stop at every church to study its art, sometimes spending hours or even whole days in every museum she could find. Her intense interest in painting and sculpture (her own artistic activities were on hold because of arthritic hands) inspired her to take half-days and sometimes all day in numerous museums.[35] She was entranced by her first trip to Europe, which took her from England to Italy, with Austria in between. In Rome, she reported, half the city was on one strike or another, and though she never met a strike she didn't like, there is no evidence of her walking in any of the picket lines.

Genora and Sol wanted to go to Spain but not while dictator Francisco Franco was in power. A Basque exile persuaded them not to wait: the Spanish people had to have contact with the outside world, he asserted, so the Dollingers reworked their travel schedules. Spain's philosophical climate manifested itself to the traveling couple one day at lunch. They struck up a conversation with a young physician, Elias, whose name was unusual, Sol thought, for a Spaniard. Elias's family had been Jewish but converted to Catholicism. Medical doctors, he said, were paid on a par with ordinary laborers because the medical profession, by and large, opposed Franco.[36] When Elias took Genora and Sol to the University of Madrid, he told them he feared to speak in public places against Franco because there were spies everywhere. Both Dollingers immediately remembered their own FBI surveillances of just a few years before.[37] One night the Dollingers stayed out late and the door of their pension was locked when they returned. They could not attract the attendant, and for a while pondered a night on the street. Then an elderly gentleman walked up to them with a key. His job was to patrol the streets and open pension doors to latecomers. "Apparently," Sol wrote, "Franco solved his unemployment problems by providing these elderly people a form of work. At the same time it was a method to demonstrate the power of the state in every block of the city."[38] The Dollingers left Spain believing they had a better understanding of the nature of dictatorship.

They returned to Europe in 1973. The most memorable part of this tour was the trip to Holland, where Genora met someone she had helped long ago. In the late 1940s, reports arrived in America of how horribly some Trotskyists had been treated in German concentration camps. Each Trotskyist chapter in the United States was asked to send food, clothing, and medicine to help these survivors get on their feet. The family assigned to Genora for help was that of Henrik Sneevliet, who had protested the German treatment of Jews in the Netherlands. He was executed, leaving behind a family, including a daughter named Bep, who later married Sal Santen.[39] Genora had gathered up and sent (sometimes barely scraping up enough for postage) huge boxes of food and cooking paraphernalia to the Sneevliet family. Now in Amsterdam, she wanted to visit this family she had never met but felt close to. It was a joyful and tearful meeting. While Genora was resting in the Santen's home one day, Bep waved an aluminum frying pan as she came into the room—it was the one Genora had sent in a shipment years before.[40]

After visiting Amsterdam and other parts of Europe, Genora and Sol traveled once more to Spain, with Franco still in office: in 1971 Genora had spent two full days in the Prado, and the only way Sol could get her to leave was to promise another trip, so here they were again. She wrote to her son from Barcelona, adding in a postscript, "We are following Watergate and enjoying developments immensely. So is everyone in Europe."[41] On another trip to Europe in 1977, they arrived in Lisbon and saw a long parade of Fiat auto workers marching out to lunch. Genora joined them in a small eatery and found that many were Socialists; she was right at home. It was the same with university students she met later that June day. Everywhere Genora went, she seemed to find people dedicated to the cause of Socialism. The couple dined with three young members of the Communist Party. The conversation was engaging until Sol noticed what he took to be some government agents trying to overhear. Later, they visited the Lisbon headquarters of the Communist Party and were flattered when one of the staff asserted that "Trotskyists are good people!" Each member present predicted that the United States would be "the last bastion of capitalism to fall."[42] This was quite a safe presentiment.

The Dollingers rented a car and traveled around the beautiful country of Portugal. As an aficionada of art, Genora was in her element. She marveled at early Roman stone walls and feudal slit windows in houses and palaces. Multicolored roofs fascinated her. It was all better than any movie she had ever seen. She observed that these scenes were like those in a Breugel painting and exulted, "How I'd love to be able to sketch and then paint all this! There are a hundred scenes, a million human stories in the near buildings and tiny enclosures of the immediate area outside my window! The sun rises daily on this ever-old, ever-new scene!"

By early July, Genora and Sol had crossed into post-Franco Spain (the dictator had died in 1975) and were happy to be back. She would "loved to have lived" in Parador San Telmo: "It's so tranquil, so restful, so satisfying for those who love nature and beauty." In Santiago de Compestela, Sol accidentally locked the car keys in the trunk. The young man who rescued them, and others at the Avis car rental office, turned out to be Socialists, another pleasing turn of events for the traveling couple.

Outside of Santiago de Compestela, Sol picked up two hitchhikers and learned that they were merchant mariners, just as he had been in World War II. They belonged to a seaman's union that had gone underground during Franco's regime; the headquarters was in Naples, Italy.

Genora and Sol were impressed that a union could have been maintained during the Franco years. "We had grave doubts," Sol said, "that an American union could have survived in similar circumstances." They picked up another hitchhiker, twenty-five-year-old Pablo Prieto Gomez and were surprised to learn that he was a Socialist, too. He regaled the two Americans with the political activity of the provinces of Asturias, Catalan, and Galicia and how they wanted political autonomy, if not complete independence, from Madrid. He predicted troublesome days ahead. Coming out of Santander, they picked up a couple named Olga and Felipe. "What a surprise!" Genora exclaims in her diary. They were Trotskyists, still illegal in Spain, and took a terrible chance by telling the Dollingers who they actually were. (Perhaps they were so talkative because at first they took the Dollingers to be French tourists.) Olga was a government employee, no less, and Felipe a university student, and both worked in close contact with the Spanish Communist Party. The Trotskyists in Spain, Olga and Felipe told the Dollingers, numbered 30,000 strong, an unbelievably large count to the Americans.

In Valladolid, a "toothless" Spanish cop hassled them until he saw that they had written down the license number of his motorcycle; this was one victory the tourists savored forever after. They drove on through this most fascinating of European countries and finally arrived in Madrid, which was "noisier" and had "more bustle" than on previous trips. They looked for the Trotskyist headquarters in Madrid; Olga, their hitchhiker, had provided the address. It turned out to be the residence of an accountant in a middle-class neighborhood. Genora rang the doorbell and a young man opened it. She explained that she and Sol were Socialists from the United States and only wanted to find the headquarters for the Trotskyists in Madrid. "At the end of a long hallway," Genora explained, "was a picture of Leon Trotsky when he was the leader of the 1905 revolution in Petrograd. . . . I was amused to think this was an underground organization operating illegally, and the accountant was giving me the address of their headquarters without checking my credentials." The Trotskyist headquarters in Madrid "was reminiscent of the SWP Headquarters in New York City" in 1939. They saw mounds of promotional pamphlets on tables throughout the room, but the young host, "while polite," showed no interest in talking to the Dollingers about the United States or the Trotskyist movement there.

By Saturday, July 16, Genora had fallen ill. She had a tightness in her chest and a sore throat. "Ain't fair!" she told her diary. There were so many things to do in Madrid, and now she was laid low. Still, she was homesick: "We think of Ron very often." Sol called for a physician (Socialist, of course), who left a prescription that eased her congestion—so much so that the next day she could go to her beloved Prado. Sol dashed from room to room in the museum, but Genora, who now knew the locations of all the famous paintings, studied them line by line, brush stroke by brush stroke, often to the protestations of her impatient husband. The next day, however, Monday the 18th, she took to her bed again. "Just as well," she thought, "because everything was closed. It was the anniversary of Franco's victory back in 1937." After a bit of thought, she realized that she had had a significant victory in 1937 as well. She stayed in bed for nearly a week, mostly reading detective stories until she "became sick of them." She had numerous conversations with a young medical assistant who came to see her throughout the week. He worked fourteen-hour shifts "but came to life when he told us he was an active socialist." The chambermaid who cleaned their room was "young, alert, and very expressive." Sol asked her about her political affiliation. "Socialist," of course, she responded. The Dollingers met all manners of people on their travels, but they did seem to have a talent for recognizing Socialists and other individuals whose political and social ideologies matched theirs.

On the day before they left, one of their cab drivers "had a dozen stickers . . . posted on parts of his dash. One looked like Che Guevara." Genora, in broken Spanish, asked him about it, and he went into a "real soap box oration" about Cuba and showed pictures of Lenin addressing the masses. "This is a different world," an astonished Genora reported. "A taxi driver doesn't have that freedom in the USA without going hungry and getting his cab turned over along with it." The next day after their conversation with the Spanish cabby, they left Spain, a country they had learned to love almost as much as Mexico. They winged their way back to Los Angeles, and Genora immediately suffered "reverse culture shock" (as Americans frequently do after an extended time abroad). "The apathy and cynicism of so many Americans is in direct contrast and the more keenly felt upon return from such an experience."[43]

Her travels in 1971, 1973, and 1977 added an international dimension to Genora's outlook on life. In many ways she learned the differences between American and European labor activities. One's labor involvement in a relatively free society can be accelerated over labor activities in despotic countries. In the United States one might receive a chastisement or perhaps a jail term; elsewhere, more likely a bullet. Genora was now both nationally and internationally "street smart," and she enjoyed the attention it brought her. In addition to being sought out by reporters and researchers, a documentary film company now expressed an interest in a movie in which she would play a major role.

A British Broadcasting Corporation (BBC) producer, Stephen Peet, wanted to make a documentary in honor of the United States' bicentennial year of 1976 and sent out researcher Jenni Pozzi to look for material. She visited a Stanford professor (Staughton Lynd?) who mentioned Genora and described her speech to the radical historians a half-dozen years before. Pozzi contacted Genora, who wanted to know her political affiliations. "Labor!" Pozzi replied. "Then I'll be happy to see you," Genora responded.[44] Ms. Pozzi stayed in the Dollinger home while she conducted her research. Filming was completed in 1976, and "The Great Sit-Down" became a part of BBC's *Yesterday's Witness* in America. Peet wrote to Genora that "the filming we did with you . . . is very good indeed. You look & sound completely relaxed. And everything you say makes very good sense."[45] The documentary shows historic newsreels of the confrontations between GM and UAW supporters, who carried signs printed with such things as "We Stand By Our Heroes in the Plants." As Genora is interviewed, scenes from the WEB breaking out the glass of tear gas–besieged Plant Nine fill the screen. The photo of Genora and her young son, Jody, standing in the picket line together gained attention in Great Britain.

Sol wrote to Peet that he had "not only opened up a hidden page of history for England, but I am sure that . . . it will have its reverberations to the far distant shores of the United States."[46] "The Great Sit-Down" aired first on BBC on Monday, October 4, 1976, and became standard fare at labor rallies and a major part of both film and labor history.

In the meantime, Genora worried about the chumminess that had developed between the UAW leadership and the executives at GM. She was not the only one with such forebodings. Her old friend Larry Jones wrote to her about the negotiations that took place in the summer of 1976 between UAW and GM. Some eight hundred UAW retirees formed a picket line. Jones expected GM officials to ignore them, but not their own president, Leonard Woodcock, and his aides, who "sneaked into the building via the private General Motors . . . entrance." Jones could not resist telling Genora that "had I been a UAW official I would have joined the picket line for a few minutes at least."[47] Genora, becoming increasingly familiar with this situation, referred to it as "tuxedo unionism," a painful reminder of the company unions that had been created in 1937 to combat the strikers. She confined her anger to a few private letters to friends, but the fortieth anniversary of the union victory over GM (February 1977) created a flashpoint for her sense of outrage. The anniversary meetings in Detroit and Flint were to be real celebrations with numerous special events. Genora received an invitation to attend a jointly sponsored UAW–General Motors cocktail party and dinner to be held at Detroit's St. Regis Hotel on the night before the general union meeting the next day in Flint (February 12). Mortified by this invitation, she quickly let Leonard Woodcock know that she would not sup with the enemy. She could not, in good conscience, "participate in a celebration under the hegemony of the very corporation which fought us at every step."[48] Many GM plants were being moved South in an effort to avoid union activities, and she wondered how Mr. UAW Woodcock could consort with the very people who would destroy him in a minute, if they had the chance. Many old-time labor leaders refused to attend. Emil Mazey wanted no part of the evening's activities, he told a newspaper reporter. Few women were present. The only participant in the sit-down to accept the invitation at the St. Regis was Victor Reuther. Nonetheless, some 200 people did attend the event and after dinner saw some newsreels of the 1937 strike, which of course had plenty of shots of Genora. "Perhaps Mrs. Dollinger did make an unknowing appearance," one reported quipped.[49]

Though avoiding Detroit, Genora did attend the annual observances in Flint. By mid-February 1977, she had committed herself to another documentary in which she played a major role, *With Babies and Banners,* released in 1978. A night before the general union conference, producer Lorraine Gray set up a surprise party for Genora. While the cameras rolled, Genora walked into the home of Delia Parrish and was astonished to see Sybil "Teeter" Walker, one of her lieutenants from the Emergency Brigade, whom she had not seen in forty years. Nellie Besson, whom she had seen on numerous occasions since the sit-down, was also present. Genora was, however, disturbed by the presence of several women who had not participated in the events of 1937, though viewers of the documentary would probably think they had. According to Gray, an African American woman was present to show that "blacks had been involved," although only one black had taken part in the sit-downs. Genora thought this and other matters misled viewers and felt Ms. Gray should have consulted her first. "I was surprised," she wrote to Gray, "when I walked into the filming [and saw] women who were never involved in the Emergency Brigade."[50] And, sure enough, according to the *Guardian* in New York, not enough explanation in the brigade's formation was given by the "one Black woman interviewed."[51] Genora had worked hard through the years to get an accurate and honest portrayal of women's roles and contributions to labor and feminism. She believed "The Great Sit-Down" started this trend and thought *With Babies and Banners* would continue this happy development. "For the first time women were using film to break new ground in interpreting history," and it was a great mistake at the beginning of this process to introduce distortions.[52] "Genora thought it was the wrong way to begin the revision process."[53] Nevertheless, she gave producer Gray and historian Lynn Goldfarb all the cooperation she could in the production of the film.

At the plenary session of the 1977 conference, Genora and a few dozen other women wore red berets, for obvious reasons. On several occasions, Genora tried to gain the floor but was not recognized by the chair, UAW regional director Don Ellis. Each time she stood, different reactions came from the audience. Some told her to hush and sit down, while others began cheering and chanting, "UAW needs an ERA." Angry women from NOW, the Ann Arbor Labor History project, and the Washington, D.C., Women's Film Cooperative "unleashed so colorful and determined a protest . . . that it . . . won Genora the right to speak."[54] Finally invited to the stage, she spoke for about fifteen minutes. She recited "Solidarity Forever" for her audience, told them about the role of women in the 1937 strike, and argued that the UAW should support the current efforts to get an ERA passed. She scolded her fellow union members because no women had officially been included in the program. "We are the foremothers of today's young women and proud of it."[55] She heard later that she had been brought to the speakers' platform by Leonard Woodcock himself. Woodcock called Ellis from the rostrum and ordered him to give Genora the floor. When Ellis stated he "couldn't" because Genora was "not on the program," Woodcock replied, "What the hell is wrong with you, Ellis? Can't you see what is happening out there?"[56] He meant, of course, that a groundswell of support and enthusiasm was developing for Genora and her feminist colleagues and the pragmatic thing to do was yield to their demands.

For the first time, in 1977 and 1978, Genora Dollinger began to look optimistically upon the possibility that women's history might finally receive the appreciation it deserved. She had never expected to see such events in her lifetime, "just as my mother and grandmother could not see the works of Lucretia Mott, Lucy Stone, [and] Susan B. Anthony . . . in their time." She could remember history classes in grade school that "reinforced my desire to be a boy or a man."

Women, she happily asserted, were becoming more than "window dressing" in her day and time. Now that the consciousness of both men and women has "been awakened, nothing can stop our progress." She said that humanity had been "limping" along for thousands of years on half its brain power. The process of equality, she argued, would produce better human beings, both men and women. Oral history projects at numerous institutions of higher education around the country were telling the feminist story, and women's self-help organizations were instilling confidence in women who had previously lacked it. Women were being interviewed now (Genora's own appointment calendar stayed full) and documentary movies made about them. All this progress, said Genora, "makes my heart sing."[57]

She probably should have known better than to get her hopes up too high. When *With Babies and Banners* was released and shown in several large cities around the country and got an Oscar nomination, Emil Mazey, now secretary-treasurer of the UAW, told a newspaper reporter that he thought the film "overrated" the role women played in the 1937 sit-down.[58] Genora, outraged at such an assertion, attributed it in large part to Emil Mazey's close friendship with Don Ellis, who had been forced to give Genora the microphone at the 1977 UAW convention. She wrote an angry letter to Emil, accompanying it with the letters by Robert Travis and Roy Reuther, written in 1937, that lauded the work of the WEB in the 1937 events.[59] She never heard back from him. Genora was so incensed that she also wrote a testy letter in October 1978 to current UAW president Douglas A. Fraser (with copies sent to the entire UAW Board) to complain about Mazey. He soothingly and condescendingly wrote back, "I do not believe the contributions the women made during the Flint sit-down can be denied nor ignored and the *New York Times* article, which you attached, testifies to the significant role they played."[60] She was mollified, to some extent, by Fraser's words.

She could not dwell on such matters for long, because she meant to move on to other things. Her crusades were more important than any quarrel with Emil Mazey, or anyone else, for that matter. She kept finding new avenues to support the causes of feminism and "radical" politics. One of them was Dr. Barry Commoner's new political organization, the Citizens Party. Its platform suited Genora's philosophy and temperament: public control of energy industries, vigorous support for human rights at home and abroad, a sharp reversal in military spending (with the money instead going to domestic educational pursuits), a guaranteed job for everyone who wanted to work, conservation with an emphasis on solar power, and adequate food, housing, and medical care for all citizens. This party promised to open a dialogue on feminism and gay rights and to get laws passed that would forbid secret FBI investigations of individuals. Blaming the long involvement in Vietnam for spiraling inflation of the late 1970s and early 1980s, the party vowed to ease the nation's economic woes. It also hoped to revive voter interest in politics: in the 1978 congressional elections, more than 100 million people stayed home. This apathy had to be reversed. And, as Commoner liked to remark, "It's time we stopped worrying about how to take over the Middle East oil fields and started working to take over the Texas oil fields."[61]

In April 1979, the Citizens Party held its nominating convention in Cleveland, Ohio. Genora (who now addressed her colleagues as "citizen" rather than "comrade") and Sol were among the 290 delegates in attendance. One of them, Jeanne Morgan, wrote to Genora a while after the convention that she was "moved to meet you and Sol again, after so many years" and to find them still dedicated to the "humanist point of view" and to social justice.[62] The party nominated Commoner to be president in the upcoming 1980 campaign and LaDonna Harris as his vice presidential candidate. The only difficulty Genora had with the Citizens Party campaign occurred when she thought Commoner was abandoning its populist characteristics and getting into narrowly defined areas of foreign policy when he was put on the program for a September 1979 conference on Palestinian human rights. Not, to be sure, that she opposed human rights; on the contrary, she had always been a firm supporter of them. The problem arose because there had been no party decision on this matter. "Are we building a populist party on principles or a sectarian party with a narrow appeal?" she rhetorically asked Commoner. If the party became involved in the Palestine-Israel conflict, there would be endless questions and debates that would keep it from addressing domestic issues.[63] The Citizens Party was "running candidates for president and vice president in 1980 to do in 1980 what the abolitionists and the Republican [P]arty did in the 1850s and 60s,"[64] and she hoped that "our new, young party won't be splitting before we get going." When she and others heard that Commoner would not, after all, appear at the Palestinian meeting, but only because he could not fit it into his time schedule, Genora angrily wrote to party official Peter Unterweger: "Does this mean if his schedule WOULD allow it he would be the featured speaker?" Such ramifications were dangerous to contemplate. She insisted, "It's either build a Populist party in this tough political system, or another sectarian party replete with slogans . . . and no strength to do anything about the serious problems facing us [i.e., Americans] or humanity."[65] Unterweger placatingly wrote back that Commoner had only been *asked* to appear before the Palestinians and that his name had appeared on the program without his consent.[66]

The party printed thousands of letters to be distributed to UAW locals around the country to urge them to support Commoner. Genora, one of the signatories of this letter, labeled herself as "Organizer." The letter campaign helped because many labor members gave Commoner their vote in 1980. Nevertheless, the Citizens Party came nowhere close to winning; it collected less than 3 percent of the total vote. Genora and Sol both knew that the Citizens Party did not stand a chance, but they worked on principle rather than expediency. After all, Genora had not collected many votes when she ran for the Senate in 1948 and the House in 1950. Yet her and Sol's affiliation with the SWP and the SUA (discussed in chapter 4) existed not for getting votes but for finding a conduit through which to express their economic, social, and political ideologies. Therefore they exuberantly endorsed Commoner and his party and would have done so again in the future if they had had the opportunity.

As the 1980s opened, Genora, for the most part, was a happy woman. Feminism became, at last, recognized and appreciated; even male historians seemed intent on correcting past omissions and inaccuracies. Her health problems continued: arthritis, heart (three pacemakers altogether), and then Meniere's syndrome, an inner ear condition that caused sudden spells of vertigo. Nevertheless, she coped, fully savoring the arrival of a new day of reform. She remained widely admired throughout the country and continued to receive correspondence from individuals in the countries she and Sol had visited, primarily Mexico,

Spain, Portugal, and the Netherlands. She cherished the encomia, but none more than the one she received from her old friend and WEB comrade in arms, Nellie Besson, who told Genora that "all my life you have been my model. Everything that I do is as close to you as I can get."[67] This letter, plus all the others, was a fine way, Genora thought, to start out the 1980s, the last full decade of her life.

Seemingly more coquettish than revolutionary, 15-year-old Genora poses for this photo in Flint, Michigan.

Lora and Raymond Albro, Genora's parents, ca. 1930, Flint, Michigan.

Family Portrait (left to right): Front row: Barbara Albro (Genora's sister), Lora (Genora's mother), Beatrice Albro (Genora's sister), Raymond Albro (Genora's father), Genora. Rear: Jarvis Albro (Genora's brother).

Right is Kermit Johnson, Genora's first husband. Left is his friend John Lamesfield.

Above in center is Genora Johnson, enrolling recruits into the famous Women's Emergency Brigade which was an important factor—on the picket lines, in the strike kitchens and elsewhere—in winning the famous sit-down strike in the General Motors plants in Flint in early 1937.

Genora (sitting) with Emergency Brigade members. Photo appeared in *Socialist Appeal,* 1938, on the occasion of Genora and Kermit joining the Socialist Workers Party.

Jarvis (Jody) Johnson at the Flint picket line, 1937. The sign he carried was published by newspapers around the world.

Genora Johnson, still youthful and full of life, ca. 1938.

The Flint Sit-Down Strike: Genora Johnson (second from right) and a group of sit-down supporters march down a street in Flint, Michigan, 1937. Photo courtesy Walter P. Reuther Library, Wayne State University.

Genora Johnson, ca. 1941.

Genora's lost boys: Jarvis (Jody) Johnson (left), killed in a cycle accident; Dennis (Denny) Johnson (right), died of what was said to be multiple sclerosis.

Genora and Sol Dollinger, around the time of their wedding, fall 1941. Photo by Ray Albro.

Genora Dollinger and son Ronald, ca. 1956.

Family photo, ca. 1970, Los Angeles (left to right): Ronald, Genora, and Sol.

Genora Dollinger, right in the middle of the 1971 teachers' strike in Los Angeles. Her home was used as headquarters for the striking teachers.

Genora Dollinger on a cold day in Red Square, Moscow, 1988.

Genora Dollinger dressed in the red beret of the Women's Emergency Brigade, speaking at UAW Convention, 1986. Her friend and fellow EB member, Nellie Besson, applauds her.

Eight **Tuxedo Unionism**

United Automobile Workers officials, particularly Larry Jones at Local 659 in Flint, wanted "historical status" for GM plants numbers one, two, and especially four, as the actions there gave the 1937 victory to the union. State and national approvals arrived in early 1980, and Genora received an invitation to participate in the gala events marking the occasion, the highlight of which would be the unveiling of bronze plaques at each of the three plants. UAW president, Douglas Fraser, wanted to emphasize the importance of this July 17, 1980, event by having the entire UAW board present, along with the mayor of Flint and the governor of Michigan. Not one of the speaking celebrities was to be from among the Flint pioneers of 1937. Genora was invited to unveil the bronze markers at the three plants but would not be among the platform guests. "But even this small token [unveiling the markers]," Genora snorted, "is awarded providing that I pay $379.00 air fare for the privilege!" She did not attend and called the affair an example of labor-capitalist cohesion that she could not countenance. (She was busy at this time promoting the fortunes of Barry Commoner's Citizens Party.) She was happy, along with Larry Jones, that workers would now be able to walk by these historic markers and read something of their past history, "But I can't help but resent that our union has produced such slimy worms who sit on our top councils."[1] It could very well have been this attitude that caused the officials not to ask her to speak in the first place.

The themes of tuxedo unionism, feminism, and the overall condition of the industrial world absorbed Genora's attention in the 1980s.

She agreed with longtime friend and poet Floyd Hoke-Miller that industrialism in the United States was being "replaced by an oriental paternalism."[2] He sent Genora this poem:

> What's good for the corporate boss
> is good for you and all the nation;
> so help him in both profit and loss
> to ensure his mammon-inspired salvation.
> Labor run unions are now out of date,
> but Papa knows best, be sure of that;
> let the 'boss-man' lead, for heaven can wait
> as the strike to win is now old hat.[3]

The poem suited Genora's mood; her beloved labor unions of 1937 and beyond had given up the fight. They appeared willing to see loyal workmen's jobs go to the American South or to Mexico, just to please the latest whims of executive overlords. Why have a strike these days when everyone knew the union leaders would capitulate before it was even half over. She told Lynn Goldfarb that "there are so few bright spots on the labor scene today . . . what a sorry role is being played by the . . . leadership."[4]

Another disadvantage for modern labor, she felt, was the "robot revolution," which constantly replaced workers, particularly women.[5] Those opposed to increased mechanization had about as much chance to stop it as had the nineteenth-century levelers in England's Industrial Revolution. The way around robotics was for workers to insist that management bring them into the decision-making process. Genora reemphasized her beliefs that government should own the means of production and distribution of basic industries. Ideally, Genora also desired the creation of a labor party in the United States, one that would truly represent the best interests of working people.[6] She told one professor and researcher after another that feminism still remained uppermost in her mind and was concerned once again (as seen in the unveiling of the plaques in Flint) that it was being ignored and downplayed. The young historians in the 1980s may have been sincere but were "incapable of doing more than collecting facts."[7] They possessed no analytical skills and therefore could not assess feminism in the context of the rise of labor unions. She repeatedly reminded journalists and historians of Kermit Johnson's and her plans for taking

Plant Four (discussed in chapter 2), only to see the story excluded from newspapers and books. Even if she had not been involved in the strategic parts of the matter, she frequently told Larry Jones, she had typed the lawyer's documentation for it and fought it through the ranks until it received official approval.[8]

These activities and observations notwithstanding, Genora joined Sol in 1983 on another European trip. In Amsterdam, she visited forty museums, and even these did not satisfy her appetite for paintings and other works of art. When the pair arrived in Lausanne, Genora found that it had no art museums, and they left quickly for Geneva. In Munich, Genora took offense at a comment by a woman gas station attendant who told the Dollingers that she had been to the United States only once—to Texas, which was, the German said, "a very bad place." Why? "Too many 'schwartzas' [African Americans]," she responded, leading Genora to conclude that the attendant was a neo-Nazi. She was saddened to realize, once again, that racial prejudice is a worldwide problem. The couple went to Dachau, walking for hours in that place of horror, studying the remnants of unspeakable cruelties. Perhaps the gas station attendant and Dachau caused Genora to write in her diary that she had ordered German food with "great trepidation." She did not know whether she was ordering "pig's snouts" or "pig's testicles."[9] She did not become anti-German on this trip, but it definitely cooled her ardor for "das Land der Mitte"(the Land in the Middle).

Her next trip abroad was to China in May 1984. She became too ill even to go to the Great Wall outside Beijing. After her health improved somewhat, she and Sol traveled to Shanghai. Here, a physician diagnosed her problems as heart troubles and told them to go home, as the Chinese hospitals did not have the equipment with which to treat her. On the way back, in Hawaii, Genora collapsed, and the first of ultimately three pacemakers was installed.[10]

Despite health problems, Genora and Sol took another trip to Europe in late summer 1984, and it made up for some of the miseries of the previous year. In Lisbon, Sol brought a copy of the *International Herald Tribune,* with the headline, "Mondale Names Ferraro as His Running Mate" blazing out. Genora felt "like shouting all over the streets of Lisbon that a woman was, for the first time, a serious candidate for vice-president of the United States!" If only her mother could have seen this headline. Women could not even vote in the United States until after Genora was born and had always been the "property of their husbands after they left their fathers' homes." If women went out on their own they were called old maids, and all kinds of jokes were made about them. "And now, today," she exulted, "a big stride has been taken." She knew that Ferraro favored a nuclear freeze, and Genora said, with some understatement, "This is a good day!" She was not so naive as to expect the Ferraro nomination to end discrimination against women or inaugurate a golden age of feminism. It was an acknowledgment by Vice President Walter Mondale that women were as capable as men in just about any field, including politics. She believed that Ferraro's elevation vindicated what she herself had sought to accomplish over the years and thought it her duty to ask any and all Americans she met about their feelings toward Ferraro. Two young girls in a shoe store had missed a day of touring just to listen to the news reports on the radio. She heard a young couple speaking "American" English on the streets and queried them: "Yippee!" they both yelled. In a cafeteria Genora again heard American English being spoken at a table where six people dined. "Their enthusiasm and support," she claimed, was "quite something to hear." The first remark came from a man of about fifty. He exclaimed, "Well, it's about time!" Genora's insistence on "American" English was due to her belief that the English "would not be excited at all" about the Ferraro nomination. After all, they had Margaret Thatcher, "the Iron Lady—a most reactionary" politician—as their prime minister.[11]

When Genora got back to her room, she wrote a lengthy and heartfelt letter to vice presidential hopeful Ferraro. On a personal level, she expressed the joy of all women at this turn of events. Congresswoman Ferraro should neither be "pressured" nor "beholden" to foreign or domestic advisors among the men now surrounding her in Washington. The vice presidential candidate, she claimed, had a constituency "greater" than any male counselors. By this statement, Genora narrowed her focus, perhaps unduly, on the presidential campaign of 1984. While Ferraro's nomination was a great day for feminism and the women's movements in general, it was as symbolic as it was real. Ferraro ran on a ticket that included feminism but did not make it the chief impetus.[12]

One would have thought that Genora Dollinger's exuberance would cause her not only to vote for the Mondale-Ferraro ticket but actively work for it as well. She did neither. Back in the states, she monitored television ads, radio announcements, and newspaper stories. Though believing that the nomination of a woman for the number two spot was a step in the right direction, she decided that the Mondale-Ferraro ticket was as "totally subordinate" as Reagan-Bush to Fortune 500 CEOs who "really rule the country."[13] Other observations confirmed her changed opinions about the Ferraro nomination. What did her candidacy mean for the United States, the Democratic Party, unionism, and women? "Not much," one poll after another indicated. Though Ferraro's nomination was a significant historical precedent, it was not—much to Genora's consternation—a "breakthrough" for American women in the context of national politics.[14]As often before, both Genora and Sol stayed home on election day; there were no fit candidates to vote for.[15]

For two years following her 1984 trip to Europe, Genora was fairly homebound. By early 1985 she was taking drugs for TB, Clinoril for arthritis, Alupent inhaler for asthma (her lung capacity, said her doctors, was only 20 to 25 percent normal), Tambocor for an irregular heartbeat, and Lanoxin and Cardizem to help her pacemaker keep things normal in her atrial chambers. Her upper esophagus was one-half flaccid, and she developed a hiatal hernia. The only organ that seemed not to bother her was her liver.[16] Did these maladies put a stop to Genora's revolutionary lifestyle and career? Emphatically, no. She maintained a stream of correspondence on the major issues of the day with individuals around the country. To her congressman, Henry A. Waxman, she lamented the Reagan administration's forays into Central America, specifically Honduras, El Salvador, and especially Nicaragua. Waxman wrote back that "this is Vietnam all over again!"[17] She strongly supported the flight attendants in their 1986 strike against Trans World Airlines (TWA) and became a fan of TV talk-show host Phil Donahue, lauding his defense of the stewardesses in their dispute with TWA.[18] She rejoiced that a pro–abortion rights rally in Los Angeles brought out 30,000 people, including Mayor Thomas Bradley.[19] She strongly opposed the U.S. bombing of Tripoli, Libya, and was disappointed when polls showed that 70 percent of Americans supported this action. In other countries, however, a similar percentage denounced the bombings.[20] The nuclear explosion in Kiev unsettled Genora, as it did most Americans. The various political organizations to which she adhered over the years had always spoken about the need for ironclad nuclear regulations, and the Ukraine incident proved—at least to her—the points she had made for years.[21]

The big event in 1986 she looked forward to, and the one she kept urging her doctors to get her in shape for, was the starting celebrations of the fiftieth anniversary of the UAW victory against GM during the sit-downs. Looking toward the August meeting, she wrote in her diary and also a notebook as early as March that "Larry Jones called to tell me I must not forget the 50th anniversary of the pioneers. . . . I am to be the main speaker."[22] As if she *could* forget. She was flattered by Jones's invitation and implied such in her notebook entries. To Jones, however, she was strident. Undoubtedly remembering the difficulty of trying to get recognized by Don Ellis during the fortieth anniversary gala, she told Jones, "If it [the fiftieth anniversary] is going to be another put-down of the women who participated in the winning of the '37 sitdown strike we women can be better prepared." Thousands of people throughout the country and the world had now learned how tough it had been to deal with industrial powers prior to unionization.[23]

The fiftieth anniversary celebrations included numerous events spread out over a few months. In late 1985, for example, about fifty young women, all members of the UAW, staged a red beret march in Flint. They arranged for two special touring cars, with Nellie Besson in the front car to head the procession. Genora received an invitation but could not attend. "If I had the names of these wonderfully independent union women I would list them all with deep gratitude. I plan to be in Flint this summer to meet them." This event, Genora wrote, was a huge "bright spot" in union affairs of the mid-1980s. Just about everything else, however, was drab. The celebrations, Genora again complained, were *jointly* arranged by GM vice president Alfred Warren and UAW president Owen Bieber. GM "fought us every step of the way . . . [and hired] thugs, goons, and Pinkerton spies who were beating the heads of men trying to organize a union. These professional goons trapped union men in alleys, cars or beer gardens, beating them badly, breaking their arms and jaws. . . . With no unemployment insurance, no money, no food and welfare, several were evicted from their homes."[24] And now, fifty years later, GM sought to cash in on a commemoration and celebration that represented one of its own darkest hours and defeat. Genora's contempt for both Warren and Bieber was obvious. No, no, she regretted, there was no redemption.

She received another telephone call from Larry Jones, giving further information about the speakers' platform in the upcoming events. He reaffirmed his wish to have Genora as a main speaker. "Well," she asked, "who else have you got?" Jones listed a number of other speakers, including Victor Reuther, but when he mentioned Henry Kraus,

Genora replied, "I will speak but I want to make sure I follow Henry Kraus. I don't care what the program is."[25] Why was she so intent on following Kraus to the podium? She had a purpose and made it clear when she stood up to speak. As the saying goes, Genora did a number on Henry Kraus. Meeting in the Flint Auditorium on Saturday, August 2, 1986, she went on for forty-five minutes in a speech that was regarded as either sensational or regrettable, depending on one's point of view. In 1947 Kraus had authored *The Many and the Few,* and that book became the focus of Genora's presentation.

She started out, after Kraus left the podium: "This book has been labeled an historical novel [by whom, she did not say]. It is undocumented and is filled with facts mixed with fantasies, distortions, character assassinations, and the magnified role of the author himself. One can read it through and find only chauvinistic references to leaderless union women performing spontaneous acts of courage. Much of the time he calls us 'the girls.'" In his book Kraus wrote about a woman at the Battle of Bull's Run who had "hysterically" castigated the police. Genora wanted to know if the men that night had been hysterical as well. "No, only that woman." And, if Henry, she told him directly, had been there that night, as he claimed, and if he took a good look at the present speaker, he would recognize that hysterical woman.

Kraus had spoken about the women gathering signatures and saying they wished to join the Emergency Brigade. There was no petition, Genora countered, only a spontaneous movement of women risking their lives by enlisting as militant strikers. She personalized her attack, accusing Kraus of having a vendetta against her when he edited the *Flint Auto Worker,* the main source of union news during the strike. Kraus, she claimed, had wanted the Emergency Brigade to be under the "immediate jurisdiction" of UAW men, even though they had their hands full fighting GM. Where could one read in Kraus's book, she asked, or "in any of the books written by male authors," of the five women "who strung themselves across the Plant #4 main gate, holding off the armed Flint police at the crucial moment before union reinforcements arrived? . . . Or of my directing the establishment of a large picket line circle in front of the entrance when reinforcements did arrive?" Coming close to calling Kraus a liar, she told him from the podium, "Henry, you weren't there but you did have a news clipping bureau." Instead, the *New York Times* was present, and she waved a tear sheet in front of Kraus. "Now anyone knows it has to be something important to get on page one of the world's most important newspaper . . . right?" Then why did Kraus ignore the role of women in the *Flint Auto Worker* and then ten years later in his book, even after the *New York Times* had written a lengthy story about the work of the Emergency Brigade?

She then went into further explanations of the women's work in the sit-downs, including the trip to Saginaw (discussed in chapter 2) to give aid and comfort to fellow unionists in that fiercely antilabor company town. She spoke about the "children's picket line" and of the photo of her and her son shown in newspapers around the world. She quoted letters she received in 1937 from Robert Travis and Roy Reuther, lauding the contributions of the Emergency Brigade in gaining the UAW victory. Saying that she and fellow Brigade members broke tradition a half-century before, she rhetorically asked, "Did we know it was the first time in labor history that women organized on a para-military basis? . . . No! . . . Did we know . . . that it was something new in labor history to be proud to be called a women's auxiliary? . . . No!" They only knew, Genora emphasized, that they were fighting the world's largest industrial corporation, and their men needed help. The Emergency Brigade symbolized women's rights everywhere, she maintained. In 1937, a woman could not serve on juries in most states. Battered women had no one to turn to in their time of troubles. A divorced woman was considered "loose." Women were expected to be in the kitchen, the laundry, the bedroom, or the nursery. The WEBs changed the world. And Kraus had the temerity to call them "the girls." According to Genora, he referred to one of the WEBs as "no flapper" but a "good housewife." But then, Genora added, men never wrote "John Brown No Ladies' man, was a good auto worker!" [*sic*].

A friend had recently told her, "History is made by the people who write it" (and she was making labor history that day!). Even historians or professors "taking oral interviews" can "slant the material they obtain, omit or enhance the importance of roles according to their own lights." For Genora, the truth of this statement was represented by Kraus's work, not only as the editor of *Flint Auto Worker* but also as the author of *The Many and the Few.* Kraus had written women out of the history of the sit-downs, and Genora let him know about it in no uncertain terms.

She mentioned the films and academic interest in the WEBs that had developed in the past decade. Genora and colleagues had been "besieged" with requests for appearances and lectures at universities, colleges, women's and labor organizations, and ethnic groups. "Women have been thirsty for this news of long ago. Why did it take so long for this history to become known?" It was, she said, because of "PR men" like Kraus who, in 1947, had all the materials at hand when he wrote *The Many and the Few.* Would it have been too "revolutionary" in historical practice to have included the significance of women in the sit-downs of 1937? Even if it had been, Genora reminded Kraus that his book had been republished in the mid-1980s, and he could have redressed this grievance. "He had a great responsibility to history and was not big enough to fulfill it!"

As she closed her speech, she addressed Kraus directly. "For 50 years I have wanted to tell you, Henry Kraus, as a representative of hundreds of departed pioneers, what an injustice you have done to the women of America and the world. For a quarter of a century you were in Paris [Kraus and his wife, Dorothy, had become permanent residents of France]. But now that you are here you know how some of us have felt for all these years."[26] Audience members felt one way or another about Genora's speech, or diatribe as some critics called it, but there were no drowsy attendees. She got hearty applause from her followers and even a standing ovation from a few, while her detractors sat in silence.

Apparently, Sol sat between Genora and Kraus at the speaker's table. When Victor Reuther took the podium after Genora finished, Kraus allegedly leaned over Sol to confront Genora. "I'm going to get even with you," he is reported to have said. "You already got even with me fifty years ago," Genora angrily answered, to which Kraus, in kind, said, "I'm going to take care of it by what I write about you in my next book. I'm going to sue you," presumably for libel and public humiliation, but for reasons known only to him, he never did. Sol tried to listen to Victor Reuther while keeping Kraus and Genora separated. He finally told Kraus, "Will you shut up and sit down?"[27] And the disgruntled author fell back into his seat.

Genora was exhausted as she and Sol flew back to Los Angeles, and as Henry and Dorothy Kraus winged their way to Paris. Both parties left behind bitter memories of the fiftieth anniversary, an event that was supposed to have brought peace and joy to all concerned. When Henry got back to his Paris home, he found tons of unanswered mail and other things to do, plus a recurrence of a painful attack of shingles. He did not get around to responding to Genora's attack on him until December 11, 1986. He wrote a long, involved letter to Larry Jones, who had coordinated the meetings in Flint. It was an "ugly affair," said

Kraus. Jones, as chairman of the meeting, had some "responsibility for what took place." At the least Jones should have "called her to order," and since he didn't, "you should have asked me if I wanted to reply to her nasty accusations." Genora's attack on Kraus was "such a mean and vulgar thing to do at such a glorious affair. Would I stoop to anything as low as that?" As Genora spoke, Kraus said, he kept looking out over the audience, trying to judge their reactions. "My impression was that they were suffering, deeply suffering, from the shock they felt in her ugly words and expressions and from the tremendous disillusionment they experienced after the great joy and pride they had shared with those who had participated with them in what was no doubt the most significant event in all our lives. Kraus knew that Jones had "a high regard for Genora," but he had let her off "quite lightly" in this entire affair. Jones had agreed just after the speech that Genora was a "high-keyed" person who "had to say" what she did. He also acquiesced, said Kraus, in the thought that she should not have used such "strident and savage" terms about a book that had been written forty years before. Kraus asked Jones and others who might be interested to read the back issues of *Flint Auto Worker* "without prejudice" and see if he had been hostile to the developing women's movements. Reading *The Many and the Few* would have revealed "verities" about "the author's overall decency." But, said Kraus, Jones had not bothered with these details and "Genora got away with her lies and the hundreds of people who heard them had no reason to doubt that they were true."[28]

Who was right—or wrong: Genora Dollinger or Henry Kraus? Neither. And both. Genora wrote later that Kraus reminded her of a "commissar character scurrying from one meeting to another," gaining confidence only in the "company of those he knew." Physically, she commented, he was short of stature and had blond white hair, "which contributed to a sense of an insecure man."[29] Just why Genora thought one's physique indicated insecurity, she never said (she was only 5'4"). Having always avoided stereotyping in her life and career, she fell victim to it on this occasion. Perhaps, as she said, she had been waiting fifty years to tell Kraus what her feelings were toward him, but it was not as though she had been silent all that time. Her friends knew all too well what her opinions were, not just of Kraus but of everything else connected with Socialist ideals.[30]

Genora could have misinterpreted the reprint of Kraus's book when she charged him with not correcting feminist omissions. In 1947 Kraus had paid the publication costs himself for his book, to which UAW secretary-treasurer George F. Addes and vice president R. J. Thompson added brief introductions. In the 1985 reprint from the University of Illinois Press, there were no changes from the 1947 text. Kraus did write a new introduction, in which he mentioned all the letters he had received from thesis and dissertation writers on the subject of women in the 1937 sit-downs. There was also an introduction by three labor historians: Neil Leighton, William J. Meyer, and Nan Pendrell. And, it must be pointed out, Kraus *did* spend about seven pages in the original of 1947 and the reprint of 1985 on the role of women in the 1937 struggles against GM. He remarked that the strike "was often to prove the beginning of life to these women, at least the beginning of a conscious social life."[31] In book publishing there is a difference between a reprint and a revised edition. With the former (which was the case with *The Many and the Few*), a writer has little or no chance of putting in new material or taking out old. With the latter, an author sometimes has this privilege, but he still has to be guided by editorial directives. Whatever the case, Kraus was not alone in any failures to document feminine participation in the sit-downs, at least as much as Genora wanted; other chroniclers failed likewise, at least until the mid-1980s. It was not just that Henry, in Genora's opinion, downplayed the role of women. He did not, in her mind, give enough credit to Roy Reuther for his work in manning the sound car and rallying the troops to the attack. She believed also that he had denigrated Kermit Johnson, her first husband. She was adamant that Kermit was the architect (discussed in chapter 2) of the plans that ultimately brought GM to its knees.[32] Genora's outburst was also the result of what had been known sub rosa in the Flint UAW for many years: before, during, and after the sit-downs, both Henry and Dorothy Kraus had been members of the Communist Party (CP). The Women's Auxiliary in which Dorothy had been active was a CP front, while the EB, led by Genora, was a Socialist Party stronghold. Genora never resorted to "red-baiting" and knew the audience would not understand why she attacked Kraus "for omission of history that was politically motivated by membership in the CP."[33]

The confrontation between Genora Dollinger and Henry Kraus was unfortunate.[34] The meeting at Union Hall 659 in Flint was supposed to be a happy occasion, one that celebrated and commemorated a wonderful event in union history. Genora and Henry were both strong-willed individuals firmly committed to principle as they saw it. Both played important roles in helping to make the country aware of the value of unionism. Several years later, Kraus won the coveted MacArthur Prize for contributions to literature. There is no evidence that Genora and Henry ever met or spoke to each other again. All things considered, that was just as well.

In one letter after another Genora continued to rail against UAW leadership, especially Owen Bieber (elected UAW president in 1986) because he was "incompetent," cozying up to GM officials and forgetting his own constituency.[35] Genora met Bieber in 1989 at the UAW annual meeting in Los Angeles. She represented a small caucus called New Directions that pushed for increased UAW independence from the executive offices at GM and for democratic leadership. Bieber refused to recognize anyone from the floor who was a New Directionist. Finally, the uproar caused him to threaten police action. Realizing how badly this move would reflect on his leadership, he did recognize some of the 150 delegates of the New Directions. At a social gathering one night, Bieber entered and Sol jokingly asked Genora if she were going to speak to him. Without saying a word, Genora coquettishly, and with a bit of bluster, walked up to Bieber and asked, "Do you know who I am?" Bieber stood six feet six inches; Genora barely reached his belt buckle. Bieber glanced down at Genora, who was wearing a large New Directions button on her lapel, but the only sound he could make was a nervous laugh.[36] Bieber quickly departed.

In the midst of these activities, Genora's health in the late 1980s remained precarious: her pacemaker had to be adjusted on occasions, and she suffered upper atrial palpitations, which "greatly lowered her heart activity."[37] Nevertheless, she and Sol traveled whenever possible, sometimes extensively. Sol retired from Technion in 1987, and in April of that year the couple traveled to New York to attend the Socialist Scholars Conference and then went on to Washington, D.C. With misgivings, the pair decided on a major undertaking, something they had always dreamed of doing: an extended visit to Moscow. Departing in August 1987, they wanted a firsthand opportunity to see *glasnost* and *perestroika* in action. Their Intourist Hotel was near Red Square, a short walk to the Kremlin, Lenin's Tomb, St. Basil's Cathedral, the War Memorial and its eternal flames, and the huge Gum Department Store.[38] (Genora was "not prepared" to see such a "paucity" of commodities—and all of poor quality).[39] They were "spellbound" by a film about Lenin—hearing a tape with his actual voice on it, they could feel the "intensity" of his effort to "draw his listeners into understanding with him." On the eighth day of their Soviet trip, and one day before they were to depart for Leningrad, where Genora wanted to visit the Hermitage, she again suffered heart failure. A physician, nurse, and medical technician rushed to her hotel room and administered emergency treatment. Then she was ordered to the main hospital in Moscow, a twenty-minute ride from the hotel. Genora explained their disillusionment: "We were prepared to see a clinic without modern Western equipment, but were totally unprepared for the ancient buildings and furnishings and the unclean facilities. A patient must bring his own gown, towel, washcloth, and toilet tissue! This was Moscow—what must the other hospitals of the USSR be like! No wonder that life expectancy is 10 years lower than ours."[40]

Genora came home in a wheel chair, disappointed but not bitter—she felt "very fortunate to have been able to see and learn about this most intriguing country and its courageous people." She was happy that a "new fresh wind" was blowing through the USSR "after 70 long years, and people are no longer afraid to talk to outsiders. . . . What an experience!—even if it was, sadly, cut short!"[41] One reason Genora was so happy about the Russian trip derived from the partial rehabilitation of Leon Trotsky's reputation in Soviet history. For sixty years Trotsky had been a "virtual curse" in Soviet orthodoxy. Prominent Soviet historian Dmitri Volkogonov wrote of Trotsky's warning that Josef Stalin would be a dictator and shared "the long-held Western belief that Trotsky was murdered in Mexico by a Soviet agent acting on Kremlin orders."[42] Events in the USSR developed rapidly: "We feel quite sure that the floodgates of the real Soviet history will now be open. Who would have thought it would happen this fast? Gorbachev deserves our support for making this possible."[43] Many people in the Soviet Union, Genora claimed, were for the first time hearing about Trotsky. Surprised when told that she and Sol were Trotskyists, some of their guides wanted to know everything about him. Strange, Genora mused, for Russians to learn about one of their major historical figures from foreigners.

With her usual routines of life, Genora continued to write letters to all sorts of people. She told a friend that "building socialism is far more complicated than we thought possible. When we were young and energetic we thought it would all be accomplished in our lifetime."[44]

To Victor Navasky, she claimed still to be a Socialist, "albeit an unaffiliated one for the past 32 years."[45] One reason she left the Socialist Party was its almost constant endorsements of the Democratic Party, becoming, as it were, "the tail of the Democratic Party kite."[46] She wrote to Navasky on a matter that greatly troubled her: union and corporate collaborations, or tuxedo unionism, as she frequently called it. There was a "headlong plunge" into the "swamp of company unionism." She wanted Navasky and others to join her in preventing the "complete emasculation" of the American labor movement. Not the least of these efforts was for workers to "mount some resistance to the course of their present leadership."[47] Even foremen had been put on salary after the war and were required to wear ties and white shirts and given special parking privileges. These were additional reasons why the unions had been weakened because, among other things, stewards had now become "referral agents" and, consequently, had lost most of the power and influence they had exercised during World War II.[48]

She "sounded off" when *Searchlight* editor Larry Jones asked her for an article to commemorate the UAW victory in 1937. Titled "UAW Revolutions in California," it attacked Bruce Lee, western regional director of the UAW. Probably for this reason, the UAW board of directors overrode editor Jones, censored the article, and did not allow its publication. Lee gave "high praise" to the "joint Japanese, General Motors, and UAW collaborations and heralded them as the signposts of a new 'team system'" where workers took control of production. Genora compared this condition with the old assembly line speedups of pre-union eras. She was incensed that Lee accused some of the "old guard unionists" of resisting this "company-union power sharing" and saw this "new" system as a ploy to "appropriate workers' knowledge to create profits for the bosses." Lee called this point of view "warmed-over academic Marxism," which only further infuriated Genora. She told would-be readers that she was one of the "old line" radicals who still thought Marx "has a lot to teach us." Our troubles and woes were caused by "the class struggle in America between capital and labor. This precept guided us and made it possible for us to win the greatest genuine revolution in labor relations [the UAW victory in 1937] that this country has ever witnessed. From it came the great benefits that permit Brother Lee to speak so condescendingly of our efforts. We made possible the good wages and benefits that he now takes credit for." Corporate America was "pitting one plant against another; one UAW region against another UAW region; one local union against another local union" and community against community as each fought to retain its local industries and keep CEOs from packing off to Mexico. The "newly found" practice of team work became a contest. If one plant did not match the productivity—and profit level—of another, its workers were laid off or the plant closed entirely. Marx said a century before that when workers are laid off, they do not generally find a new profession that paid them as much as the one they had been required to leave. For Genora, this remained as true in the twentieth century as it had in the nineteenth. Under Lee's "team work," Genora penned, seniority ceased to exist. Many of the production jobs demanded young and strong novices. Thus Lee and his colleagues, Genora charged, "made it possible for workers in their early 40s to be discarded by the corporation without recourse and without pension benefits." It was a pity, she felt, that the union had joined with the corporation in altering workers' benefits—especially after so many years of struggle to attain them. Present day UAW leaders, from Bieber to Lee, Genora believed, wanted unions with no problems, "roses with no thorns." Workers of the past had run the gauntlet to achieve success. They believed that their sacrifices would create humane workplaces for those who followed them. Modern-day workers had little or no "historical sense" of "how and why the union built guarantees into the union contracts." Genora suggested that Lee collaborate with Roger Smith, chairman of the board at GM, to keep any more plants from being built in low-wage countries. Those plants already moved to foreign parts should be disassembled, brought home piece by piece, and American jobs should be restored in America. She closed her article by asserting, "It is sad to see the great institution of labor, which we old radicals made possible with our sweat and blood, destroyed by this new breed of sanctimonious, class-collaborating union leaders."[49] Genora had not been quite so worked up since the lambasting she gave Henry Kraus back in 1986.

In August 1989, Genora and Sol got what they considered stark confirmation of the views Genora expressed in her unpublished article for *Searchlight:* they returned to Flint for a sit-down commemoration, only to find plants standing idle and empty, the old Chevrolet sign missing, and "forlorn and worried looks on the faces of men and women in anticipation of further industrial decline" because of a union that had been "diminished in strength and vitality."[50]

"Runaway" plants were located in Mexico, Taiwan, Korea, the Philippines, and Puerto Rico. How could this have happened, Genora wanted to know, without protests from the current union leadership? Were the union, the company, and the workers all in collusion to dismantle American industry? Were we observing the demise of industrial unionism in America? So it would seem, at least to Genora and her followers. It was a sad and forlorn thought to the woman whose life and career had been shaped so decidedly by the sit-downs of 1937 and the subsequent negotiations that gave labor in this country some comfort and dignity.

Genora Dollinger had every right to settle down, enjoy her grandchildren (Kenneth Vincent Dollinger joined Danielle Genora in Ron's growing family), and be feted and honored after so many years of struggle. Nothing of the sort even crossed her mind. As the new decade opened and she reached her seventy-seventh birthday, she was more determined than ever to make a difference in the world.

The first opportunity came from the heart of Genora's life and experiences. Dan La Botz wrote a book for Labor Notes (a labor conscious press in Detroit) titled *A Troublemaker's Handbook: How to Fight Back Where You Work—and Win,* and he asked Genora to write a foreword, just up her alley. The book's topic was the exact motif to which she had dedicated her life so many years ago. She attacked unions as they expressed themselves in 1991 rather than in 1937. Most unions acquired bloated budgets to the extent that, "if finances were the measure, the big established unions would pass muster with flying colors." Unions had changed since "the feisty days of the 1930s. Many seem arthritic, with recurring symptoms of Alzheimer's." Present day (1991) union leadership had lost its will to lead and showed no imagination and certainly no boldness because they sup with employers and "forget what is fundamental to unionism—that management and labor are on opposing sides." The odds against labor were "just as formidable" in 1991 as they had been in 1937, perhaps even more so. In 1991 women made up almost 50 percent of the workforce in the United States, yet they routinely and scandalously failed to receive equal pay for equal work. Neither the corporations nor the unions had incorporated the full interests of the workingwoman into their schemes of management. Over the years labor had become too close to the Democratic Party, and this alliance was a big reason for "thousands of factories and millions of jobs being transported to foreign shores." Not only must this industrial flight be stopped, but also a national health care plan, adequate pensions, and child care centers for working parents were necessary for the workplace to become decent. There was a "current stagnation" in the labor movement that either "could not last much longer" or would destroy the hopes of working people once and for all.[51] She hoped La Botz's militant frame of mind would create a new labor impetus throughout the country. Such was not to be. The decline and deterioration of labor interests continued throughout the remainder of the 1990s.

As her body weakened, her mind quickened. She yielded to the spirit of the times and bought a computer; this caused her written output to increase considerably. An anthology on the labor movement came out in 1991, and Genora, two years before, had been asked by UAW Local 659 in Flint to contribute to it. She sent some articles but never heard from the editors. Her articles were not included in the book, which "perpetuated many inaccuracies" about the role of women in the 1937 strike. The anthology, she told *Labor History* editor Daniel Leab, exaggerated the role of the CP in the sit-downs, to the detriment of the Socialist Party, one that did make contributions, she believed, to the successful outcome of the strike.[52]

She got a lesson in the capricious world of publishing when she sent an article to *Labor History,* "Shedding Light on Some Unrecorded Pages of History." Leab accepted the article and sent his approval to Genora in November 1993.[53] In June 1994, however, he had to tell her that "my initial enthusiasm was not seconded by the editorial readers." He meant, of course, "peer review," which, in her case, he thought would "only be a formality."[54] He sent everything back to her, and that was that. There exist few, if any, appeals of editorial judgments. Leab did not even tell her what the outside readers said about her article. Genora attributed the negative response to her article as a rejection "of a contrary view" of the 1937 sit-downs by—of all things—a labor journal! She had long rallied against tuxedo unionism, and to her, this was additional evidence that labor and management were hand in glove. She believed her article was a "lost page of history" that "deserves to be in print."[55] Alas, Genora never found an editor to agree with her, so her article remained unpublished.

Her feelings were assuaged in late 1994, when she was inducted into the Michigan Women's Hall of Fame and received a Lifetime Achievement Award from the Women's Studies Association, headquartered in Lansing. She could not attend either event because of illnesses. She sent greetings to the Hall of Fame dinner audience on October 20, 1994. One attendant wrote to Genora that "we are so pleased you are being honored and recognized for the wonderful work you have done for working people over the years, and continue to do so."[56] Victor Reuther's wife, Sophie, sent a letter to the Hall of Fame, saying that it "honors itself" as well as the honoree by Genora's induction, which "advances and elevates the continuing struggle of women for equal rights, equal recognition . . . and equal remuneration for their contributions." Genora, Sophie asserted, was of the "great tradition of Mother Jones." Genora was to the auto workers what Mother Jones had been to the mine workers. The 1937 settlement with GM was "more than a Union victory." It was a "small revolution in the continuing struggle of women for equality and justice." All who had fought in that long-ago struggle "owe an enormous debt of gratitude to Genora."[57] Sue Ann Connolly said that Genora devoted herself to helping others realize their rightful life of dignity and security and had "a knack for teaching people they have rights." She inspired them to use their unrealized powers to protect and preserve those rights.[58] The Hall of Fame sent a huge bouquet of roses to Genora in Los Angeles. She received letters of congratulations from all over the country, along with tapes and other memorabilia from the celebration. "This whole experience," she happily exclaimed, "has been quite overwhelming."[59]

Despite ill health, Genora remained ambulatory and managed to be present at one very important event in Los Angeles. She wrote to a friend that "in 1994 the disgust with the two-party system has skyrocketed across the nation."[60] She was therefore a charter member of a new attempt to build a bona fide national labor party. The group making this effort was the Labor Party Advocates (LPA). "We need to form our own political party," she told an interviewer. "What have we got today? We won a great number of economic gains [in the Socialist and Socialist Workers Party] but politically we never did anything to secure them," making them vulnerable to legislative destruction. "I have always been in favor of a Labor Party for working people."[61]

In December 1994, Genora attended the organizational meeting of the LPA. Receiving two standing ovations, she told the crowd that this gathering reminded her of an old-time revival meeting. In the beginning was the Word, and that Word was "Organize!"[62] The workingman would not receive any protection—from either government or management—"until we get back into our original mold" of solidarity. The North American Free Trade Agreement (NAFTA), she argued, was bad news for the laboring classes in the United States. Jobs were exported overseas, primarily to Mexico, where the wages were 10 percent of those found in this country.[63] Corroborating her opinions here, another factory laborer lamented that "corporations want the American worker to tread water or sink so other workers around the world can catch up with us."[64]

Nonetheless, Genora objected to an anti-Japanese "Made in Japan" advertisement issued by the International Ladies' Garment Workers Union. Since moving to California, Genora had made many new friends of Japanese ancestry and knew of the "genuine horror they went through in the days of World War II." The individual Japanese worker should not be attacked for taking American jobs. The blame should be placed where it belonged: on big U.S. corporations whose cost-cutting strategies had led to much human misery. Some kind of labor party must succeed, she believed, "for our children's future" and, indeed, for the sake of humanity. Behind the podium where Genora spoke was a large sign that read, "The bosses have two parties; We need one of our own."[65] The party she sought to build is still in existence today (as of 2007) but has no chance in the national arena and very little, if any, in the local.

At the onset of 1995, Genora Dollinger suffered from exhaustion and illness. She told Studs Terkel, for his book *Coming of Age,* that, "sure, my body has slackened off, but my interest hasn't diminished." She still hoped, even at this late date, that "we'll see a decent society, without greed, without plundering other nations, without war, and with the salvation of the earth, for crying out loud." There was a pause in her speech and, significantly, she remarked, "I better take that pill now."[66] These were laudable thoughts that no well-meaning individual could easily refute, but they were idealistic—maybe too idealistic for human beings to attain.

All her life Genora suffered from one malady or another. Tuberculosis, asthma, heart problems, Meniere's syndrome, and high blood pressure, not to mention the traumatic effects of the beating she endured in the 1940s. She wrote to Michigan governor John Engler to solicit his views about Dr. Jack Kevorkian and assisted suicide, a big issue in the news at that time. Although there is little evidence that the thought of suicide ever crossed her mind (she did get to a point where she *wanted* to pass on), she did "profoundly support" Kevorkian's "right to die" activities.[67] The governor's answer to Genora was tactful: "The whole question of death and dying involves profound and complex ethical questions." Neither Kevorkian nor any other individual had the right to "decide who lives and dies in our state."[68]

The week of October 9, 1995, opened the way most of Genora's weeks had for the past three years since 1992, when she had become chronically ill. Her wasted body belied the sharpness of mind she still possessed. On Wednesday, October 11, she quietly passed away at the Cedar Sinai Medical Center in Los Angeles. She was eighty-two years old. Obituaries appeared in newspapers over the next several days. The *Flint Journal*'s Bruce Dickmeyer said that Genora stood out "as a leader" in the UAW labor movement and in the fight for women's equality.[69] The *Detroit Free Press* lauded her courage in forming the Women's Emergency Brigade in 1937 that was so significant in the fight against GM.[70] The *Los Angeles Times* spoke of her as a "pioneering female labor leader."[71] The *New York Times* said that Genora "rallied support for the hard-fought strike that gave the United Auto Workers Union its foothold at the General Motors Company in 1937."[72] Labor journals throughout the country, including *Searchlight* and *Headlight,* paid tribute to their fallen comrade. The North American Labor History Congress, meeting in Detroit, "could not proceed without a tribute to so magnificent a labor pioneer as Genora."[73] The Labor Museum in Flint, along with the Women's Coalition, sponsored a memorial for Genora in December 1995: "Celebration of the Lifework of Genora Johnson Dollinger." A friend wrote to Sol that the memorial was "impressive." She could "just hear" Genora "telling folks what should be done! She was some kind of gal!"[74]

Condolences arrived at Sol's home from all over the world. Melvyn Bloom spoke about how Genora was one of the great heroines of the American labor movement.[75] Janice Hassett Bedayn said she had been privileged to learn a "significant piece" of history "from the woman who made it."[76] Genora had always been the great role model for Patricia Butler, who wrote to Sol that "the world is a little darker, a little colder without her light to warm and inspire us."[77] From Mexico, the Dollingers' old friend Max Shein spoke of Genora's "nobility of character and kindliness of heart."[78] Genora's great-niece by marriage, Jessica Johnson, had always wanted to ask Genora "what gave her the drive to give so much of herself to many causes" and regretted her failure to do so.[79] Verena and Robert Walter admired Genora's "radiating" optimism and "willingness to put up a good fight" and hoped that workers' and women's rights "won't gradually get lost in this world ruled by mighty mammon."[80] On and on these heartfelt tributes came to Sol in memory of a beloved wife, mother, friend, and social activist extraordinaire.[81]

From the heyday of union activity in the late 1930s to its virtual demise in the mid-1990s, Genora Dollinger was on the scene of labor and social reform. If it took physically risking her life, as in 1937, to gain rights for workers and women, so be it. In the ensuing years she never hesitated to give her thoughts and opinions, whether or not she was asked for them, of labor conditions in the United States and around the world. She was the constant questioner, the tireless worker for things she deemed right, just, and proper. Her legacy should not be forgotten, even by those who disdain the labor movement. She was at the heart of the labor and women's rights movements in this country for much of the twentieth century, and her memory extends well into the twenty-first.

Nine An Assessment

Genora Albro Johnson Dollinger's life can be considered revolutionary on many levels. Her early family life did not point the way later on for "radical" Trotskyism: she taught Sunday school in a Methodist church and availed herself of all the trappings of a middle-class family. Carl Johnson, her father-in-law, had more ideological influence on her life than her own father, Raymond Albro, and showed her the way of Socialism.

Nevertheless, there was nothing incremental in her life; she was either one thing or the other. This does not mean that Genora was impetuous—at least, always—though sometimes her statements appeared so. She studied the philosophical assortments proffered to her and, because of the 1937 sit-downs and the Oak Park demonstrations the next year, concluded that involvement from the federal government was essential to alleviate human suffering when state governments could not or would not do whatever was necessary.

Genora's forming of the Women's Emergency Brigade and her subsequent activities in it provided the next level of her developing revolutionary involvement. No one could have predicted, based on her earlier life, that she would become this militant. To be sure, she had a reputation among family and friends for stridency on several issues, but, until 1937, militarism was not one of them. Though connecting the sit-downs of 1937 with the beginnings of the modern women's movement, she and her colleagues were more pragmatic than idealistic when they formed the EB to protect, defend, and fight—if necessary—for the men inside the plants. During the dramatic events of

1937 and her subsequent extensive speaking tours on the East Coast, Genora increasingly evoked a women's rights agenda within the context of union—union all the way. "Organize" was her call, after which was "solidarity" and these calls included both men and women in the labor movement.

The sit-downs of 1937 and the union victory were the formative events in Genora's life. In one way or another in the future, whatever she spoke about—political ideology, social justice, educational systems, racial bigotries, abortion, the right to die, and a host of other major issues of her day and time—was in the context of the conjoined union-feminist movement of 1937. Audiences always knew that if her subject was not the EBs of 1937, they were at least on her mind. This made her speeches popular with many listeners and tiresome to some. She inadvertently practiced the old speech-class adage that people come to orations not to learn anything new but to reconfirm what they already know.

Genora was also revolutionary in her avid participation—along with that of her husband, Sol—in the SWP. She read a wide range of Socialistic books, pamphlets, and articles and put this acquired knowledge to use during World War II as she increasingly included a feminist element to her pleas for workers' advancement. A Woman's Department became a part of the United Auto Worker's Union in 1944, the last full year of World War II. Genora had dealings with this department because she was a steward at Briggs during the war, and her unionist-feminist militarism continued to grow. She noticed the brutish behavior of some male workers toward women in the various Flint and Detroit plants and committed herself to doing something about it.

War emergencies caused more women than ever to be hired at armaments factories and other plants that produced war materiels. One week before Pearl Harbor, 25.3 percent of women over the age of fourteen had public jobs (i.e., outside the home). During the war this figure climbed to 36.1 percent, for a wartime peak of 19.5 million female employees.[1] As Genora personally learned on many occasions—and she was in the company of thousands of other women—even in wartime, women's presence in factories created jealousies and resentments, not just among management but among union workers as well. A woman's place was in the home, and that was all there was to it. For most male workers, "family wages," or the "sum necessary to sustain family members" meant "reserved for men only."[2]

These attitudes by both labor and management inspired Genora to work toward uniting the interests of workers and feminism. She never objected to a woman staying at home through choice; in fact, she lauded such a course. It was only if a woman were denied employment simply on the grounds of gender that became a major spur of Genora's social commitments. Immediately after the war an "intensification of propaganda" sought to indoctrinate the American woman back into "her place" of "happy housewife." This struggle between the "establishment" and women's rights groups "had to be dealt with in some way."[3] And Genora took up her own role in these matters.

From 1929 onward, Genora was a Socialist, though for much of that time not formally affiliated with any particular party. After a stint in the SWP and the Social Union of America, she avoided political factions until near the time of her death in 1995, when she worked to establish an American Labor Party. Whatever causes she supported, her work was always within the framework of a Socialist philosophy—not particularly Trotskyist after she left the SWP in 1953, and never Stalinist. Too many factions developed in these persuasions, to the point that workers' interests were buried beneath intellectual jargon. She became, in effect, a freelance Socialist, always maintaining that the philosophies of Karl Marx remained viable.

Genora was a high school dropout who at first did not comprehend theory, then tired of it quickly as she gained a clear understanding. (Theory is wonderful, but you can't put it on your dinner table.) She wanted action and was impatient and frustrated that so many times she did not get it—at least as she wanted it.

She would have agreed with Elizabeth Faue's observation that women workers had been ignored "by a labor movement that failed to acknowledge the . . . importance of women's work to the family economy . . . and the connections between the community and the workplace."[4] Genora also liked Ann Gordon's 1971 statement that "the new women's history seeks to bring the lives of ordinary women to the foreground and to understand them in the largest context" and hoped such statements would encourage studies that included women in all stages of life and occupations.[5] The workingwoman would surely be included in such a sweep.[6]

Genora helped propel the second wave of feminism that occurred primarily after World War II, but she came to reject the idea of many second wavers that they had "rekindled a struggle that had been dormant since the suffrage victory in 1920."[7] She held this thought to be absurd because it totally ignored women's efforts for political and labor equality throughout the 1920s and 1930s and, especially, the important work of 1937 and the WEB.[8] She was in good company here: in 1972 author Eleanor Flexner told an interviewer that one of the things that bothered her was that many women's liberation spokeswomen didn't give any credit to the people who laid the foundation for them.[9]

Like many colleagues, Genora came to the point where she did not try to separate feminist activism from union activism and linked the two groups through their mutual interests.[10] As historian Sherry Lee Linkon asserts, "Cultural Studies [which includes feminism] and labor history have not usually made a comfortable pair. They are distant cousins, with Marx as a common ancestry."[11] Genora's life proposed to close that gap; she was a "new woman" who "experimented with new forms of public behavior and new gender roles."[12]

Coming out of the mid to late 1980s was another feminist movement, generally referred to as the third wave. These women identified less with the political arena than their earlier counterparts and more with questions of abortion, eating disorders, and domestic abuse.[13] Third wave proponents rejected the influence of past movements because they saw feminism not as a growing and changing movement but as a dialogue of the past that "conjures up images of militantly bell-bottomed women's libbers."[14] While Genora was sympathetic in many ways to the third wave, she faulted them, as did other individuals, for neglecting, even ignoring, the past. As one author put it, "Having no sense of how we got here condemns women to reinvent the wheel and often blocks us from creating a political strategy." The third wave must understand the "first two waves of feminism in America to continue and move forward" in allowing women to make their own choices between and among career, family, and education.[15] The third wave was still in progress when Genora died in 1995.

Beyond giving her thoughts on the third wave, Genora also used letters, speeches, symposia, seminars, and, eventually, the movies to publicize her principles and philosophies. In the process, she became a heroine of the labor movement, as well as of feminism, social reform, and legal justice. She did not reach national prominence the way individuals such as Ralph Nader, Barry Commoner, Betty Friedan, and a few others did, but she greatly helped them on their way to the top. The most famous movie Genora had a part in was *With Babies and Banners*, which depicted Genora's and other women's roles in the 1937 sit-downs. In 1999 professor Lauren Coodley of Napa Valley College in

California showed this movie to her history students. She asked them two questions: "What do you want to remember from the movie?" and "How can women be written into history?" Admittedly, these questions encouraged favorable student responses, but because they were hearing about Genora Dollinger for the first time in their lives, the reactions did contain some intellectual analyses. Here are some responses.

Roberta Morovic admired Genora's "spunkiness."[16] Angelina Rodriquez believed that if "people get together and organize, things can be accomplished."[17] Laurie Thompson was impressed with Genora's strength and power that "changed history" in the sit-downs and afterward and "set an example for other women." Genora, Laurie said, was "tricky, cunning, and overall, very smart."[18] Genora had "the courage to speak up for what she believed in," asserted Maria Villafuerte; she "struggled to break the old stereotypes" of women belonging "only in the kitchen."[19] Genora exemplified the thought, Peggy David wrote, that "if you feel passionate about something you will find the way to make it work."[20] When the sit-down strike started, Genora and the other women probably did not have any specific notions of what they were going to do, but "she found the voice she needed to get the victory she desired."[21] According to Karen Gratton, Genora "stepped up and voiced what many of the women felt. She organized them so they could feel they were . . . helping and partaking in the livelihood of their families."[22] Emily Palana was grateful that Genora and her followers "put their lives on the line" for future generations. They "walked the extra mile" and deserved the "respect and acknowledgment" of posterity.[23] Genora and colleagues offered a "good example" of how effective and peaceful civil protest can be, wrote student E. Wolfe.[24] And Bernadine Garcia, remarking on the importance of the past, asked, "How can we learn from it if we are only taught part of it?"[25] These responses in Professor Coodley's class urged an increased awareness of women's roles in the past and a better understanding of how their activities contributed to the betterment of not only their status but men's as well. Genora would have been thrilled with these observations and comments from such bright young people. To be sure, one might argue, showing this movie to young, impressionable minds might have elicited expected comments; it was nevertheless a film in which the unfamiliar Genora Dollinger spoke to them about very familiar contemporary matters.

The essays also touched on the cherished internationalism that Genora, James P. Cannon, and the SWP championed for so long. Interestingly, however, the internationalism they envisioned came not because of any workers' uprisings but because of capitalistic manipulations, expressed in part through NAFTA. Genora lamented the loss of U.S. jobs to overseas markets and argued that this kind of internationalism was confrontational rather than cooperative. She was depressed by this situation and would not have agreed with Howard Zinn, Dana Frank, and Robin D. G. Kelley that "the union movement has been re-infused with the fighting spirit that working class neighborhoods have nurtured for so long."[26] She would undoubtedly have said, "Bring back the jobs and then we'll talk about working-class neighborhoods." A major event of early 2006, however, might have given her a reason to be heartened by Zinn, Frank, and Kelley's statement. Poll results emanating from the New York City transit strike of 2006 indicated that the public, despite the hardships imposed on them by the strike, favored the union. One poll, conducted by Survey USA on the first day of the strike, asked, "In the transit strike, whose side are you on?" and 52 percent of respondents said the union while only 40 percent said the Metropolitan Transit Authority (MTA). A poll by a local radio station, WWRL, "found that 71 percent of respondents blamed the MTA for the strike and 14 percent blamed the union."[27] So it may well have been that union and management practiced tuxedo unionism, but the relationship between union and the general public appeared to be on a sounder and friendlier basis than was commonly thought.

Genora would have been pleased with celebrations in Flint on February 11, 2003, with UAW president Ron Gettelfinger as the featured speaker. A handful of the ever-dwindling number of sit-down survivors attended this White Shirt Day. The luncheon featured only bean soup and bread because this was the "simple fare that the sit-down strikers ate during their 44-day confrontation with General Motors."[28] White shirts and beans were reminders of the events of 1937 that caused Genora to agitate one labor, feminist, social, and economic question after another.

Genora's revolutionary spirit can also be seen in the way she dealt with her physical condition. She exemplified the thought that if you want to live a long time, find yourself a "nice" disease—"nice" here meant "treatable"—and develop a lifestyle compatible with the degree and extent of your malady. Her illnesses accentuated her zest for life. She knew there was a timetable; therefore it was incumbent upon her to get as much out of life as she could. Would her revolutionary activities have been greater and more widespread if she had remained perfectly healthy? Probably not. In fact, they could very well have been less because of other activities and interests. Her illnesses focused her attention. She did not put off the important things of life: family, union, feminism, and social justice—all within a framework of Socialism.

Was Genora a professional agitator? Emphatically, yes! Within the context of political, social, and economic conditions in the United States and the world, her life was one long reform movement. She had detractors, not limited to the Kraus faction of the workers' movements. They included the intellectuals with advanced degrees who look down on someone who proposed to contribute to their fields without what they considered the proper credentials. Many times, especially in later life, she was accused of inconsistency, of saying something, for example, in 1990 that negated her words of 1940. Apart from Ralph Waldo Emerson's statement that "foolish consistency is the hobgoblin of little minds," one can argue that creative people are frequently inconsistent, especially over a long span of years. As famed historian Richard Hofstadter puts it, "Any man who makes written commitment year after year on difficult public questions, will live to find some of his views evanesced and embarrassing and to see his own words quoted with telling effect against himself."[29] Besides, Genora could fire right back at the experts, becoming, as it were, an intellectual bully. "You're the one with the degree," she told some of her detractors, especially if their opinions turned out to be incorrect on a significant question. She was not, however, an anti-intellectual. On the contrary, her reading list was longer than that of many who denigrated her. She sometimes expressed an interest, even after reaching an elevated position in the labor-feminist movement, of going back to high school and getting a diploma or acquiring a General Equivalency Diploma (GED).

Genora Dollinger's life was a statement of ideals and ideologies that—in her own thoughts at least—put her into an underdog status. This caused her to support programs to end racism and poverty and elevate the lives of working men and women to a level of comfort and dignity. The nobility of work was an idea she pushed most of her life, believing that workers deserved better than they usually received. These are the main thoughts and philosophies that propelled Genora on her pathway to a lifetime of revolutionary activities and accomplishments:

She opposed capital punishment and argued that it did little to prevent homicides; instead she believed in long or lifetime incarceration. She believed in the right to die with dignity, supporting Dr. Jack Kevorkian, who argued that states frequently impose a painful death on the terminally ill. She favored a woman's right to choose and objected to the damage and destruction of abortion clinics throughout the country.

She believed in freedom of religion, which included opting out if one so chose. As noted in chapter 1, she went from being a devout Methodist to an ideological Marxist. She favored women's rights, believing that women's accomplishments over the years had been scandalously ignored. She continued to criticize male historians who neglected women, but at the same time, inconsistently, argued that men could not really understand women; thus she strongly supported female historians when it came to writing histories of the feminist movements in the United States. She supported—as seen by her longtime work with the NAACP and the ACLU—all those she considered to be downtrodden, whether they were African American, immigrant workers, or unskilled laborers.

She sought causes to fight within a Socialistic context and found plenty of them, all the way from unionism to feminism and the connection between the two movements, to the Citizen's Party, and beyond. Genora Dollinger, in any way one wishes to view her, positively or negatively, truly did live a revolutionary life.

Appendix **A Chronology of Genora Dollinger's Life**

1913	Born in Kalamazoo, Michigan.
1914	Moves with mother and father to Flint, Michigan.
1920s	Attends elementary and junior high school in Flint. Attends Central High School. Active in the Methodist Church.
1929	Joins Young People's Socialist League (YPSL) in Flint. Thought influenced by Socialist Carl Johnson.
1930	Elopes with Kermit Johnson to Bowling Green, Ohio.
1931	Son Dennis (Denny) is born.
1936	Participates in the Flint sit-down strikes against General Motors (GM).
1937	Joins with other United Auto Workers (UAW) workers in celebrating UAW victory over GM; is sent by UAW on a speaking tour. Travels to New York, Philadelphia, and several other eastern cities to lecture on unionism and Socialism.
1938	Participates in "Death Watch" in Flint. Is expelled from the Socialist Party, along with Kermit. Joins the Socialist Workers Party (SWP).
1941	Is blacklisted from all the Flint factories. Nevertheless works at Budd Wheel and becomes a shop steward at Briggs factory during the war; meets Sol Dollinger in New York while separated from Kermit Johnson.
1942	Divorces Kermit Johnson; marries Sol Dollinger.
1942–45	Exchange of letters between Genora and Sol, who is away from home most of the time in the Merchant Marines. Genora suffers from health problems, primarily tuberculosis.

1945	Genora and Sol beaten in their Detroit home on October 15, Genora almost fatally, presumably by corporate thugs.
1946	Odd jobs in the Detroit area. Genora still active in Local 212, Sol in Flint recruiting for SWP. Son Jarvis ("Jody") is killed in a cycle accident in September.
1947–48	Odd jobs; still active in SWP and Local 212. Senatorial candidate, 1948, for SWP.
1949	Tours New York; attends numerous SWP rallies.
1950	Congressional candidate, SWP. Father, Ray Albro, dies. Son Dennis dies.
1951	Genora renews her union and political activities. Comes under the scrutiny of the FBI.
1952	Son Ronald is born.
1953	Dollingers expelled from the SWP. Join Bert Cochran's Socialist Union of America (SUA).
1957	SUA dissolved. American Socialist Clubs formed.
1959–early 1960s	Dollingers grow increasingly aloof from Trotskyist organizations.
1960	Genora active with the National Association for the Advancement for Colored People (NAACP) in Flint. Becomes involved in the Monroe (NC) case.
1961	Dollingers begin traveling fairly often to Mexico. Become involved in Detroit with the American Civil Liberties Union (ACLU).
1963–64	Becomes totally opposed to U.S. buildup in Southeast Asia.
1966	Dollingers move to Los Angeles. Genora immediately becomes involved in educational reforms, anti-Vietnam rhetoric, and race reform. Joins People's Lobby.
1967	Death of Genora's first husband, Kermit Johnson.
1970	Lauds the election in Chile of President Salvadore Allende. Strongly supports the Los Angeles teachers' strike. Opens her home on Queen Anne Place to the teachers. Appears before the Organization of American Historians (OAH) meeting in Los Angeles.
1970s	Strong supporter of the equal rights amendment (ERA) to the Constitution.
1971	Trip to Europe.
1973	Trip to Holland, meeting friends Genora had helped during the war.
1976	Film *With Babies and Banners* features Genora. Also, another film, *The Great Sit Down.*
1977	Trips to Europe; meets many Socialists; health problems.

1978 Criticizes and condemns tuxedo unionism.

1979 Believes history is catching up with the events of the sit-downs. Sit-downs finally being written about "correctly," largely by women historians. Works with Dr. Barry Commoner's Citizen Party.

1983 European trip; contact with Socialists.

1984 Trip to China; falls ill.
Trip to Europe. Thrilled at Geraldine Ferraro's nomination for vice president.

1986 Celebrations for the fiftieth anniversary of the start of the GM sit-downs. Genora unhappy that the events are *jointly* sponsored by GM and UAW.
Attacks Henry Kraus for his book of 1947, *The Many and the Few.* Causes uproar at UAW annual meeting.

1987 Trip to Moscow; disillusionments. Soviets have not heard about Trotsky's "repatriation."

1989 Writes introduction to Dan La Botz book, *A Troublemaker's Handbook: How to Fight Back Where You Work—and Win.*

1990–93 Speaks endlessly about women's and labor's rights; writes articles, some of which are published.

1994 Inducted into the Michigan Women's Hall of Fame.
Becomes involved in trying to form a labor party in the United States. Labor Party Advocates (LPA) formed. Opposes NAFTA and the continuing loss of jobs to overseas plants and factories.

1995 Interviewed by Studs Terkel for his book *Coming of Age;* supports Jack Kevorkian.
Dies at the Cedar Sinai Medical Center in Los Angeles in October at eighty-two years of age.

Notes

Preface

1. Joseph H. Parks, *Felix Grundy: Champion of Democracy* (Baton Rouge: Louisiana State Univ. Press, 1940), xii.
2. John P. Diggins, *The American Left in the Twentieth Century* (New York: Harcourt, Brace, and Jovanovich, 1973), 108.
3. Fred Feldman, "Some Historical Background to the 1939–40 Struggle in the SWP," in *Background to "The Struggle for a Proletarian Party,"* ed. George Clarke, James P. Cannon, and Leon Trotsky (New York: Pathfinder, 1979), 4.
4. Ibid., 6.
5. Arlie Russell Hochschild, "A Generation Without Public Passion," *Atlantic Monthly,* Feb. 2001, 62.
6. "Labor Dips in Private Sector," *Bowling Green Daily News* (Bowling Green, Ky.), Jan. 21, 2001.
7. Carlton Jackson, *Hounds of the Road: A History of the Greyhound Bus Company,* rev. ed. (Bowling Green, Ohio: Popular Press, 2001), 189.
8. Carlton Jackson, *J. I. Rodale: Apostle of Nonconformity* (New York: Pyramid, 1974), 19.

An Introduction

1. Dorothy Sue Cobble, "Recapturing Working-Class Feminism: Union Women in the Postwar Era," in *Not June Cleaver: Women and Gender in Postwar America, 1945–1960,* ed. Joanne Meyerowitz (Philadelphia: Temple Univ. Press, 1994), 58.
2. Joanne Meyerowitz, introduction, *Not June Cleaver,* 6.

3. Sherna Berger Gluck, *Rosie the Riveter Revisited: Women, the War, and Social Change* (Boston: Twayne, 1987), 7.
4. Ibid., 8.
5. John W. Jeffries, *Wartime America: The World War II Home Front* (Chicago: Ivan Dee, 1996), 7.
6. Nancy A. Naples, *Grassroots Warriors: Activist Mothering, Community Work, and the War on Poverty* (New York: Routledge, 1998), 114.
7. Sidney Fine, *Sit-Down: The General Motors Strike of 1936–1937* (Ann Arbor: Univ. of Michigan Press, 1969), 200. Also quoted in Philip S. Foner, *Women and the American Labor Movement: From World War I to the Present* (New York: Free Press, 1980), 305.
8. Howard Zinn and Anthony Arnove, eds., *Voices of a People's History of the United States* (New York: Seven Stories, 2004), 346.

1. Genesis of a Revolutionary

1. Harold Meyerson, "The Women Just Came Out of Their Homes . . . ," *Dissent* (Fall 1985): 21, 23. An interview with Genora Dollinger on May 11, 1986.
2. Nan Enstad, "Fashioning Political Identities: Cultural Studies and the Historical Construction of Political Subjects," *American Quarterly* 50.4 (Dec. 1998): 745.
3. Kevin Boyle, review of *Community of Suffering and Struggle: Women, Men, and the Labor Movement in Minneapolis, 1915–1945,* by Elizabeth Faue, *Journal of Urban History* 23.1 (Nov. 1996): 120–25.
4. Meyerson, "Women," 465.
5. *Columbia Encyclopedia,* 5th ed., s.v. "Flint, Michigan." For further discussions of Flint and its "working class," see Ronald Edsforth, *Class, Conflict, and Cultural Consensus* (New Brunswick, N.J.: Rutgers Univ. Press, 1987), 79–84, 87–88, 95–96.
6. Genora Johnson Dollinger, interview with Sherna Berger Gluck, University of Michigan, 1 (hereafter cited as Gluck interview). Gluck conducted a series of eight interviews with Genora between May 21, 1976, and April 28, 1977.
7. Genora to Jack Johnson, Apr. 23, 1958, Dollinger Collection, Los Angeles.
8. Gluck interview, 16
9. Myerson, "Women," 464.
10. Casey Henry Waite to Genora, Jan. 3, 1992, Dollinger Collection, Los Angeles.
11. Gluck interview, 10.
12. Sol Dollinger, "The Formative Years: Memories of Conversations with Genora," unpublished essay, Dollinger Collection, Los Angeles, 9.

13. Gluck interview, 4.
14. Sol Dollinger, "Formative Years," 7.
15. Sol Dollinger to the author, June 29, 1999.
16. Ibid.
17. Ibid.
18. Ibid.
19. Ibid.
20. Gluck interview, 19.
21. Ibid., 27.
22. Ibid., 29.
23. Larry Jones, "Hall of Fame for Genora Dollinger," *Searchlight,* Sept. 1994, 6.
24. Ronda Hauben, "Carl Johnson: A Pioneer Labor Journalist," unpublished essay, 1, Dollinger Collection, Los Angeles.
25. Janice Hassett, "Never Again Just a Woman: Women of the Auxiliary and Emergency Brigade in the General Motors Sit-Down Strike of 1937" (senior thesis, Mills College, 1994), 14.
26. Jones, "Hall of Fame for Genora Dollinger."
27. M. Kent Jennings, "Women in Party Politics," in *Women, Politics, and Change,* ed. Louise A. Tilly and Patricia Guren (New York: Russell Sage Foundation, 1990), 55.
28. Alice Kessler-Harris, "Where Are the Organized Women Workers?" in *A Heritage of Her Own: Toward a New Social History of American Women,* ed. Nancy Cott and Elizabeth H. Pleck (New York: Simon & Schuster, 1979), 347.
29. Oscar Ameringer (1870–1943) was born in Germany and arrived in Oklahoma in 1907. The greatest influences on his young life were the reformers Henry George and Edward Bellamy. Werner Sombart's book *Socialism and the Socialist Movement in the Nineteenth Century* was also important to Ameringer, as was Eugene Debs. In his autobiography *If You Don't Weaken* (New York: Greenwood Press, 1940) Ameringer said of him, "Gene Debs was the dreamer, poet, and prophet of the weary and heavy-laden." In Oklahoma, Ameringer held meetings wherever there might be socialist-inclined people: "Gathering my little flock together, I started preaching Marxism. At every meeting pamphlets were sold, subscriptions and applications for membership taken" (267).
30. Sol Dollinger, "Formative Years," 12.
31. Sol Dollinger to the author, June 29, 1999.
32. Genora to Lora Albro, n.d., Dollinger Collection, box 2, folder 2, Walter P. Reuther Library, Wayne State University, Detroit, Michigan (hereafter cited as Reuther Library).
33. Genora's notes, Dollinger Collection, Los Angeles.

34. Gluck interview, 38.

35. Genora to Lora Albro, n.d., Dollinger Collection, box 2, folder 2, Reuther Library. Showing that she still disdained her father, Genora put this postscript to her letter: "I remembered dad's birthday and almost sent him a card but do you know I couldn't give him the satisfaction of thinking I remembered it because of the way he treated you on your birthday." The author is grateful to Sol Dollinger for sharing this story and many others about Genora, his wife of more than fifty years.

36. Brenda Fowler, "History and a Name in a Vienna Project," *New York Times*, July 11, 1991.

37. Sol Dollinger, interview with the author, Oct. 31, 1997.

38. Genora Dollinger, interview at UCLA, May 1976, Dollinger Collection, Los Angeles.

39. Robert Kilroy-Silk, *Socialism Since Marx* (New York: Taplinger, 1972), 122–23.

40. Bertram D. Wolfe, *Marxism: One Hundred Years in the Life of a Doctrine* (New York: Dial Press, 1965), 20. See also Joseph M. Schwartz, *The Permanence of the Political: A Democratic Critique of the Radical Impulse to Transcend Politics* (Princeton, N.J.: Princeton Univ. Press, 1995), 23–24.

41. Sol Dollinger [Jerry Kirk, pseudo.], position paper; Sol Dollinger to the author, June 29, 1999.

42. Sol Dollinger, interview with the author, Oct. 31, 1997.

43. She told Victor Reuther in 1988, "I am still a Socialist (albeit an unaffiliated one for the past 32 years)." Genora to Victor Reuther, July 25, 1988, Dollinger Collection, box 2, folder 7, Reuther Library.

2. Genora and Friends—Standing By Their Men

1. Carlton Jackson, "The 1930s," in *The Columbia Companion to American History on Film: How the Movies Have Portrayed the American Past*, ed. Peter Rollins (New York: Columbia Univ. Press, 2003), 22.

2. Arthur M. Schlesinger, *The Crisis of the Old Order* (Boston: Houghton Mifflin, 1957), 8.

3. See *Striking Flint: Genora (Johnson) Dollinger Remembers the 1936–37 General Motors Sit-Down Strike*, with Susan Rosenthal (Chicago: L. J. Page, 1996), 9–10.

4. Jennifer Johnson, "Women's Auxiliary: Unsung Heroes of the Battle of Bull's Run," *Flint Journal*, Jan. 11, 1987.

5. According to author Stephen Franklin, the first major sit-down in the United States was by the Rubber Union in Akron, Ohio. In the mid-

1930s rubber workers sat down many times, "protesting line speed-ups, wage cuts, and racist intimidations." See Stephen Franklin, *Three Strikes: Labor's Heartland Losses and What They Mean for Working Americans* (New York: Guilford Press, 2001), 118. In this same vein, Dana Frank reports that Michigan governor Frank Murphy claimed "that the masons for the pharaohs of Egypt used 'sit-downs' to express grievances" (82). Also, in 1715 workers on the Lille Cathedral in France staged a sit-down, English workers tried the sit-down technique in 1817, and in Cincinnati in 1884 workers at the Jackson Brewery barricaded themselves behind beer barrels for sixty-five hours to get better working conditions. See Dana Frank, "Girl Strikers Occupy Chain Store, Win Big: The Detroit Woolworth's Strike of 1937," in *Three Strikes: Miners, Musicians, Salesgirls, and the Fighting Spirit of Labor's Last Century,* ed. Howard Zinn, Dana Frank, and Robin D. G. Kelley (Boston: Beacon Press, 2001), 82.

6. Patricia Bergman to the author, Aug. 6, 1998.
7. Gluck interview, 76.
8. For a close look at Governor Murphy's role in the sit-down, see Sidney Fine, "The General Motors Sit-Down Strike: A Reexamination," *American Historical Review* 70.3 (Apr. 1969): 699–713.
9. Patricia Yeghissian, "Women's Emergency Brigade: Flint Sit-Down Strike of 1936–37 (senior honors thesis, Univ. of Michigan, 1974), 35.
10. *Life,* Jan. 18, 1937.
11. Genora Dollinger, interview with Jack W. Skeels, July 31, 1960, Univ. of Michigan–Wayne State University, Reuther Library, 20 (hereafter cited as Skeels interview).
12. Christiane Diehl-Taylor, "Partners in the Struggle: The Role of Women's Auxiliaries and Brigades in the 1934 Minneapolis Truck Drivers' Strike and the 1936/37 Flint General Motors Sit-Down Strike" (research paper, Univ. of Minnesota, 1990), 6.
13. Skeels interview, 20.
14. Genora Dollinger, speech to Chevrolet Local 659, 1971, Flint, Michigan, Dollinger Collection, Los Angeles.
15. See Helen Drusine, "*Just* a Housewife!?" in *Sisterhood Is Forever: The Women's Anthology for a New Millenium,* ed. Robin Morgan (New York: Washington Square Press, 2003), 342.
16. Nancy Gabin, *Feminism in the Labor Movement: Women and the United Auto Workers, 1935–1975* (Ithaca, N.Y.: Cornell Univ. Press, 1990), 18.
17. Johnson, "Women's Auxiliary."
18. Gluck interview, 85.
19. Hassett, "Never Again," 21.
20. Skeels interview, 21.

21. Joel Seidman, *"Sit-Down"* (New York: League for Industrial Democracy, 1937), 3–4.
22. Quoted from the Genora Johnson Dollinger memorial service, Oct. 1995. Victor Reuther recounts this story in *The Brothers Reuther and the Story of the UAW* (Boston: Houghton Mifflin, 1976), 156–57.
23. Fine, *Sit-Down,* 6.
24. Foner, *Women and the American Labor Movement,* 306.
25. Genora Dollinger memorial service, Oct. 1995.
26. Fine, *Sit-Down,* 3–11.
27. In later years, Genora told Fine that his documentation "sets forth the events logically and objectively." Genora to Sidney Fine, Jan. 20, 1987, Dollinger Collection, box 2, file 17, Reuther Library. Seven years later, however, Genora had changed her mind. She wrote to Larry Jones that "Sidney Fine was so careless in his research. . . . [H]e traveled to L. A. to interview Bob Travis living out here but . . . did not try to locate me or any other member of the Auxiliary Number Ten." Genora to Larry Jones, ca. 1994, Dollinger Collection, Los Angeles. Henry Kraus, the only eyewitness ever to write a book about the Flint sit-downs, *The Many and the Few: A Chronicle of the Dynamic Auto Workers,* 2d ed. (Urbana: Univ. of Illinois Press, 1985), says that he gave the fight with the policemen its name of "Battle of Bull's Run." Victor Reuther, he claims, was probably the principal creator of the title. Certainly Kraus was on the mark when he wrote that the event was too significant to spend the next fifty years arguing over who coined the phrase. Henry Kraus, "Facts and Fact," unpublished essay, Kraus Files, folder 2, Reuther Library. Another description of the "Battle of Bull's Run" can be found in Gabin, *Feminism in the Labor Movement,* 42.
28. Sol Dollinger, interview with the author, Oct. 31, 1997.
29. In a 1985 interview with Harold Meyerson, however, Genora referred to the incident as the "Battle of Running Bulls." See Meyerson, "Women," 465.
30. Sol Dollinger, "Formative Years," 20–21.
31. Ibid.
32. Quoted in Fine, *Sit-Down,* 8–9.
33. Collection of Parodies, Dollinger Collection, box 1, file 36, Reuther Library.
34. Hassett, "Never Again," 29. Also, Mary Heaton Vorse, "The Emergency Brigade at Flint," *New Republic* (Feb. 17, 1937): 38.
35. Quoted in Hassett, "Never Again," 30.
36. Fine, *Sit-Down,* 201. Also quoted in Foner, *Women and the American Labor Movement,* 309.
37. Genora would not call the group the Ladies Auxiliary, as in Minneapolis and the rest of industrial America, because "ladies" went to tea and

indulged in other "polite" manners. The Women's Auxiliary of Flint "had no interest in politeness or other such inconsequential matters." Diehl-Taylor, "Partners in the Struggle," 12.

38. Henry Kraus, *Many and the Few,* 235. See also Hassett, "Never Again," 25.
39. Henry Kraus, column, *Flint Auto Worker,* Jan. 12, 1937.
40. Skeels interview, 35.
41. Genora to the Reverend Keith Pohl, Mar. 11, 1986, Dollinger Collection, file 3, folder 21, Reuther Library.
42. Flint was such a company town that this story was frequently heard: During the holiday season a father told his son the Christmas story. The son's reaction was, "Jesus Christ? Jesus Christ? What plant does he work in?" Genora Dollinger, interview with Hy Fish, May 31, 1975, Dollinger Collection, file 2, folder 18, Reuther Library, 2.
43. Elizabeth M. Howe, "The Sitdowns" (unpublished paper, Univ. of Michigan, 1993).
44. Sol Dollinger, "Formative Years," 22.
45. Skeels interview, 47.
46. Robert S. McElvaine, *The Great Depression: America, 1929–1941* (New York: Three Rivers Press, 1993), 291–92.
47. Skeels interview, 47.
48. Ibid., 19.
49. Gluck interview, 97.
50. Rosenthal, *Striking Flint,* 17.
51. Genora Dollinger, speech to Local 659, 1974, in Flint, Michigan, Dollinger Collection, box 4, folder 37, Reuther Library.
52. Skeels interview, 41.
53. Gluck interview, 72.
54. Genora Dollinger, speech to Local 659, 1974.
55. Yeghissian, "Emergency Brigade," 26.
56. "Auto Women Advance," *Women's Auxiliary* pamphlet, Local 156, Flint, Michigan, Apr. 1937, 2.
57. *Detroit Evening News,* Jan. 20, 1937.
58. Ibid.
59. Meyerson, "Women," 466, 465.
60. Howard Zinn, *The Twentieth Century* (New York: Perennial, 2003), 128.
61. Cornelia Bryce Pinchot, speech to the EB, Dollinger Collection, Los Angeles.
62. Ellen Wilkinson, speech to the EB, 1937, Dollinger Collection, box 2, folder 2, Reuther Library; also in the Dollinger Collection, Los Angeles.
63. Christine Collette, "The Jarrow Crusade," BBC online, June 1, 2002,

http://www.bbc .co.uk/ history/british/britain_wwone/jarrow_03.shtml (accessed Sept. 27, 2005). A previous hunger march in England was sponsored by the National Unemployed Workers' Movement (NUMWM), and 200 blind people converged on London, also in 1936.

64. Patricia Bergman to the author, Aug. 6, 1998.
65. General UAW Collection, Reuther Library.
66. Alfred P. Sloan Jr. to the workers of Flint, Jan. 5, 1937, Kraus Collection, box 9, file 1, Reuther Library.
67. This parody can be found in the UAW Collection, Reuther Library. Two employees of Chevy Four (generally called the "hell hole" because of its dreadful working conditions), Gilliland and Beck, are credited with writing these lines.
68. Sibyl N. Walker, "Wishie Washie," Dollinger Collection, box 4, file 3, Reuther Library.
69. Roger Keeran, *The Communist Party and the Auto Workers Union* (Bloomington: Indiana Univ. Press, 1980), 149.
70. Homer Martin to Alfred J. Sloan Jr., Jan. 6, 1937, Kraus Collection, box 9, file 1, Reuther Library.
71. Kraus Collection, box 9, file 1, Reuther Library. This letter and the ones following were written between factory and home and home and factory from late January to mid-February 1937.
72. Rosenthal, *Striking Flint,* 17.
73. Ibid.
74. Robert M. LaFollette, Committee on Violations of Free Speech and Rights of Labor, Subcommittee of the Senate Committee on Education and Labor, 75th Cong., 1 sess., 1937, 2520.
75. Skeels interview, 38.
76. Ibid., 40.
77. Ibid., 19.
78. Yeghissian, "Emergency Brigade,"42.
79. Ibid., 43.
80. Rosenthal, *Striking Flint,* 20.
81. Yeghissian, "Emergency Brigade," 43.
82. Rosenthal, *Striking Flint,* 20.
83. Ever since the event, union people and their historians have disputed who actually conceived of the plan to feign an attack on Number Nine while actually intending to take Number Four. Robert Travis, local Flint UAW official, said that he and author Henry Kraus "worked out the details of the movement." Roy Reuther remembered that "it was a kind of a joint thing in which four to five people sort of refined and developed the idea" (Yeghissian, "Emergency Brigade," 44). It seems, however, that Kermit Johnson, in consort with his wife, Genora (who did all the typ-

ing—no mean feat in those days!), was the principal architect. He and Genora held several meetings in their own home to discuss strategies and maneuvers. Kermit Johnson, like his wife, has been neglected by history. For yet another version, see Keeran, *Communist Party.*

84. Skeels interview, 26. Nevertheless, when the action started, Walter Reuther apparently had a change of heart. "As the fighting progressed, Walter joined in, bringing a west-side caravan to Flint. See Nelson Lichtenstein, *The Most Dangerous Man in Detroit: Walter Reuther and the Fate of American Labor* (New York: Basic Books, 1995), 78–79.
85. Keeran, *Communist Party,* 165.
86. Rosenthal, *Striking Flint,* 21.
87. Sol Dollinger to the author, June 28, 1999.
88. Rosenthal, *Striking Flint,* 21.
89. Skeels interview, 27.
90. Rosenthal, *Striking Flint,* 20–21.
91. Ibid., 22.
92. Irving Howe and B. J. Widick, *The UAW and Walter Reuther* (New York: Random House, 1949), 59.
93. "Women's Brigade Uses Heavy Clubs," *New York Times,* Feb. 1, 1937.
94. Rosenthal, *Striking Flint,* 22.
95. Gluck interview, 106. Genora thought the term might have been coined during the IWW ("Wobbly") movements of a few years before.
96. Rosenthal, *Striking Flint,* 22.
97. Yeghissian, "Emergency Brigade," 47.
98. Ibid. See also Skeels interview, 31.
99. Skeels interview, 31.
100. Ibid.
101. Kermit Johnson to Robert Travis, Sit-Down, 1937, UAW Collection, Reuther Library.
102. Ibid., Feb. 4, 1937, UAW Collection, Reuther Library.
103. Bud Simon to Robert Travis and the Flint Auto Workers, Feb. 6, 1937, UAW Collection, Reuther Library.
104. Hassett, "Never Again," 12.
105. Yeghissian, "Emergency Brigade," 49.
106. Gluck interview, 67, 101.
107. Yeghissian, "Emergency Brigade," 49.
108. Ibid.
109. Ibid., 51.
110. Genora Dollinger, "A Dance in Front of Fisher #1," unpublished article, Dollinger Collection, box 3, folder 7, Reuther Library.
111. Sol Dollinger to the author, June 28, 1999.
112. Genora Johnson, interview with Kathryn Kish, ca. 1987.

113. Unsigned telegram to Henry Kraus, Feb. 12, 1937, Kraus Collection, box 9, folder 14, Reuther Library.

114. Patricia Murolo and A. B. Chitty, *From the Folks Who Brought You the Week-End: A Short, Illustrated History of Labor in the United States* (New York: New Press, 2001), 207.

115. McElvaine, *Great Depression,* 294.

116. Fine, *Sit-Down,* 201.

117. Yeghissian, "Emergency Brigade," 59.

118. Genora Dollinger, speech to Local 659, 1974, Flint, Michigan, Dollinger Collection, Los Angeles.

119. Quoted in Yeghissian, "Emergency Brigade," 59.

3. The Lure of Trotskyism

1. *Congressional Record,* 49 Cong., 2d sess., 1875, 1887. Quoted in Carlton Jackson, *Presidential Vetoes: 1792–1945* (Athens: Univ. of Georgia Press, 1967), 153.

2. Sol Dollinger, "Formative Years," 19.

3. Sol Dollinger, interview with the author, Oct. 19, 1997.

4. Sol Dollinger, "Formative Years," 27, 29. See also Skeels interview, 37

5. Roger Keeran, in *The Communist Party and the Auto Workers' Union,* 169, credits Dorothy Kraus with setting up a "chiseling committee" to "obtain food from sympathetic grocers . . . and impor[t] Max Gazan" to cook at the strike kitchen. He also gives Dorothy credit for staging the play about the sit-downs, *The Strike Marches On,* which she claimed she helped to write. Even today there are strong supporters of Dorothy in the sit-downs as opposed to Genora. It is quite possible for partisans of either group to become downright emotional in their quest to identify the most important woman in Flint during the sit-downs.

6. With her trepidations about public speaking, she was anticipating Gloria Steinem, who said that "women speakers are . . . likely to get some version of 'You have a good point, but you're not making it effectively,' or 'Your style is too aggressive/weak/loud/quiet.' It is with such criticism . . . that [men] often dismiss the serious message of a female colleague." See Gloria Steinem, *Outrageous Acts and Everyday Rebellion,* 2d ed. (New York: Henry Holt, 1995), 200.

7. Genora Dollinger, diary entry, Apr. 28, 1937, Dollinger Collection, Los Angeles.

8. Ibid., May 1, 1937, Dollinger Collection, Los Angeles.

9. Sol Dollinger, "Formative Years," 27.

10. Genora Dollinger, diary entry, May 3, 1937, Dollinger Collection, Los Angeles.

11. Ibid., May 4, 1937, Dollinger Collection, Los Angeles.
12. Ibid., May 11, 1937, Dollinger Collection, Los Angeles.
13. Ibid., May 15–17, 1937, Dollinger Collection, Los Angeles.
14. Skeels interview, 41.
15. Sol Dollinger, "Formative Years," 39.
16. Gluck interview, 93.
17. Skeels interview, 52.
18. Sol Dollinger to the author, June 28, 1999.
19. Jack Palmer, "His Priceless Gift to 659: Kermit Johnson, 1911–1967," in *Searchlight,* Feb. 5, 1975, 2.
20. Another person who was foreclosed on was Raymond Albro. He had gone "up to his eyeballs" in mortgages on his photographic studios and a grapefruit orchard he wanted to start in Texas. Genora said that he threatened suicide, he was so distraught. In the last years of his life, he worked as a janitor at Buick. Sol Dollinger, "Festival Gaiety," 2, Dollinger Collection, Los Angeles.
21. Rosenthal, *Striking Flint,* 29.
22. Palmer, "Kermit Johnson," 4.
23. Sue Connolly, remarks on the occasion of Genora Johnson Dollinger's induction into the Michigan Women's Hall of Fame, Oct. 29, 1994, Dollinger Collection, box 4, folder 39, Reuther Library.
24. James R. Green, *The World of the Worker: Labor in Twentieth-Century America* (New York: Hill and Wang, 1980), 96.
25. Linda Gordon, *Pitied but Not Entitled: Single Mothers and the History of Welfare, 1890–1935* (New York: Free Press, 1994), 234.
26. Martin Glaberman, ed., *Marxism for Our Times: C. L. R. James on Revolutionary Organization* (Jackson: Univ. Press of Mississippi, 1999), 11–12. See also Martin Glaberman, *Wartime Strikes: The Struggle Against the No-Strike Pledge in the UAW During World War II* (Detroit: Bewick Editions, 1980), 73–74.
27. Robert A. Alexander, *International Trotskyism 1929–1985: A Documented Analysis of the Movement* (Durham, N.C.: Duke Univ. Press, 1991), 27.
28. A copy of this declaration by Kermit and Genora Johnson is in the Dollinger Collection, Los Angeles.
29. Bruce Sloan to George Clarke, Dollinger Collection, Los Angeles.
30. Alexander, *International Trotskyism,* 1.
31. Ibid., 762.
32. Jack Barnes, *James P. Cannon: A Political Tribute* (New York: Pathfinder, 1981), 5.
33. Constance Ashton Myers, *The Prophet's Army: Trotskyists in America, 1928–1941* (Westport, Conn.: Greenwood Press, 1977), 145.

34. Ibid., 14.

35. George Breitman, "The Liberating Influence of the Transitional Program," in *Revolutionary Traditions of American Trotskyism* (New York: Fourth International Tendency, 1988), 25.

36. Barnes. *James P. Cannon,* 9.

37. Sol Dollinger, "Festival Gaiety," 3.

38. Riley E. Males to Genora, Dec. 18, 1939, Kraus Collection, folder 2, Reuther Library.

39. A copy of this poem was found in the Dollinger Collection in Los Angeles.

40. Ibid.

41. Kermit ultimately went back to the Johnson family farm in Humboldt, South Dakota, where he lived until his death on May 7, 1967, at the age of fifty-five.

42. Sol Dollinger, "Festival Gaiety," 5.

43. Ibid., 7.

44. Ibid., 9.

45. Sol Dollinger to Margaret Raucher, Mar. 2, 1999, author's collection.

46. Sol Dollinger, "Formative Years," 2.

47. Ibid., 3.

48. Sol wrote scathingly about the war to Genora in April 1942. "[War] is a curse to millions. No one wants it and yet you can't avoid it. . . . It is like the dregs of quicksand. You're lost once it grips you" He remarked that FDR "wants to find a name for the war." Sol nominated this title: "The Vulture's Feast." Dollinger Collection, box 1, folders 3–6, Reuther Library.

49. Sol to Genora, Mar. 4, 1942, Dollinger Collection, box 1, folders 3–6, Reuther Library.

4. Genora's War

1. Ruth Milkman, *Gender at Work: The Dynamics of Job Segregation by Sex during World War II* (Urbana: Univ. of Illinois Press, 1987), 37, 39.

2. An instructive article on this topic is in Olga Domanski, "Women Workers in the Auto Industry: The Immediate Post–World War II Experience," unpublished essay, n.d., 1–2. A copy of this essay can be found in the Dollinger Collection, box 2, folder 15, Reuther Library, and in the Dollinger Collection, Los Angeles.

3. Angela G. Dorenkamp, et al., eds., *Images of Women in American Popular Culture,* 2d ed. (Ft. Worth, Tex.: Harcourt Brace, 1995), 293.

4. Sol to Genora, Mar. 15, 1942, Dollinger Collection, box 1, folders 3–6, Reuther Library.

5. Ibid., Mar. 17, 1942, Reuther Library.
6. Ibid., Mar. 11, 1942, Reuther Library.
7. Ibid., May 2, 1942, Reuther Library.
8. Genora to Sol, Sept. 20, 1942, Dollinger Collection, box 1, folders 3–6, Reuther Library.
9. Genora Dollinger, "Today," Dollinger Collection, Los Angeles.
10. Ibid.
11. Ibid.
12. Sol Dollinger, "Escape from the Black List," unpublished essay, n.d., 1, Dollinger Collection, Los Angeles.
13. Ibid.
14. Sol and Genora Dollinger, interview with Neil Leighton, Oct. 21, 1993, Dollinger Collection, Los Angeles (hereafter Leighton interview).
15. Sol Dollinger, "Escape," 3.
16. Ibid.
17. Rosenthal, *Striking Flint,* 33.
18. Sol Dollinger, "Escape," 5.
19. Leighton interview, Oct. 21, 1993.
20. Rosenthal, *Striking Flint,* 33.
21. Sol Dollinger, "Escape," 5.
22. Interview by Socialist Worker Party of Genora Dollinger, Oct. 20, 1993, Dollinger Collection, box 4, folder 31, Reuther Library (hereafter SWP interview).
23. Nelson Lichtenstein, "Auto Workers Militancy and the Structure of Factory Life, 1937–1955," in *Journal of American History* 67.2 (Spring 1980): 339.
24. Sol Dollinger, "Escape," 6. See also Judith Stephen-Norris and Maurice Zeitlin, *Left Out: Reds and America's Industrial Unions* (Cambridge: Cambridge Univ. Press, 2003), 101–7, for a discussion of other caucuses.
25. Lichtenstein, "Auto Workers," 336, 337.
26. Sol to Genora, Dollinger Collection, box 2, folder 30, Reuther Library.
27. Ibid.
28. Kermit Johnson to Genora, Apr. 9, 1943, Dollinger Collection, box 2, folder 32, Reuther Library.
29. Sol to Genora, with enclosed note to Denny, Apr. 5, 1942, Dollinger Collection, box 1, folders 3–6, Reuther Library.
30. Ibid., Sept. 13, 1942, box 1, folders 10–11, Reuther Library.
31. Genora to Sol, Feb. 18, 1944, Dollinger Collection, box 1, folder 7, Reuther Library.
32. Harriett Arnow, *The Dollmaker* (New York: Macmillan, 1954).
33. Sol Dollinger, "Escape," 7.

34. Charles Denby, *Indignant Heart: A Black Worker's Journal* (Detroit: Wayne State Univ. Press, 1978), 168.

35. Genora to Sol, Feb. 11, 1945, Dollinger Collection, box 1, folder 9, Reuther Library.

36. Sol Dollinger describes this procedure quite thoroughly in "Escape."

37. Leighton interview, Oct. 20, 1993.

38. Keeran, *Communist Party,* 243–44.

39. Rosenthal, *Striking Flint,* 34.

40. To become a foreman it helped considerably if you were above average in size and tended not to remember or accentuate your own time on the line. Former linemen tended to be "cruel," unlike in later years when they were "college trained" and taught how to deal tactfully with fellow employees. Orvel Simmons, interview with Kenneth B. West, Feb. 28, 1980, University of Michigan–Flint Labor History Project, Genesee Historical Collections Center, Flint, Michigan.

41. Rosenthal, *Striking Flint,* 34.

42. "Report of Genora Dollinger, Chief Steward," Dept. 15, May 1–5, 1945, Dollinger Collection, box 4, folder 7, Reuther Library.

43. *On Guard* no. 4, published by the Educational Committee of Local 212 UAW-CIO, Dollinger Collection, box 4, folder 7, Reuther Library.

44. Genora to Sol, Feb. 12, 1946, Dollinger Collection, box 1, folders 12–16, Reuther Library.

45. Sol to Genora, Aug. 19, 1945, Dollinger Collection, box 1, folder 1, Reuther Library.

46. Genora to Sol, Aug. 25, 1945, Dollinger Collection, box 1, folder 9, Reuther Library.

47. Leila Rupp and Verta Taylor, *Survival in the Doldrums: The American Women's Rights Movements 1945 to the 1960s* (New York: Oxford Univ. Press, 1987), 12.

48. Elaine Tyler May, *Homeward Bound: American Families in the Cold War Era* (New York: Basic Books, 1988), 198.

49. Linda Kerber and Jane Sherron DeHart, *Women's America: Refocusing the Past,* 4th ed. (New York: Oxford Univ. Press, 1995), 453.

50. Sara Evans, *Born for Liberty: A History of Women in America* (New York: Free Press, 1989), 223.

51. Sherna Berger Gluck, *Rosie the Riveter,* 8.

52. Ibid., 11.

53. William Henry Chafe, *The American Woman: Her Changing Social, Economic, and Political Roles, 1920–1970* (New York: Oxford Univ. Press, 1972), 190.

54. Genora to Sol, Sept. 4, 1945, Dollinger Collection, box 1, folder 9, Reuther Library.

55. Ibid., Aug. 19, 1945, Reuther Library.
56. Rosenthal, *Striking Flint*, 39.
57. Meyerson, "Women," 465.
58. Genora Dollinger, notes and letters to Genora, Dollinger Collection, box 4, folder 7, Reuther Library.
59. Rosenthal, *Striking Flint*, 38.
60. SWP interview, Oct. 21, 1993, Dollinger Collection, Los Angeles.
61. Elaine Roseland to Genora, Oct. 25, 1945, Dollinger Collection, box 4, file 7, Reuther Library.
62. Genora Dollinger, notes and letters to Genora, Dollinger Collection, box 4, folder 7, Reuther Library.
63. Genora to Lora Albro, n.d., Dollinger Collection, box 2, files 2–4, Reuther Library.
64. Rosenthal, *Striking Flint*, 39.
65. Genora Dollinger, "I Warned Reuther," *The America Socialist*, Feb. 1954.
66. Leighton interview, Oct. 21, 1993.
67. Genora Dollinger, notes, Mar. 13, 1951, Dollinger Collection, Los Angeles.
68. U.S. Senate Special Committee Investigation of Organized Crime in Interstate Commerce, Kefauver, 82 Cong., 1st sess., vol. 979, 1951, 606. See also Dollinger Collection, box 4, folder 20, Reuther Library.
69. Genora to Sol, Mar. 18, 1946, Dollinger Collection, box 1, folder 9, Reuther Library.
70. Ibid., Sept. 10, 1945, Dollinger Collection, Reuther Library.
71. Ibid., Jan. 21, 146, Dollinger Collection, box 1, Dollinger Collection, Reuther Library.
72. Ibid., Jan. 20, 1946, Dollinger Collection, box 1, folders 12–16, Reuther Library.
73. Ibid., Apr. 9, 1946, Dollinger Collection, Reuther Library.
74. Ibid., Apr. 10, 1946, Dollinger Collection, Reuther Library.
75. Ibid., Apr. 15, 1946, Dollinger Collection, Reuther Library.
76. Ibid., May 6, 1946, Dollinger Collection, Reuther Library.
77. Ibid., May 7, 1946, Dollinger Collection, Reuther Library.
78. Ibid., May 8, 1946, Dollinger Collection, Reuther Library.
79. Ibid., May 13, 1946, Dollinger Collection, Reuther Library.
80. Sol to Genora, May 14, 1946, Dollinger Collection, Reuther Library.
81. Ibid., May 15, 1946, Dollinger Collection, box 1, folders 17–22, Reuther Library.
82. Genora to Sol, May 18, 1946, Dollinger Collection, box 1, folders 12–16, Reuther Library.
83. Ibid., Apr. 23, 1946, Dollinger Collection, Reuther Library.

84. Sol to Genora, June 2, 1946, Dollinger Collection, box 1, folders 17–22, Reuther Library.
85. Genora to Sol, June 23, 1946, Dollinger Collection, box 1, files 12–16, Reuther Library.
86. Sol Dollinger, interview with the author, Oct. 31, 1997.
87. Ernie Mazey to Genora, Sept. 19, 1946, Dollinger Collection, box 3, folder 30, Reuther Library.
88. Arthur? and Roy? Letter of condolence to Genora, ca. Sept. 1946, Dollinger Collection, box 2, folder 30, Reuther Library.
89. *UAW Solidarity* (Jan.–Feb. 2003): 23.
90. Genora to Sol, May 2, 1949, Dollinger Collection, box 1, folder 24, Reuther Library.
91. Ibid., May 14, 1949, Dollinger Collection, Reuther Library.
92. Ibid., May 6, 1949, Dollinger Collection, Reuther Library.
93. Ibid., May 7, 1949, Dollinger Collection, Reuther Library.
94. Sol to Genora, May 12, 1949, Dollinger Collection, box 1, file 24, Reuther Library.
95. Ibid., May 13, 1949, Dollinger Collection, Reuther Library.

5. Trials and Tragedies

1. *Red Channels: The Report of Communist Influence in Radio and Television* (New York: Counterattack, 1950), 215.
2. *Counterattack* 6:39 (Sept. 26, 1952): n. p.
3. Genora Dollinger, senatorial campaign speech, ca. 1948, Dollinger Papers, Los Angeles. See also Dollinger Collection, box 4, folder 11, Reuther Library.
4. Sol Dollinger, e-mail to the author, Jan. 20, 2000.
5. Gluck interview, 362–63.
6. Sol Dollinger, interview with the author, Oct. 31, 1997.
7. Genora Dollinger, campaign article, *Flint Journal,* Mar. 6, 1950.
8. "Genora Dollinger Is SWP Candidate for Congress," *Militant,* Aug. 28, 1950, 4.
9. Ibid., Mar. 5, 1951.
10. Sol Dollinger, interview with the author, Oct. 31, 1997.
11. FBI report on Genora Dollinger, 1953.
12. Genora Dollinger, letter to the editor, *Flint Journal,* Oct. 30, 1952.
13. "How the Trucks Act Was Passed: Genora Dollinger Blames Major Parties for Reactionary Statute," *Militant,* Apr. 28, 1952, 2.
14. FBI report on Genora Dollinger, 1953.
15. Sol Dollinger, interview with the author, Oct. 31, 1997.
16. FBI report on Genora Dollinger, 1951.

17. Sol Dollinger, interview with the author, Oct. 31, 1997.
18. Ibid.
19. "Goodbye, My Son," *Militant,* Jan. 15, 1951, 3, Dollinger Collection, box 1, folder 27, Reuther Library.
20. Genora to Sol, Jan. 31, 1951, Dollinger Collection, box 1, folder 27, Reuther Library.
21. Condolence letters to Genora, Jan. 21, 1951, Dollinger Collection, box 2, folder 30, Reuther Library.
22. Genora to Sol, 1951, Dollinger Collection, box 1, folder 27, Reuther Library.
23. Speech to UAW 659, Jan. 1951, Dollinger Collection, box 4, folder 11, Reuther Library.
24. Genora to Sol, Jan. 16, 1951, Dollinger Collection, box 1, folder 27, Reuther Library.
25. Sol to Genora, Jan. 24, 1951, Dollinger Collection, box 1, folder 1, Reuther Library.
26. Genora to Sol, Jan. 19, 1951, Dollinger Collection, box 1, folder 27, Reuther Library.
27. Ibid., Jan. 25, 1951, Dollinger Collection, Reuther Library.
28. Sol to Genora, Feb. 2, 1951, Dollinger Collection, box 1, folder 28, Reuther Library.
29. Genora to Sol, Jan. 16, 1951, Dollinger Collection, box 1, folder 27, Reuther Library.
30. Ibid., Jan. 25, 1951, Dollinger Collection, Reuther Library.
31. FBI reports on Genora and Sol Dollinger, 1951, Dollinger Collection, box 5, folders 11–13, Reuther Library.
32. Ibid.
33. Ibid.
34. Genora to Sol, Feb. 10, 1953, Dollinger Collection, box 1, folder 29, Reuther Library.
35. Ronald Dollinger to Sol, Jan. 31, 1956, Dollinger Collection, box 1, folder 29, Reuther Library.
36. Genora to Sol, Jan. 31, 1956, Dollinger Collection, box 1, folder 30, Reuther Library.
37. Ibid., Oct. 5, 1953, Reuther Library.
38. Sol Dollinger, e-mail to the author, Jan. 29, 2000.
39. Sal Santen to Sol Dollinger, June 1954, Dollinger Collection, box 2, folder 51, Reuther Library. Sol's friend, Sal Santen, was "sure" that America would be the base from which "Trotsky will conquer the whole world." It would start in Latin America and then spread north. He told Sol that if you he and Genora "remain faithful to the International movement, the Trotskyists will be in the United States."

40. Peter Rachleff, "Organizing 'Wall to Wall': The Independent Union of All Workers, 1933–37," in *We Are All Leaders: The Alternative Unionism of the Early 1930s*, ed. Staughton Lynd (Urbana: Univ. of Illinois Press, 1996), 60. On trade unions, Farrell Dobbs argued that each of them is "a tiny mirror which reflects a small though distorted image of the whole class." Trade unions, he believed, had been "deceived by false education, poisoned by vicious propaganda, and chained to the wheel of capitalist propaganda." See Farrell Dobbs, *Trade Union Problems* (New York: Pioneer Publishing, n.d. [1940?]), quoted in *U.S. Labor in the Twentieth Century: Studies in Working-Class Struggles and Insurgency*, ed. John H. Hinshaw and Paul Le Blanc (Amherst, N.Y.: Humanity Books, 2001), 156–57. A dated but still useful book on trade unions, especially their relationship to women workers, is Alice Henry, *The Trade Union Woman* (New York: Burt Franklin, 1915).
41. Donald Drew Egbert et al., eds., *Socialism and American Life*, vol. 2 (Princeton, N.J.: Princeton Univ. Press, 1952), 59–60, 154–55.
42. Ibid., 10.
43. Sol Dollinger, e-mail to the author, Jan. 29, 2000. C. L. R. James joined the SWP minority with a dim view of Cannon. He wrote to Martin Glaberman that "to this day [1962] he [Cannon] has been totally unable to adapt Marxism to the American scene. And to the particular age in which we live." Glaberman, *Marxism*, 69. For other views of the Cannonites, see Egbert and Persons, *Socialism*, 221, 288.
44. Alexander, *International Trotskyism*, 836.
45. FBI report on Sol Dollinger, ca. 1958, Dollinger Collection, box 5, folders 11–15, Reuther Library.
46. Sol Dollinger, e-mail to the author, June 8, 2000. Sol stated positively that this was not the first such incident with the FBI, nor the last.
47. FBI report on Genora Dollinger, ca. 1958, Dollinger Collection, box 5, folders 11–15, Reuther Library.
48. For additional descriptions of this trend, see Warren Lerner, *A History of Socialism and Communism in Modern Times: Theorists, Activists, and Humanists*, 2d ed. (Englewood Cliffs, N.J.: Prentice Hall, 1994), 214.
49. FBI report on Genora Dollinger, ca. 1958, Dollinger Collection, box 5, folders 11–15, Reuther Library.
50. Ibid.
51. Sol Dollinger to the author, Nov. 30, 1997.
52. Genora to Jack Johnson, Apr. 23, 1958, Dollinger Collection, Los Angeles.
53. Genora to Charles Wilderspin, July 4, 1958, Dollinger Collection, Los Angeles.
54. Sol Dollinger, e-mail to the author, June 8, 2000.

55. FBI report on Sol Dollinger, Nov. 22, 1954, Dollinger Collection, box 5, folders 11–15, Reuther Library.
56. Ibid., ca. winter 1956, Dollinger Collection, Reuther Library.
57. Ibid., ca. summer 1957, Dollinger Collection, Reuther Library.
58. Ibid., May 12, 1958, Dollinger Collection, Reuther Library.
59. Sol Dollinger, "Festival Gaiety," 7.
60. Betty Friedan, *The Feminine Mystique* (New York: Norton, 1963), 36.

6. California Girl

1. Sarah Evans, *Personal Politics: The Roots of Women's Liberation in the Civil Rights Movement and the New Left* (New York: Knopf, 1979), 15.
2. Kathleen O'Nan, "The Role of Women, and of Radicals in the First Sit-Down Strikes: An Interview with Genora Dollinger," in *U.S. Labor in the Twentieth Century: Studies in Working-Class Struggles and Insurgency,* ed. John H. Hinshaw and Paul Le Blanc, 163.
3. Flint NAACP report, Dec. 4, 1959, Dollinger Collection, Los Angeles.
4. Flint NAACP, undated newsletter, Dollinger Collection, Los Angeles.
5. Ibid.
6. Sol Dollinger, "Formative Years," 7.
7. Conrad J. Lynn, *Monroe, North Carolina . . . Turning Point in American History,* pamphlet, 1962, Labadie Collection, University of Michigan Library, Ann Arbor, 1–27. See also Lynn, *There Is a Fountain: The Autobiography of Conrad Lynn* (Brooklyn, N.Y.: Lawrence Hill Books, 1993), 141–55; Truman Nelson, *People with Strength: The Story of Monroe, N.C.* (Durham, N.C.: Duke Univ. Press, 1962), 1–37. The most brilliant book written about Monroe during this time is Timothy B. Tyson, *Radio Free Dixie: Robert F. Williams and the Roots of Black Power* (Chapel Hill: Univ. of North Carolina Press, 1999).
8. Nelson, *People with Strength,* 13.
9. Berta Green to Sam Duncan, of Flint, Michigan, Jan. 19, 1961, Dollinger Collection, box 5, folder 8, Reuther Library.
10. Berta Green to Genora, Jan. 19, 1961, Dollinger Collection, box 5, folder 8, Reuther Library.
11. Berta Green to Sam Duncan, Jan. 19, 1961, Dollinger Collection, box 5, folder 8, Reuther Library.
12. Ibid.
13. Genora Dollinger, notes, n.d., Dollinger Collection, box 5, folder 8, Reuther Library.
14. Genora Dollinger, "The Iron Curtain of Dixie," unpublished writing, ca. 1962, Dollinger Collection, box 4, folder 24, Reuther Library.

15. Genora Dollinger, “To Whom It May Concern,” Oct. 22, 1963, Dollinger Collection, box 4, folder 49, Reuther Library.

16. See Larry Jones, “Hall of Fame for Genora Dollinger,” in *The UAW Local 659 Searchlight,* Sept. 23, 1994.

17. Sol Dollinger, “Formative Years,” 43.

18. Ibid., 44.

19. Sol Dollinger, interview with the author, Nov. 1, 1997.

20. Sol Dollinger, “Formative Years,” 45.

21. Sol Dollinger, interview with the author, Nov. 1, 1997.

22. O’Nan, “Role of Women,” 176.

23. David Herreshoff, “On Genora,” unpublished writing, Apr. 23, 1965, Dollinger Collection, box 4, Reuther Library.

24. Sol said later that the “average life of a fund raiser . . . was five years.” He stayed with the Technion Society of America for nineteen years. Although no specific records were ever reported, he estimated that altogether he raised between forty-five and fifty million dollars.

25. Genora to Sol, n.d., Dollinger Collection, box 1, folder 1, Reuther Library.

26. Genora to Helen Travis, Apr. 21, 1966, Dollinger Collection, box 1, folder 39, Reuther Library.

27. Ernest Mazey to Eason Monroe, Apr. 4, 1966, Dollinger Collection, box 1, folder 39, Reuther Library. As if to underscore these remarks, just a few weeks later Genora received a grateful letter from Cary T. Cook, thanking her for helping him to obtain his freedom from jail.

28. Genora Dollinger, “The Joint (Mr. & Mrs.) Membership and the Important Role of Women,” ACLU pamphlet, n.d., Dollinger Collection, box 4, folder 49, Reuther Library.

29. Ernest Mazey to Genora and Sol, Dec. 24, 1966, Dollinger Collection, box 4, folder 49, Reuther Library.

30. Ed Galligan to Genora, Apr. 21, 1966, Dollinger Collection, box 2, folder 21, Reuther Library.

31. Walter Bergman to Genora, June 20, 1966. Dollinger Collection, box 2, folders 6–7, Reuther Library.

32. Sol to Genora, May 15, 1966. Dollinger Collection, box 1, folders 31–32, Reuther Library.

33. Ibid., May 18, 1966, Dollinger Collection, Reuther Library.

34. Ibid., May 17, 1966, Dollinger Collection, Reuther Library.

35. Ibid., June 2, 1966, Dollinger Collection, Reuther Library.

36. Ibid., May 23, 1966, Dollinger Collection, Reuther Library.

37. Larry Jones to Sol and Genora, Sept. 18, 1967, Dollinger Collection, Los Angeles.

38. Larry Jones to Genora, Sept. 18, 1967, Dollinger Collection, Los Angeles.

39. Ibid., Oct. 10, 1967, Dollinger Collection, Los Angeles.

40. Genora to "Ray," Sept. 7, 1970, Dollinger Collection, box 2, folder 5, Reuther Library.
41. Sol Dollinger, "Formative Years," 45.
42. Sol describes one meeting of the Peace and Freedom organization. Black Panthers came to the door where the meeting was in progress but would not enter until the whites present emptied their pockets of change and cigarettes. An attendee protested that this was not the way to enter into an accommodating relationship. Sol recorded that the "parlor pink whites voted her down."
43. Sol Dollinger to the author, Nov. 30, 1997.
44. Sol Dollinger, e-mail to the author, July 9, 2000.
45. Sol Dollinger, "Formative Years," 45.
46. Sol Dollinger, e-mail to the author, June 18, 1999.
47. Genora to Sol, Dec. 7, 1968, Dollinger Collection, box 1, folder 33, Reuther Library.
48. Stanyo Kaminski to Genora, May 21, 1968, Dollinger Collection, Los Angeles.
49. Sol Dollinger to the author, Mar. 23, 1998.
50. Sol Dollinger, e-mail to the author, June 18, 1999.
51. Genora to (sister?) Barbara, Apr. 26, 1968, Dollinger Collection, Los Angeles.
52. Sol Dollinger, interview with the author, Nov. 1, 1997.
53. Studs Terkel, *Coming of Age* (New York: New York Press, 1997), 519.
54. Sol Dollinger, interview with the author, Nov. 1, 1997.
55. Ronald Dollinger to Genora [ca. 1970?], Dollinger Collection, box 2, folder 14, Reuther Library.
56. Ibid., Sept. 27, 1971, Dollinger Collection, Reuther Library.
57. Tape recording made for Sol and Ron Dollinger at Genora's "homecoming" party in Detroit, fall 1970, Dollinger Collection, Los Angeles.
58. Ibid.

7. "It Makes My Heart Sing"

1. Los Angeles High School Community Advisory Council publication, Nov. 7, 1977, Dollinger Collection, box 4, folder 42, Reuther Library.
2. Genora Dollinger, pamphlet, ca. 1970, Dollinger Collection, box 3, folder 26, Reuther Library.
3. Ibid.
4. *Agenda,* People's Lobby Newsletter 71, vol. 2, Jan. 1971, Dollinger Collection, box 4, folder 44, Reuther Library.
5. Genora Dollinger in *Los Angeles Highlights* (newsletter), Oct. 18, 1971, Dollinger Collection, box 4, folder 44, Reuther Library.

6. Ibid. The teachers wanted collective bargaining rights. The city agreed, but a group known as the Professional Educators/Los Angeles brought a lawsuit in accordance with the Winton Act that prohibited any collective bargaining. It was not until 1976 that the teachers won full rights of bargaining. Raymond Butler, e-mail to the author, July 18, 2000.
7. Genora Dollinger, speech to the Organization of American Historians (OAH), Apr. 1970, Dollinger Collection, box 3, folder 34, Reuther Library.
8. Genora Dollinger, speech to "Pioneers Reunion," UAW Local 659, Aug. 2, 1987, Dollinger Collection, box 3, folder 32, Reuther Library.
9. Genora to Larry Jones, May 17, 1974, Dollinger Collection, box 2, folders 33–36, Reuther Library.
10. Foner, *Women and the American Labor Movement,* 1.
11. Gluck, *Rosie the Riveter,* 7, 8.
12. Foner, *Women and the American Labor Movement,* 306, 309.
13. Karen Anderson, *Wartime Women: Sex Roles, Family Relations, and the Status of Women during World War II* (Westport, Conn.: Greenwood Press, 1981), 174.
14. Genora Dollinger, untitled writing, Feb. 1974, Dollinger Collection, box 2, folder 33, Reuther Library.
15. On the subject of interviews, Genora knew that the Skeels's 1960 interview of her was stored in the archives at Wayne State University. She learned that the interview was not available to students except under certain circumstances. Genora asked why, wanting the widest coverage possible of what she had said to Skeels. Representing the archives, Philip Mason wrote back to Genora that the interview had to be restricted because of some of the "libelous" material in it. The Skeels interview, he said, was going to be used for "scholarly" purposes only, with no "sensationalism." Genora scoffed at such "timidity," but there was nothing she could do about it. Genora to Philip Mason, Apr. 23, 1972; and Philip Mason to Genora, Apr. 27, 1972, Dollinger Collection, box 2, Reuther Library.
16. Genora to Larry Jones, May 17, 1974, Dollinger Collection, box 2, folders 33–36, Reuther Library.
17. Genora to Julius and Phyllis Jacobson, May 30, 1993, Dollinger Collection, box 2, Reuther Library.
18. Genora to Pauline and Bernie Goodman, Aug. 16, 1977, Dollinger Collection, box 2, folders 23–24, Reuther Library.
19. Joe Rosenthal to Genora, June 15, 1973, Dollinger Collection, box 2, folder 49, Reuther Library. Apparently, Rosenthal was correct in his theory. By 1999, only 26 percent of women surveyed said that they liked the word "feminism." Two years later, in 2001, the percentage rate had

dropped by one point. See Ariel Levy, *Female Chauvinist Pigs: Women and the Rise of Raunch Culture* (New York: Free Press, 2005), 86.

20. Sheila McCoy, e-mail to the author, Nov. 26, 1999.
21. Patricia Ireland, *What Women Want* (New York: Penguin, 1996), 70. Seven years, however, was the normal waiting time for states to decide constitutional amendments.
22. Genora Dollinger, "The Spirit of 1976 and 1937," *Searchlight*, Feb. 5, 1976, 5.
23. Annelise Orleck, *Common Sense and a Little Fire: Women and Working-Class Politics in the United States, 1900–1965* (Chapel Hill: Univ. of North Carolina Press, 1995), 303.
24. Marcia Cohen, *The Sisterhood: The Inside Story of the Woman's Movement and the Leaders Who Made It Happen* (New York: Fawcett Columbine, 1988), 359, 360.
25. Nancy A. Naples, *Grass Roots Warriors*, 141.
26. Nancy Gabin, "Time Out of Mind: The UAW's Response to Female Labor Laws and Mandatory Overtime in the 1960s," in *Work Engendered: Toward a New History of American Labor*, ed. Ava Barton (Ithaca, N.Y.: Cornell Univ. Press, 1993), 372.
27. Dorothy Sue Cobble, *Dishing It Out: Waitresses and Their Unions in the Twentieth Century* (Urbana: Univ. of Illinois Press, 1991), 11.
28. Blanche Wiesen Cook, *Women and Support Networks: Women Against Economic and Social Repression: The Two-Front Challenge* (New York: Out and Out Books, 1979), 9.
29. Daniel Horowitz, *Betty Friedan and the Making of* The Feminine Mystique: *The American Left, the Cold War, and Modern Feminism* (Amherst: Univ. of Massachusetts Press, 1998), 127. The ERA's major objectives were equal pay, government-sponsored daycare centers, an end to lynching and racial discrimination, national health insurance, leadership for women in unions, and respectful representation of women in the media. For additional discussions of the pros and cons of the ERA, see Kathleen A. Laughlin, *Women's Work and Public Policy: A History of the Women's Bureau, U.S. Department of Labor, 1945–1970* (Boston: Northeastern Univ. Press, 2000), 35–37.
30. Rupp and Taylor, *Survival in the Doldrums*, 144.
31. Genora to Senator Edward W. Brooke, July 1, 1969, Dollinger Collection, box 4, folder 42, Reuther Library.
32. Genora to Senator Edward Kennedy, July 2, 1969; also, letter to "Ray," July 7, 1970, Dollinger Collection, box 4, folder 42, Reuther Library.
33. Genora to Ron Dollinger, June 16, 1971, Dollinger Collection, Los Angeles.
34. Ibid., July 6, 1971, Dollinger Collection, Los Angeles.
35. Sol Dollinger, interview with the author, Oct. 19, 1997.

36. Sol Dollinger, "Franco and Beyond," unpublished paper, Dollinger Collection, Los Angeles, 4.

37. On February 6, 1976, Genora used the Freedom of Information Act to obtain her files from the FBI, only to be told that the FBI had received 17,469 requests, with a present backlog of 6,350. By January 11, 1977, Genora had not received a report from the federal agency. She did some quick math: "Since according to this information, you completed approximately eleven thousand requests . . . why is it that I have not received the information in my case over a year after my original request" when their backlog was under 10,000? Finally, on May 16, 1977, the FBI wrote to her, "We have now searched our records and find numerous references to you in which you were not the subject of the investigation." Her disdain for the FBI and the CIA continued.

38. Sol Dollinger, "Franco and Beyond," 5.

39. Sol Dollinger, e-mail to the author, July 1, 2000; Sol Dollinger, interview with the author, Oct. 31, 1997.

40. Sol Dollinger, interview with the author, Oct. 31, 1997.

41. Genora to Ronald Dollinger, July 19, 1973, Dollinger Collection, Los Angeles.

42. This and other references to Genora and Sol's 1977 trip to Europe are, unless otherwise noted, from Genora's diary entries between June and July 1977, Dollinger Collection, Los Angeles.

43. Sol Dollinger, interview with the author, Oct. 31, 1997.

44. Sol Dollinger and Genora Dollinger, *Not Automatic: Women and the Left in the Forging of the Auto Workers' Union* (New York: Monthly Review Press, 2000), 63. This book was compiled after Genora's death, and Sol added Genora's byline as a loving tribute to his wife of more than a half-century. Reviewer Collete A. Hyman, said, "Two thirds of the book focuses far more on left-wing politics specifically on the battles among male politicos—than on women." Nevertheless, Sol includes "class-conscious militants," one of whom was Genora, "who played an 'inspiring, complex and intrepid role' in the labor movement." See Colette A. Hyman, "Heroines and Homemakers: Views from Across the Disciplines," in *National Women's Studies Association Journal* 13:3 (2001): 189–98, http://muse.jhu.edu/journals/nwsa_journal/ vo13.3hyman.html

45. Stephen Peet to Genora, Nov. 13, 1975, Dollinger Collection, Los Angeles.

46. Sol Dollinger to Stephen Peet, Oct. 12, 1976, Dollinger Collection, Los Angeles. The Dollingers and the Peets stayed in contact with each other over the next several years. Peet asked Genora for film ideas. She believed he should make a documentary on the integration struggle in the United States and what remained to be done before full equality was

realized; the "hillbillies" who had come up from the South to work in the Flint auto plants would make a good subject, as would the establishment of the twelve missions in California by the Jesuits.

47. Larry Jones to Genora, Aug. 25, 1976, Dollinger Collection, box 2, folders 33–36, Reuther Library.
48. Genora to Leonard Woodcock, Feb. 4, 1977, Dollinger Collection, box 3, folder 19, Reuther Library.
49. Sol Dollinger, "Good Housekeeping Seal of Approval," unpublished paper, n.d., 12, Dollinger Collection, Los Angeles. The reporter Sol quoted was John R. Emshwiller of the *Wall Street Journal.*
50. Genora to Lorraine Gray, May 19, 1979, Dollinger Collection, Reuther Library.
51. Sol Dollinger, "Good Housekeeping," 16.
52. Ibid., 13–14.
53. "N&L," pamphlet, Mar. 1977, Dollinger Collection, Los Angeles.
54. David Vizard, "Documentary Lauds Women's Roles in Flint Sit-Down Strike," *Flint Journal,* May 14, 1978.
55. Ibid.
56. Larry Jones to Genora, Feb. 25, 1977, Dollinger Collection, box 2, folders 33–36, Reuther Library.
57. Genora Dollinger, interview with Neil Leighton, ca. 1978, Dollinger Collection, Los Angeles.
58. Sol Dollinger, "Mazey Labels Dinner Class Collaboration," unpublished essay, n.d., Dollinger Collection, Los Angeles, 6–7.
59. See chapter 1 for further references to these letters.
60. Douglas A. Fraser to Genora Dollinger, Oct. 10, 1978, Dollinger Collection, Los Angeles. See chapter 1 for further reference to this article.
61. Citizen's Party position paper, Apr. 1979, Dollinger Collection, box 5, folder 3, Reuther Library.
62. Jeanne Morgan to Genora, ca. 1979, Dollinger Collection, box 5, folder 3, Reuther Library.
63. Genora to Barry Commoner, Aug. 22, 1980, Dollinger Collection, box 5, folder 3, Reuther Library.
64. Citizen's Party position paper, Apr. 1979, Dollinger Collection, box 5, folder 3, Reuther Library.
65. Genora to Peter Unterweger, Aug. 18, 1980, Dollinger Collection, box 5, folder 3, Reuther Library.
66. Unterweger to Genora Dollinger, Aug. 27, 1980, Dollinger Collection, box 5, folder 3, Reuther Library.
67. Nellie Besson to Genora, Nov. 1, 1978, Dollinger Collection, box 2, folder 8, Reuther Library.

1. Genora Dollinger, untitled unpublished paper, 1980, Dollinger Papers, Los Angeles, 1. See also Robert L. Bruce to Genora Dollinger, June 23, 1980, Dollinger Collection, box 2, folder 28, Reuther Library.
2. Genora to Floyd Hoke-Miller, June 15, 1984, Dollinger Collection, box 2, folder 28, Reuther Library.
3. Floyd Hoke-Miller, "A Laborer Looks at Life, Then and Now," in *Poems from the Shop Floor,* Dollinger Collection, box 2, folder 28, Reuther Library.
4. Genora to Lynn Goldfarb, Feb. 5, 1984, Dollinger Collection, box 3, folder 18, Reuther Library. For a different perspective, see Ruth Milkman, *Farewell to the Factory: Auto Workers in the Late Twentieth Century* (Berkeley: Univ. of California Press, 1997). See particularly chapter 2, "Prisoners of Prosperity: Autoworkers in the Postwar Period," 22–51.
5. An instructive article about automation, decentralization, corporate mergers, and so forth is in Nancy Gabin's "Time Out of Mind," 354.
6. Genora Dollinger note, ca. 1980, Dollinger Collection, Los Angeles.
7. Genora to Floyd Hoke-Miller, June 15, 1984, Dollinger Collection, box 2, folder 28, Reuther Library.
8. Genora to Larry Jones, Aug. 14, 1981, Dollinger Collection, box 2, folders 33–36, Reuther Library.
9. Genora Dollinger, diary entries, June–July 1983, Dollinger Collection, Los Angeles.
10. Sol Dollinger, e-mail to the author, Nov. 5, 2000.
11. Diary, July 1983, Dollinger Collection, Los Angeles.
12. Ibid.
13. Ibid.
14. An instructive article on this subject is M. Kent Jennings, "Women in Party Politics," in *Women, Politics, and Change,* ed. Tilly and Gurin, 244.
15. She did vote, at least from time to time, for the Peace and Freedom Party, which, among other things, wanted "a socialist economy, one where industries, financial institutions, and natural resources are owned by the people as a whole and democratically managed by the people who work in them and use them." California Peace and Freedom Party, "What Positions Does the Peace and Freedom Party Take?" California Peace and Freedom Party, www.peaceandfreedom.org/what_is.htm.
16. Genora Dollinger, "Weekly Minder," notebook, Dollinger Collection, Los Angeles.
17. Henry A. Waxman to Genora Dollinger, n.d., Dollinger Collection, Los Angeles.
18. Genora Dollinger, notebook, Feb. 1986, Dollinger Collection, Los Ange-

les. She was apparently a notary public, because she speaks frequently in this notebook about various individuals coming to her house at Queen Anne Place to get papers notarized.

19. Ibid., Mar. 14, 1986, Dollinger Collection, Los Angeles.
20. Ibid., Apr. 20, 1986, Dollinger Collection, Los Angeles.
21. Ibid., May 4, 1986, Dollinger Collection, Los Angeles.
22. Ibid., Mar., 27, 1986, Dollinger Collection, Los Angeles.
23. Genora to Larry Jones, May 8, 1985, Dollinger Collection, box 2, folders 33–36, Reuther Library.
24. Genora Dollinger, "Hail to the Red Berets of 1985," *Searchlight,* Feb. 6, 1986, 17.
25. Sol Dollinger, interview with the author, Oct. 31, 1997.
26. Genora Dollinger, speech to UAW-GM on the fiftieth anniversary of the 1937 sit-down strike, Aug. 2, 1986, Dollinger Collection, box 3, folder 33, Reuther Library.
27. Sol Dollinger, interview with the author, Oct. 31, 1997.
28. Henry Kraus to Larry Jones, Dec. 11, 1986, Dollinger Collection, box 2, folders 33–36, Reuther Library. Also in the Dollinger Collection, Los Angeles.
29. Genora Dollinger, "Thumb-Nail Sketch of Communist Party Leaders in 1937—Flint," unpublished paper, Mar. 8, 1994, Dollinger Collection, Los Angeles.
30. Sol says of this point, "Of course Genora's friends knew what she thought of Kraus but his book was sold in large numbers wherever the Cpers (Communist Party) in the union could influence sales in the country." Sol Dollinger, e-mail to the author, Nov. 5, 2000.
31. Kraus, *The Many and the Few,* 234–41. Kraus's book could be evaluated as having been written and published in the midst of the 1947 fight for control of the UAW and as a factional document designed to celebrate the role of Communists and their allies and denigrate that of the SP and the Reutherites.
32. Genora to Fania [?], Sept. 28, 1986, Dollinger Collection, box 2, folder 46, Reuther Library.
33. Sol Dollinger, e-mail to the author, Nov. 5, 2000.
34. Sol Dollinger disagrees with the author on the word *unfortunate.* Genora, he says, had been on a program in Detroit ten years earlier where Kraus was supposed to speak. He was a no-show and thus "deprived Genora the opportunity of making the historical correction [in person] of the record for another decade."
35. Genora to Don and Sylvia Dotzert, Sept. 7, 1987, Dotzert Collection, Tecumseh, Ontario.
36. Sol Dollinger to the author, Nov. 12, 1997.

37. Genora Dollinger, diary entry, ca. 1988, Dollinger Collection, Los Angeles.
38. Sol and Genora to Don and Sylvia Dotzert, Dec. 1988, Dotzert Collection, Tecumseh, Ontario.
39. Genora to Don and Sylvia Dotzert, Oct. 29, 1988.
40. Ibid.
41. Genora to Don and Sylvia Dotzert, Oct. 29, 1988, Dotzert Collection, Tecumseh, Ontario. After returning from Russia, Genora saw an array of physicians once a week. Her cardiologist tried to reactivate one segment of her heart by drug therapy. Her prescription bill ran to $250 a month and the state-of-the art equipment her doctors used ranged from $159 to $219 for each visit. "Thank the gods," she proclaimed, "we have private insurance covering the latter." She stored her wheelchair in the family garage and refused to use it until shortly before her death in 1995.
42. Michael Parks, "After 60 Years, Soviets Air New View of Trotsky's Role," *Los Angeles Times,* Sept. 10, 1988.
43. Genora to Don and Sylvia Dotzert, Sept. 10, 1988, Dotzert Collection, Tecumseh, Ontario.
44. Genora to Bernie and Pauline Goodman, June 2, 1989, Dollinger Collection, box 2, folders 23–24, Reuther Library.
45. Genora to Victor Navasky, July 25, 1989, Dollinger Collection, Los Angeles.
46. Sol to Nelson Lichtenstein, Oct. 20, 1989, Dollinger Collection, box 2, folder 38, Reuther Library.
47. Genora to Victor Navasky, Feb. 12, 1989, Dollinger Collection, Los Angeles.
48. See Lichtenstein, "Auto Workers' Militancy and the Structure of Factory Life, 1937–1955," 351.
49. Genora Dollinger, "UAW Revolutions in California," unpublished paper, Dollinger Collection, Los Angeles, 1–12.
50. Genora to Jack Rosenthal, Mar. 3, 1990, Dollinger Collection, box 2, folder 49, Reuther Library.
51. Genora Dollinger, foreword to *A Troublemaker's Handbook: How to Fight Back Where You Work—and Win,* Dan La Botz (Detroit, Mich.: Labor Notes, 1991).
52. Genora to Daniel Leab, ca. 1991, Dollinger Collection, box 1, folder 44, Reuther Library.
53. Daniel Leab to Genora, Nov. 1993, Dollinger Collection, Los Angeles. Genora signed the agreement on Nov. 14, 1993.
54. Ibid., June 2, 1994, Dollinger Collection, Los Angeles.
55. Genora to Molly McGarry, June 16, 1994, Dollinger Collection, Los Angeles; also in the Dollinger Collection, box 4, folder 39, Reuther Library.

56. "Joyce" to Genora Dollinger, Oct. 1994, Dollinger Collection, box 4, folder 39, Reuther Library.
57. Sophie Reuther to the Michigan Women's Hall of Fame, Oct. 4, 1994, Dollinger Collection, box 4, folder 39, Reuther Library.
58. Sue Ann Connolly, remarks at the Michigan Women's Hall of Fame dinner, Oct. 29, 1994, Dollinger Collection, box 4, folder 39, Reuther Library. Connolly had written a play, *Down in the Hole,* about the contributions of women to the victory in 1937. The play was performed in Flint at the Buckham Alley Theatre in 1994.
59. Genora to Wendy Wendland, Oct. 1994, Dollinger Collection, box 4, folder 39, Reuther Library.
60. Genora to Margaret Guttshall, Oct. 3, 1994, Dollinger Collection, box 4, folder 39, Reuther Library.
61. O'Nan, "Role of Women," 177.
62. Genora Dollinger, speech to LPA, Dec. 1994, Dollinger Collection, Los Angeles. This was the last public speech Genora gave.
63. When the SWP had been formed several years before, Genora had enthusiastically embraced its programs and philosophies. James P. Cannon had frequently mentioned that "internationalism" was the central principle of SWP ambitions. It may have appeared that Genora was refuting some of the earlier stances by opposing NAFTA. It must be remembered that at this time (1994), she did not belong to the SWP or, for that matter, any political party. Even if she had, Cannon had offered a way out of any inconsistencies. Internationalism, he had argued, meant collaboration "of those people in all countries who recognize . . . our historical problems." Barnes, *James P. Cannon,* 17. In Genora's opinion, NAFTA did not promote collaboration. On the contrary, it engendered capitalistic competition, and therefore she could not support it.
64. Stephen Franklin, "Wages Falling for Factory Workers," in *Park City Daily News* (Bowling Green, Kentucky), Feb. 5, 2006.
65. Dana Frank, *Buy American: The Untold Story of Economic Nationalism* (Boston: Beacon Press, 1999), 141.
66. Terkel, *Coming of Age,* 520. Sol Dollinger believes Terkel "took liberties" with his interview of Genora, who "would never suggest she had to take a pill in front of company." Sol Dollinger, e-mail to the author, Nov. 5, 2000.
67. Sol Dollinger, e-mail to the author, Oct. 9, 2000.
68. John Engler to Genora, Jan. 6, 1994, Dollinger Collection, Los Angeles.
69. *Flint Journal,* Oct. 14, 1995.
70. *Detroit Free Press,* Oct. 17, 1995.
71. *Los Angeles Times,* Oct. 14, 1995.
72. *New York Times,* Oct. 14, 1995.

73. Olga Domanski to Sol Dollinger, Nov. 4, 1995, Dollinger Collection, Los Angeles.
74. Ruth Van Zandt to Sol Dollinger, Dec. 4, 1995, Dollinger Collection, Los Angeles.
75. Melvyn H. Bloom to Sol Dollinger, Oct. 18, 1995, Dollinger Collection, Los Angeles.
76. Janice Hassett Bedayn to Sol Dollinger, Nov. 1995, Dollinger Collection, Los Angeles.
77. Patricia Butler to Sol Dollinger, Oct. 16, 1995, Dollinger Collection, Los Angeles.
78. Max Shein to Sol Dollinger, Oct. 13, 1995, Dollinger Collection, Los Angeles.
79. Jessica Johnson to Sol Dollinger, Nov. 1995, Dollinger Collection, Los Angeles.
80. Verena and Robert Walters to Sol Dollinger, Nov. 1995, Dollinger Collection, Los Angeles.
81. Sol himself wrote an article, "The Unrelenting Genora Dollinger," for *Against the Current* (Jan./Feb. 1996): 43.

9. An Assessment

1. Sheila Tobias and Lisa Anders, "What Really Happened to Rosie the Riveter? Demobilization and the Female Labor Force," in *Women's America: Refocusing the Past,* ed. Linda Kerber and Jane Mathews (New York: Oxford Univ. Press, 1980), 178.
2. Cobble, *Dishing It Out,* 5.
3. Rupp and Taylor, *Survival in the Doldrums,* 144.
4. Elizabeth Faue, *Community of Suffering and Struggle: Women, Men, and the Labor Movement in Minneapolis, 1915–1945* (Chapel Hill: Univ. of North Carolina Press, 1991), xiv.
5. Ann D. Gordon, Mari Jo Buhle, and Nancy E. Schrom, "Women in American Society: An Historical Contribution," *A Heritage of Her Own: Toward a New Social History of American Women,* ed. Cott and Pleck, 16.
6. Kate Weigand, *Red Feminism: American Communism and the Making of Women's Liberation* (Baltimore: Johns Hopkins Univ. Press, 2001), 139.
7. Ibid., 140.
8. Ibid., 139.
9. Ellen Fitzpatrick, foreword to *Century of Struggle: The Woman's Rights Movement in the United States,* ed. Eleanor Flexner and Ellen Fitzpatrick (Cambridge, Mass.: Belknap Press, 1975), vii–xviii.

10. An early California reformer, Frances Nacke Noel, had also connected labor and the suffrage movement. See Patricia Loughlin, "In Search of Capable Allies: Frances Nacke Noel and Women's Labor Activism in Los Angeles," *Southern California Quarterly* 88.3 (Dec. 2001): 61–74.
11. Sherry Lee Linkon, "A Marx Family Reunion: Cultural Studies and Labor History on Common Ground," *American Quarterly* 52.3 (Sept. 2000): 555.
12. Leslie Fishbein, review of *Female Spectacle: The Theoretical Roots of Modern Feminism,* by Susan A. Glenn, *Journal of American History* 88.3 (Dec. 2001): 1110.
13. See Leslie Heywood and Jennifer Drake, *Third Wave Agenda: Being Feminist, Doing Feminism* (Minneapolis: Univ. of Minnesota Press, 1997), 5. See also Stephanie Gilmore, "Looking Back, Thinking Ahead: Third Wave Feminism in the United States," *Journal of Women's History* 12.4 (Winter 2001): 215.
14. Heywood and Drake, *Third-Wave Agenda,* 23.
15. Michelle Jensen, "Riding the Third Wave," *Nation* 271, no. 19 (Dec. 11, 2001): 24. See also Jennifer Baumgardner and Amy Richards, *Manifesta: Young Women, Feminism, and the Future* (New York: Farrar, Straus and Giroux, 2000).
16. The author is grateful to Professor Coodley for furnishing these essays for my research. I received copies of them from Sol Dollinger. They are used here with the permission of Lauren Coodley.
17. Essays, Angelina Rodriguez, Apr. 1, 1999.
18. Ibid., Laurie Thompson, Apr. 1, 1999.
19. Ibid., Maria Villafuerte, Apr. 1, 1999.
20. Ibid., Peggy David, Apr. 1, 1999.
21. Ibid.
22. Ibid., Karen Gratton, Apr. 1, 1999.
23. Ibid., Emily Palana, Apr. 1, 1999.
24. Ibid., E. Wolfe, Apr. 1, 1999.
25. Ibid., Bernadine Garcia, Apr. 1, 1999.
26. Howard Zinn, Dana Frank, and Robin D. G. Kelley, eds., *Three Strikes: Miners, Musicians, Salesgirls, and the Fighting Spirit of Labor's Last Century* (Boston: Beacon Press, 2001), 1.
27. Christopher Hayes, "In Search of Solidarity," *In These Times,* Feb. 3, 2006, http://www.inthesetimes.com/site/main/print/in_search_of_solidarity.
28. Todd Seibt, "UAW Leader to Visit Flint on Feb. 11," *Flint Journal,* Jan. 29, 2003.
29. Richard Hofstadter, *The Progressive Historians: Turner, Beard, Parrington* (New York: Alfred A. Knopf, 1968), 345.

Bibliography

Manuscript Sources

Dollinger Collection, 1942–94. Walter Reuther Library, Wayne State University, Detroit, Michigan. This repository contains 52 years of letters, interviews, press clippings and releases, speeches, notes, and so on pertaining to the life and times of Genora Dollinger.

Dollinger Collection. Los Angeles, California. This is a private collection in the papers of Sol Dollinger. It contains essays, both published and unpublished, about Genora Dollinger and her work and Genora's diaries for the years 1937, 1977, 1983, 1984, and 1988.

Dotzert Collection. Tecumseh, Ontario, Canada. This is a private collection, consisting mostly of correspondence between Genora and Sol Dollinger and Donal Dotzert.

Kraus Collection. Walter Reuther Library, Wayne State University, Detroit, Michigan. This collection contains notes, articles, and letters dealing with the life and career of Henry Kraus.

UAW Collection. Walter Reuther Library, Wayne State University, Detroit, Michigan. This is a massive collection of articles, newspaper accounts, and so on dealing with the UAW from 1937 to the present.

Published Sources

Alexander, Robert A. *International Trotskyism 1929–1985: A Documented Analysis of the Movement.* Durham, N.C.: Duke University Press, 1991.

Ameringer, Oscar. *If You Don't Weaken.* New York: Greenwood Press, 1940.

Anderson, Karen. *Wartime Women: Sex Roles, Family, Relations, and the Status of Women During World War II.* Westport, Conn.: Greenwood Press, 1981.

Arnow, Harriett. *The Dollmaker.* New York: Macmillan, 1954.

Auto Women Advance. Flint, Mich.: *Women's Auxiliary,* Local 156, Apr. 1937.

Barnes, Jack. *James P. Cannon: A Political Tribute.* New York: Pathfinder, 1981.

Barton, Ava, ed. *Work Engendered: Toward a New History of American Labor.* Ithaca, N.Y.: Cornell University Press, 1993.

Baumgardner, Jennifer, and Amy Richards. *Manifesta: Young Women, Feminism, and the Future.* New York: Farrar, Straus and Giroux, 2000.

Boyle, Kevin. Review of *Community of Suffering and Struggle: Women, Men, and the Labor Movement in Minneapolis, 1915–1945,* by Elizabeth Faue. *Journal of Urban History* 23.1 (Nov. 1996): 120–25.

Breitman, George. "The Liberating Influence of the Transitional Program." In *Revolutionary Traditions of American Trotskyism.* New York: Fourth International Tendency, 1998.

Cannon, James P. "A Letter to Trotskyists Throughout the World." 25th Anniversary Plenum of the National Committee of the Socialist Workers Party, November 7–8, 1953. www.marxist.org/history/etol/document/swp-us.htm. Accessed July 2007.

———. "The Revolutionary Party: Its Role in the Struggle for Socialism." In *50 Years of World Revolution (1917–1967).* New York: Merit Publications, 1968.

———. "Speech at the First Workers Party Convention." December 1921. Marxists Internet Archive. www.marxists.org/cannon/works/21fwpc.htm. Accessed July 2007.

Chafe, William Henry. *The American Woman: Her Changing Social, Economic, and Political Roles, 1920–1970.* New York: Oxford University Press, 1972.

———. *Women and Equality: Changing Patterns in American Culture.* New York: Oxford University Press, 1977.

Clarke, George, James P. Cannon, and Leon Trotsky. *Background to "The Struggle for a Proletarian Party."* New York: Pathfinder, 1979.

Cobble, Dorothy Sue. *Dishing It Out: Waitresses and Their Unions in the Twentieth Century.* Urbana: University of Illinois Press, 1991.

———. "Recapturing Working-Class Feminism: Union Women in the Postwar Decades." In Joanne Meyerowitz, ed. *Not June Cleaver,* 57–83.

Cochran, Bert. *Labor and Communism: The Conflict that Shaped American Unions.* Princeton, N.J.: Princeton University Press, 1977.

Columbia Encyclopedia. 5th ed. New York: Columbia University Press, 1993.

Cook, Blanche Wiesen. *Women and Support Networks: Women Against Economic and Social Repression: The Two-Front Challenge.* New York: Out and Out Books, 1979.

Cott, Nancy, and Elizabeth H. Pleck, eds. *A Heritage of Her Own: Toward a New Social History of American Women.* New York: Simon & Schuster, 1979.

Denby, Charles. *Indignant Heart: A Black Worker's Journal.* Detroit: Wayne State University Press, 1978.

Dollinger, Genora. Foreword to Dan La Botz, *A Troublemaker's Handbook: How to Fight Back Where You Work—and Win.* Detroit, Mich.: Labor Notes, 1991.

Dollinger, Sol. "The Unrelenting Genora Dollinger." *Against the Current* (Jan./Feb. 1996): 43.

Dollinger, Sol, and Genora Dollinger. *Not Automatic: Women and the Left in the Forging of the Auto Workers' Union.* New York: Monthly Review Press, 2000.

Dorenkamp, Angela G., John F. McClymer, Mary M. Moynihan, and Arlene C. Vadum, eds. *Images of Women in American Popular Culture.* 2d ed. Fort Worth, Tex.: Harcourt Brace, 1995.

Edsforth, Ronald. *Class, Conflict, and Cultural Consensus.* New Brunswick, N.J.: Rutgers University Press, 1987.

Edwards, P. K. *Strikes in the U.S.* New York: St. Martin's Press, 1981.

Egbert, Donald Drew, et al., eds. *Socialism and American Life.* Vol. 2. Princeton, N.J.: Princeton University Press, 1952.

Enstad, Nan. "Fashioning Political Identities: Cultural Studies and the Historical Construction of Political Subjects." *American Quarterly* 50.4 (Dec. 1998): 745–82.

Evans, Sara. *Born for Liberty: A History of Women in America.* New York: Free Press, 1989.

Faue, Elizabeth. *Community of Suffering and Struggle: Women, Men, and the Labor Movement in Minneapolis, 1915–1945.* Chapel Hill: University of North Carolina Press, 1991.

Fine, Sidney. "The General Motors Sit-Down Strike: A Reexamination." *American Historical Review* 70.3 (Apr. 1969): 699–713.

———. *Sit-Down: The General Motors Strike of 1936–1937.* Ann Arbor: University of Michigan Press, 1969.

Fishbein, Leslie. Review of Susan A. Glenn, *Female Spectacle: The Theoretical Roots of Modern Feminism. Journal of American History* 88.3 (Dec. 2001): 1110.

Flexner, Eleanor. *Century of Struggle: The Woman's Rights Movement in the United States.* Rev. ed. Cambridge, Mass.: Harvard University Press, 1975.

Foner, Philip S. *Women and the American Labor Movement: From World War I to the Present.* New York: Free Press, 1980.

Fowler, Brenda. "History and a Name in a Vienna Project," *New York Times,* July 11, 1991.

Frank, Dana. *Buy American: The Untold Story of Economic Nationalism.* Boston: Beacon Press, 1999.

———. "Girl Strikers Occupy Chain Store, Win Big: The Detroit Woolworth's Strike of 1937." In Howard Zinn et al., eds. *Three Strikes,* 57–118.

———. *Purchasing Power: Consumer Organizing, Gender, and the Seattle Labor Movement 1919–1929.* Cambridge: Cambridge University Press, 1994.

———. "Symposium on Tera Hunter: *To 'joy My Freedom—The Labor Historian's New Clothes.*" *Labor History* 39.2 (May 1998): 1–3.

Franklin, Stephen. *Three Strikes: Labor's Heartland Losses and What They Mean for Working Americans.* New York: Guilford Press, 2001.

Friedan, Betty. *The Feminine Mystique.* New York: Norton, 1963.

Gabin, Nancy. *Feminism in the Labor Movement: Women and the United Auto Workers, 1935–1975.* Ithaca, N.Y.: Cornell University Press, 1990.

———. Review of *Community of Suffering and Struggle,* by Elizabeth Faue. *Journal of American History* 79.1 (June 1992): 311–12.

Gilmore, Stephanie. "Looking Back, Thinking Ahead: Third Wave Feminism in the United States." *Journal of Women's History* 12.4 (Winter 2001): 215.

Glaberman, Martin, ed. *Marxism for Our Time: C. L. R. James on Revolutionary Organization.* Jackson: University Press of Mississippi, 1999.

———. *Wartime Strikes: The Struggle Against the No-Strike Pledge in the UAW During World II.* Detroit: Bewick Editions, 1980.

Glickman, Lawrence. Review of *Community of Suffering and Struggle,* by Elizabeth Faue. *Labor History* 34.2–3 (Spring 1993): 387–89.

Gluck, Sherna Berger. Interview of Genora Dollinger, May 21, 1976–April 28, 1977. Ann Arbor: University of Michigan.

———. *Rosie the Riveter Revisited: Women, the War, and Social Change.* Boston: Twayne, 1987.

Gordon, Ann D., Mari Jo Buhle, and Nancy E. Schrom. "Women in American Society: An Historical Contribution." In Cott and Pleck, eds. *A Heritage of Her Own,* 15.

Gordon, Linda. *Pitied but Not Entitled: Single Mothers and the History of Welfare, 1890–1935.* New York: Free Press, 1994.

Green, James R. *The World of the Worker: Labor in Twentieth Century America.* New York: Hill and Wang, 1980.

Henry, Alice. *The Trade Union Woman.* New York: Burt Franklin, 1915.

Heywood, Leslie, and Jennifer Drake. *Third Wave Agenda: Being Feminist, Doing Feminism.* Minneapolis: University of Minnesota Press, 1997.

Hofstadter, Richard. *The Progressive Historians: Turner, Beard, Parrington.* New York: Alfred A. Knopf, 1968.

Hollows, Joanne. *Feminism, Femininity, and Popular Culture.* New York: Manchester Press, 2000.

Horowitz, Daniel. *Betty Friedan and the Making of* The Feminine Mystique: *The American Left, the Cold War, and Modern Feminism.* Amherst: University of Massachusetts Press, 1998.

Howe, Irving, and B. J. Widick. *The UAW and Walter Reuther.* New York: Random House, 1949.

Hunter, Tera W. *To 'Joy My Freedom: Southern Black Women's Lives and Labors after the Civil War.* Cambridge, Mass.: Harvard University Press, 1997.

Hyman, Colette A. Review of *Ladies of Labor,* by Nan Enstad. *Journal of American History* 87.4 (Mar. 2001): 1526–27.

Jackson, Carlton. "The 1930s." In Peter C. Rollins, ed. *The Columbia Companion to American History on Film: How the Movies Have Portrayed the American Past.* New York: Columbia University Press, 2003.

———. *Hounds of the Road: A History of the Greyhound Bus Company.* Rev. ed. Bowling Green, Ohio: Popular Press, 2001.

———. *J. I. Rodale: Apostle of Nonconformity.* New York: Pyramid Books, 1974.

———. *Presidential Vetoes, 1792–1945.* Athens: University of Georgia Press, 1967.

Jeffries, John W. *Wartime America: The World War II Home Front.* Chicago: Ivan Dee, 1996.

Jensen, Michelle. "Riding the Third Wave." *Nation* 271.19 (Dec. 11, 2001): 24.

Keeran, Roger. *The Communist Party and the Auto Workers Union.* Bloomington: Indiana University Press, 1980.

Kerber, Linda, and Jane Sherron DeHart. *Women's America: Refocusing the Past.* 4th ed. New York: Oxford University Press, 1995.

Kilroy-Silk, Robert. *Socialism Since Marx.* New York: Taplinger, 1972.

Kraus, Henry. *The Many and the Few: A Chronicle of the Dynamic Auto Workers.* 2d ed. Urbana: University of Illinois Press, 1985.

La Botz, Dan. *A Troublemakers Handbook: How to Fight Back Where You Work–and Win.* Detroit: Labor Notes, 1991.

Laughlin, Kathleen A. *Women's Work and Public Policy: A History of the Women's Bureau, U.S. Department of Labor, 1945–1970.* Boston: Northeastern University Press, 2000.

Le Blanc, Paul, ed. *Revolutionary Traditions of American Trotskyism.* New York: Fourth International Tendency, 1998.

Lerner, Warren. *A History of Socialism and Communism in Modern Times: Theorists, Activists, and Humanists.* 2d ed. Englewood Cliffs, N.J.: Prentice Hall, 1994.

Levy, Ariel. *Female Chauvinist Pigs: Women and the Rise of Raunch Culture.* New York: Free Press, 2005.

Lichtenstein, Nelson. "Auto Workers Militancy and the Structure of Factory Life, 1937–1955." *Journal of American History* 67.2 (Spring 1980): 335–53.

———. *The Most Dangerous Man in Detroit: Walter Reuther and the Fate of American Labor.* New York: Basic Books, 1995.

Linkon, Sherry Lee. "A Marx Family Reunion: Cultural Studies and Labor History on Common Ground." *American Quarterly* 52.3 (Sept. 2000): 555–61.

Loughlin, Patricia. "In Search of Capable Allies: Frances Nacke Noel and Women's Labor Activism in Los Angeles." *Southern California Quarterly* 82.1 (Dec. 2001): 61–74.

Lynd, Staughton, ed. *We Are All Leaders: The Alternative Unions of the Early 1930s.* Urbana: University of Illinois Press, 1996.

Lynn, Conrad J. *Monroe, North Carolina . . . Turning Point in American History.* Privately Published Pamphlet, 1962. Labadie Collection. Ann Arbor: University of Michigan Library.

———. *There Is a Fountain: The Autobiography of Conrad Lynn.* Brooklyn, N.Y.: Lawrence Hill Books, 1993.

McElvaine, Robert S. *The Great Depression: America, 1929–1941.* New York: Three Rivers Press, 1993.

Meyerowitz, Joanne, ed. *Not June Cleaver: Women and Gender in Postwar America, 1945–1960.* Philadelphia: Temple University Press, 1994.

Meyerson, Harold. "The Women Just Came Out of Their Homes . . . " An Interview with Genora Dollinger, *Dissent* 32.4 (Fall 1985), 464–67.

Milkman, Ruth. *Farewell to the Factory: Auto Workers In the Late Twentieth Century.* Berkeley: University of California Press, 1997.

———. *Gender at Work: The Dynamics of Job Segregation by Sex During World War II.* Urbana: University of Illinois Press, 1987.

———. "Gender and Trade Unionism in History Perspective," in Louise A. Tilly and Patricia Gurin, eds. *Women, Politics, and Change.*

———, ed. *Women, Work, and Protest: A Century of Women's Labor History.* Boston: Routledge, Keegan, Paul, 1985.

Morgan, Robin, ed. *Sisterhood Is Forever: The Women's Anthology for a New Millenium.* New York: Washington Square Press, 2003.

Murolo, Priscilla, and A. B. Chitty. *From the Folks Who Brought You the Week-End: A Short, Illustrated History of Labor in the United States.* New York: Free Press, 2001.

Myers, Constance Ashton. *The Prophet's Army: Trotskyists in America, 1928–1941.* Westport, Conn.: Greenwood Press, 1977.

Naples, Nancy A. *Grassroots Warriors: Activist Mothering, Community Work, and the War on Poverty.* New York: Routledge, 1998.

Nelson, Truman. *People with Strength: The Story of Monroe, N.C.* Durham, N.C.: Duke University Press, 1962.

O'Nan, Kathleen. "The Role of Women and of Radicals in the First Sit-Down Strikes: An Interview with Genora Dollinger." In John H. Hinshaw and Paul Le Blanc, eds. *U.S. Labor in the Twentieth Century: Studies in Working-Class Struggles and Insurgency.* (Amherst, N.Y.: Humanity Books, 2001). 162–77.

On Guard. Bulletin No. 4. Detroit, Mich.: Educational Committee, Local 212 UAW-CIO, 1945. Copy found in Wayne State University, Reuther Library.

Orleck, Annelise. *Common Sense and a Little Fire: Women and Working-Class Politics in the United States, 1900–1965.* Chapel Hill: University of North Carolina Press, 1995.

Rachleff, Peter. "Organizing 'Wall to Wall': The Independent Union of All Workers, 1933–37." In Staughton Lynd, ed. *We Are All Leaders: The Alternative Unionism of the Early 1930s,* Urbana: University of Illinois Press, 1996. 60–66.

Red Channels: The Report of Communist Influence in Radio and Television. New York: *Counterattack, The Newsletter of Facts to Combat Communism,* 1950.

Reuther, Victor. *The Brothers Reuther and the Story of the UAW.* Boston: Houghton Mifflin, 1976.

Rupp, Leila, and Verta Taylor. *Survival in the Doldrums: The American Women's Rights Movements 1945 to the 1960s.* New York: Oxford University Press, 1987.

Schlesinger, Arthur M. *The Crisis of the Old Order.* Boston: Houghton Mifflin, 1957.

Schwarz, Joseph M. *The Permanence of the Political: A Democratic Critique of the Radical Impulse to Transcend Politics.* Princeton, N.J.: Princeton University Press, 1995.

Scott, Anne Firor, Sara M. Evans, Susan K. Cahn, and Elizabeth Faue. "A Conversation Across Three Generations: Parts 1 and 2." *Journal of Women's History* 11.1/2 (1999): 9–30, 199–220.

Seidman, Joel. *"Sit-Down."* New York: League for Industrial Democracy, 1937.

Skells, Jack. Interview of Genora Dollinger, July 31, 1960. Detroit, Mich.: Wayne State University.

Sombart, Werner. *Socialism and the Social Movement in the Nineteenth Century.* London: J. M. Dent & Co., 1909.

Steinem, Gloria. *Outrageous Acts and Everyday Rebellion.* 2d ed. New York: Henry Holt, 1995.

Stephen-Norris, Judith, and Maurice Zeitlin. *Left Out: Reds and America's Industrial Unions.* Cambridge: Cambridge University Press, 2003.

Terkel, Studs. *Coming of Age.* New York: New Press, 1997.

Tilly, Louise A., and Patricia Guren, eds. *Women, Politics, and Change.* New York: Russell Sage Foundation, 1990.

Tyson, Timothy. *Radio Free Dixie: Robert F. Williams and the Roots of Black Power.* Chapel Hill: University of North Carolina Press, 1999.

Ware, Susan. *Holding Their Own: American Women in the 1930s.* Boston: Twayne Publishers, 1982.

———. *Modern American Women: A Documentary History.* New York: McGraw-Hill, 2002.

Wolfe, Bertram D. *Marxism: One Hundred Years in the Life of a Doctrine.* New York: Dial Press, 1965.

Zinn, Howard, and Anthony Arnove, eds. *Voices of a People's History of the United States.* New York: Seven Stories, 2004.

Zinn, Howard, Dana Frank, and Robin D. G. Kelley, eds. *Three Strikes: Miners, Musicians, Salesgirls, and the Fighting Spirit of Labor's Last Century.* Boston: Beacon Press, 2001.

Newspapers

The American Socialist
Bowling Green Daily News
Detroit Evening News
Detroit Free Press
Flint Journal
In These Our Times
Los Angeles Times
The Militant
New York Times
Park City (Ky.) Daily News
Searchlight (UAW Local 659)

Unpublished Sources

Diehl-Taylor, Christiane. "Partners in the Struggle: The Role of Women's Auxiliaries and Brigades in the 1934 Minneapolis Truck Drivers Strikes and the 1936/37 Flint General Motors Sit-Down Strike." Research paper, University of Minnesota, 1990.

Hassett, Janice. "Never Again Just a Woman: Women of the Auxiliary and Emergency Brigade in the General Motors Sit-Down Strike of 1937." Senior thesis, Mills College, 1994.

Yeghissian, Patricia. "Women's Emergency Brigade: Flint Sit-Down Strike of 1936–37." Senior honors thesis, University of Michigan, 1974.

Index